Tom Stobart

I TAKE
PICTURES
FOR ADVENTURE

DOUBLEDAY & COMPANY, INC.

Garden City, New York 1958

Library of Congress Catalog Card Number 58–10042
Copyright © 1958 by TOM STOBART
All Rights Reserved
Printed in the United States of America

But we feel it is a great moment in our lives—in fact one of the best we have ever experienced. We think that something is going to happen; we hope devoutly that something will happen; yet at the same time we do not want to be hurt or killed. What is it then that we do want? It is that lure of youth—adventure, and adventure for adventure's sake. You might call it tomfoolery.

SIR WINSTON CHURCHILL—*My Early Life*

I TAKE PICTURES
FOR ADVENTURE

chapter 1

I SHOULD think that in 1937 the film industry was one of the hardest in the world to get into—unless you knew the right people, which I did not. I didn't even know the first thing about films. All I knew was what I wanted to do, and it was a kind of job that did not yet exist.

The whole thing started one day in Cambridge when I went to a lecture at the Polar Research Institute. They were showing a film made by some expedition in Iceland, and it was lousy. Because I belonged to a generation brought up with the movies, I knew instinctively just where the camera should have been pointing when it was not. I had been turning over all the possible things I could do with my life and was in the usual youthful muddle with a thousand attractive alternatives, when I suddenly saw quite clearly that this was just what I should like to do—make films about wild places, especially about expeditions.

It was all very well to think about it, even to discuss it with a few chosen friends, but it was another matter to make it a reality. It would have been bad enough wanting to change to a sensible job—I mean one considered sensible in the scientific circle to which I belonged—because I held a Colonial Office Scholarship, was a highly qualified zoologist, and many people had a vested interest in keeping me on the straight and narrow path. But proposing some crack-brained scheme like going into films was dreadful, and I was on very shaky ground.

9

"You'll never get started," they told me; and then, as they saw a pigheaded glitter in my eye, "Or if you do, you'll never get to filming expeditions. Who's interested? Not the public. All the public wants is "LURVE.""

It was odd to find professors and super-mammoth producers in agreement, but as for myself, I did not believe it. I too was not averse to a spot of *lurve*, but I also liked a good full-blooded adventure which could surely be none the worse for being true. How many boys lapped up Everest and Captain Scott? When Ginger Rogers flew into their lives, did Shackleton fly completely out? Surely films of true adventure would be popular if they could be made good enough, but to do that, one had to become a specialist, and this was the job that did not exist.

I was scared and uncertain, so I had to dive straight in. I deliberately failed my examinations and burned my boats. The horrified silence was rather like letting a banger off in church.

It is very hard to convince people that your forte is making films unless you look the part. A beard, a velvet coat, and a Rolls-Royce are helpful props. Moreover, nobody wants to employ a man who looks healthy. He must be all body if he is not all soul, and I had just come back from the Alps. The sound of closing inquiry hatches was as brisk as a machine gun. It began to look as if the pessimists were right. In six months I had never even seen the inside of a studio, and so far the I-told-you-sos were winning hands down. I lived on odd jobs which I kept to myself, like posing for an art school when the model across the hall had a cold (being smart, I wore a bathing suit), and in between times reviewing "quota quickies" for the Film Institute which nobody else would sit through.

However, it was indirectly through the thankless little reviews I did that I at last got my first chance. I was reading through the *Film Institute Journal* one day, admiring my work in print, when I came on an article outlining the production plans of the Dartington Hall Film Unit. I had never heard of it, but a number of geographical films were listed in the schedule, including one on nomads in Russia. I did not know that this was only going to be edited out of existing material for the film *Turksib*. It sounded exactly what I was looking for; among other places, I had always wanted to go to Russia—well, of course anywhere, so long as it was travel.

Dartington Hall was an estate in Devonshire where a social experiment in rural rehabilitation was going on, a community inspired a little by Rabindranath Tagore's *Shantiniketan*, and a beautiful home for the arts in the English countryside. It had been founded as a trust by an American millionairess, Dorothy Elmhirst, and had attracted a number of advanced and energetic people who had naturally pushed their own interests far beyond the needs of the original project. This makes a short description difficult. It contained a modern school for children, a school of ballet, painting, music—everything a young artist might require, or even dream about. Apparently, also a film unit. I wrote, asking if I could go there as a student.

It so happened that the timing of my letter was exactly right. The Film Unit consisted of one master at the school, the late Bill Hunter, one of the pioneers of the educational film. Bill had the help and encouragement of Robert Flaherty, whose children he had been teaching, and in between his work as geography master he was making 16-mm. films of a very high caliber. His films were just achieving recognition, and someone's writing and asking to work under him as a student seemed a feather in his cap indeed. I did not tell him till later that I had never heard of him before and that I had read the notice quite by chance.

I met Bill on his next visit to London and liked him at sight. He was young and full of enthusiasm. He did not, however, hold out much hope. He would need a grant of one hundred pounds for film stock if he took me as a student, and to add to the difficulties, I needed to have some job to support me while I studied. I was therefore surprised and enormously relieved a few weeks later when I received a letter saying it was all arranged. I was in.

Dartington Hall Estate lay in a bend of the River Dart in that fat Devon countryside that bursts its seams with vegetable growth. On the top of the hill, near the tower of the old church, was an ancient manor house of gray stone. The buildings surrounded a large courtyard and had been largely restored with splendid oak beams from the estate. The plumbing was perfect. Everything was lovely in the garden, which was one of the most beautiful I have ever seen.

Some distance away were the new buildings of the school where I worked. There was no special room available for films, and the editing had to be done at the back of Bill's classroom. Quite apart from the fact that Bill was a fine photographer with a great feeling for motion pictures, the films grew up in the room where the children were taught and could hardly fail to be right for the job they were intended to do.

My official job, for which I earned two pounds a week, was acting as assistant guide on the estate. Because it was the home of a *modern* experiment, there were many visitors, but most of the work came during the holidays, and if nobody turned up for the conducted tour I was free to go back to my studies. Bill, who was an excellent teacher, had simply thrown a roll of film at me—it was material on canning fish in Norway—and told me to get on with it.

To be honest, I did not find photography an interesting occupation. People have two sorts of interests, the primary one which fascinates them because they enjoy it for itself alone and like playing with the materials, and secondary interests acquired in order to pursue better the primary ones. Here enjoyment may give way to the determination to get a boring task done. It was rather like this with my photography. My first interest always lay in the subject itself, which I hoped would one day be expeditions; my second, in the direction and editing. A long way in the rear came photography, and I looked with envy at those people who took photographs because they enjoyed it. To me a camera was a bore and photography something that had to be done but got in the way of the full enjoyment of the scene and surroundings. How lucky a writer is; free of apparatus, he has only to use his eyes and let the impressions soak in.

Film work came very easily to me, and it was fine training to operate on such a small scale that one literally had to do everything. I do not much believe in the departmentalization that is the rule in our century, and certainly not that if I attained my ambition to become a film director I should know nothing and have no interest in anybody's job but my own.

It was not long before Bill suggested I was ready to start work on a film that was absolutely mine, and I chose the subject of *Rivers*, which was not only useful in teaching geography but also gave me the chance to begin to travel, to film in the mountains and the wilds, off the beaten track.

As soon as the autumn rush of visitors was over and I again had time to devote to my studies, I planned an excursion up to Scotland. There was so little money that I had to hitchhike. This suited me well, as it meant that I had to carry all the equipment on my back, which was good practice if I wanted one day to get my camera into unusual places. The fact that I started off in this way and got used to managing on a shoestring was to stand me in good stead later on. With a different sort of start I might have been lured by the big cameras and large units with which the usual documentary work was being done at that time and still is.

It was midwinter when I worked up into the Cairngorms, and there were some bad blizzards. There are people who do not realize it can reach arctic ruggedness in Scotland and that every year rash or inexperienced people die there of exposure.

The cold on the peaks was so intense that it stopped my camera and gave me a first taste of the kinds of difficulties I have since had to face so often.

It was on my return just after New Year's, 1939, that fate grabbed me and set me off on my first travels—which were almost immediately interrupted by the Second World War. During the next six years there were interesting moments in Rumania, Turkey, and Arabia, but the big adventures still lay ahead. By 1945 I was in India.

chapter 2

IN INDIA I had an enormous stroke of luck. I met
Brigadier Desmond Young, now known to the world as the
author of *Rommel,* and within a short time found myself in
uniform, charged with the task of founding a unit and
making films for the General Staff. It was not quite what I
wanted; I had hoped to return to the Middle East as a correspondent, but that was not allowed.

"Yours is a much more important job," said the Colonel
when I hesitantly broached the subject. "Don't you like
it?"

"Yes, I know, but . . ."

"There aren't any *buts* young fellah, you're in the Army
now." I was still sufficiently green to believe him.

There was such a frantic rush to train troops and I was
kept so busy that for two years I scarcely had a Sunday
free, let alone leave. Yet I traveled far and wide, learned
my trade by practice in a way impossible in peacetime.
For so many of my friends the time spent in the Army
was wasted, and I was lucky indeed to get those two years.
What happened afterward is another story. (It is a pity
that in the Army so many one would like to shoot are
technically on your own side!)

But all the time I was acutely conscious of a presence
to the north, like a Geiger counter being nudged by a
concealed nugget of uranium. In short, the Himalayas
were there if I could only get to them.

My chance came at last when I landed in the military

hospital suffering from overwork and jaundice. The hospital was the kind to get out of quickly, for to my certain knowledge the floors had not been properly cleaned for six months, and what with the dirt and flies, we all got dysentery in addition to our original complaint.

When I finally escaped, I was given six weeks' leave and told to go somewhere cool to rest, so I resurrected my old climbing boots and bought a ticket for Kathgodam, railhead for the mountain district of Kumaon. I was free once more.

After a day and two nights on the train, I woke at dawn to find we were running through the jungles of the Terai. This is a strip of dense malarious forest that stretches along the base of the Himalayas, between the foothills and the plains.

Although it was only March, it was stifling hot, and when the hills first came in sight they only showed like blue shadows through the dusty haze. But as we came closer, they became defined into forests and gorges. At their bases were huge gravel washouts made by the rivers. Tigers, elephant, even rhino, lived in this tangle of country, and it was an exciting place, with strange flowers and a promise of excitement in every bush.

Outside the station at Kathgodam waited a line of dirty old buses with small, unglazed windows like cattle trucks. Already people were fighting to get in, but it was over an hour before the luggage was piled on top, and all the passengers somehow squeezed into the narrow seats. They were made of wood and were going to be hard on the bottom.

After six hours in that bus without food or water (which I had not had the sense to bring), I was thankful to reach Almora, the town nearest the high mountains. My liver had begun to hurt again and I could feel it grumbling under my ribs. It was not a very good start to a strenuous holiday, but I knew I had been right to come.

A ragged coolie with a loop of rope seized my box and slung it on his back. His calf muscles bulged below homespun jodhpurs. I followed him past the cottage-industry tweed factory to a small hotel. It was dark and a few flakes of snow swirled in the air, but there was a fire inside. The other occupants were an English girl and a young Indian. They were huddled near the flames to keep warm.

"Good evening. How fine it feels to be cold again, to need a fire." Nobody who has not spent several years in a winterless climate can realize that cold may be as welcome as sun.

The English girl had rosy cheeks, but the Indian was gray with cold. He was a student, and the floor by his chair was piled with books.

"What have you come up here for?" they asked.

"I am going on up into the mountains."

"But it is too early in the year—and even if it wasn't, of course you cannot go *alone*." They spoke with authority, as guests who have been in residence a few days longer than you always do.

This was disappointing if it was true, and everyone agreed it was, but on inquiry, what they really meant was, "No one ever did," or "No one ever had," and it was this which made it impossible.

Almora is one of the great cultural centers of India, and among the many artists and sages living there were several who had connections with Dartington Hall and to whom I had introductions.

There was Boshi Sen, a famous Indian scientist, and his American wife, Gertrude, who was busy on a history of India. Boshi was a biologist and was experimenting on how to improve the hillmen's crops, but he was also able to fill me with fascinating and stimulating tidbits of information about exploration in Tibet to the north. Up there was the sacred mountain, Kailas, on the path around which pilgrims went measuring their length the whole way. It was forbidden to Europeans, although some had done the trip in disguise. Boshi told me of an Indian who had had a metal boat carried up for the exploration of Lake Manasarowar. How I longed to pierce that curtain myself, but alas, in six weeks . . .

Nearer, seventy miles away, was Nanda Devi, the highest mountain in the Commonwealth, and at that time the highest mountain that had ever been climbed, 25,500 feet, or approaching five miles high.

Nanda Devi is a very special mountain. It stands in a secret basin, walled in by peaks that descend lower than 20,000 feet only at one place, and that where the drainage water has cut a stupendous gorge through the barrier. The first entry by Shipton and Tillman into this basin through the gorge and out over the wall into the Sunderhunga was one of the classics of mountaineering. This was followed a few years later by a brilliant expedition that reached the top.

Nanda Devi had a particular interest for me, since my father used to climb with one of the men who had scaled it, N. E. Odell. I could still remember looking at the expedition photograph in his house at Cambridge, and how he had said, "It's steeper than it looks," which was not true, because it looked awful. Odell had been a frequent visitor at our house when I was a child. I used to creep in my pajamas to the top of the stairs and listen to the singing that was stimulated by our home-brewed cider, and the conversations overheard, along with mysterious departures laden with ropes, were partly to blame for the fact that during my schooldays it had been more attractive to dream of climbing Everest than of driving an engine.

Of course any real climbing now—alone and so early in the year—was entirely out of the question, but there was a summer treck to the Pindar Glacier, between a peak called Nanda Kot and the Nanda Devi Basin, which might provide some fun in winter. I intended to try.

I brooded over this when I occasionally glimpsed the distant peaks through the window of Boshi's laboratory or walked through the snow, admiring the enormous fragrant lemons that grew in his garden. Boshi had been near the Pindar in summertime, collecting rare flowers. He said it was delightful, wonderful, beautiful, but he didn't think it was wise to go in winter either.

Uday Shankar had his school of Indian dance just around the hill. His musician, Shirali, and I had been close friends when he had studied in England, and I spent several fascinating days sitting on the floor, watching the classes. Under normal circumstances I should have been content to be endlessly enthralled, but now, restless and a little nostalgic, I had only one thought: How soon could I set off into the mountains?

When I wasn't scouring the bazaar for canned foods, I walked in the surrounding hills with the Indian student. I found he had studied yoga, and one day he stopped to demonstrate how it was possible for a man to balance himself horizontally on the tips of his fingers. This was a prodigious feat of strength, but still no more than the turn of a good circus acrobat.

"No doubt if I am lucky enough to meet a full-fledged yogi one day, I shall learn something sensational, like how to sit in the nude in a blizzard," I told him. "That trick would be rather useful for a mountaineer, and would save a lot of money when I get home."

"Well," he replied, taking me seriously, "that's not impossible, you know. I am afraid you are skeptical."

"Well, yes, to be quite honest, I am."

The efforts to dissuade me continued all during my preparations for the trip. Friends pointed out that I was recovering from a serious illness and ought to rest; that under the circumstances it was unwise to go; that I would

19

certainly never get there. They only succeeded in making the project sound like even more fun, although I was now expecting it to be pretty tough. So, with these dire warnings in my ears, I took the bus up to the roadhead and set off on foot for Bageshwar, a village some twelve miles along the path, where there was a resthouse.

The track led up a valley adorned with terraces of young rice, surely the most startling green of any in the world. The sun was hot, and I stopped frequently to rest. This suited my coolies admirably. They were ordinary bazaar coolies, unused to long trecks, and they carried only forty pounds each, as opposed to the usual eighty, but they were the best I could find.

The valley rose to a narrow pass at the top, and I stopped there for lunch. On an outcrop of rocks a few rhododendrons were in bloom, the dark red flowers of the lower altitudes. A spring of water flowed into a tank from the mouth of a carved head, and it looked good to drink. A supply of good drinking water is a constant worry to the traveler in the East who likes to avoid a belly-ache. I had a canvas bottle of boiled water, but that was warm and tasted of smoke. I risked the spring, a foolish thing to do.

I lay on the ground resting and looking at the rhododendrons. Behind them a haze hid the big mountains, or so I thought until I happened to glance above at a cloud. Then I could not believe my eyes. Higher, higher than was possible and right up in heaven, was a penciled face of ice, a little paler and more delicate than the sky. I watched it grow into the stupendous precipices ringing the basin of Nanda Devi. The red flowers, a gnarled tree, and those fantastic mountains. It was the most wonderful picture I have ever seen—my first glimpse of the Himalayas soaring high into the heavens—and I thought of what was said in the Ramayana:

"He who thinks on Himachal, though he should not

20

behold him, is greater than he who performs all worship in Benares.

"In a thousand ages of the gods, I could not tell thee of the wonders of Himachal, where the Ganges falls from the foot of Vishnu like the slender thread of a lotus flower."

What if I did have blistered feet and a knife in my liver?

"And all things that in dying look upon those snows are freed from sin."

Then as I gazed upon the vision, the haze came in again, and the ice vanished as softly as it had come, so that there was only a pale luminous sky. I rubbed my eyes in disbelief.

I had that disturbing feeling we all get—a dream or whatever it is—that I had seen it all before, except that there should have been a bird all gold and blue, like a peacock, but not a peacock. It upset me because it made me wonder about life and death and all those things which it is more comfortable to banish from our everyday thoughts. I was no longer sure I was my own master, but wondered if perhaps we were at the whim of something else. I shook the thoughts off and got up to go on. I remembered that as a child I was told of a certain explorer who did not believe in God, and I could not understand then how he dared climb in the Himalayas, defying the spirits alone.

Below the pass a forest fire had crossed the track. Although it must have gone by weeks ago, some of the larger trees were still smoldering. One tottered and crashed, and I had to sprint to get out of the way. Perhaps these mountains did not like to be disturbed. My feet hurt and I began to get blisters. A blue jay laughed raucously at me from a high branch. "Brother, why can't you fly?"

At the end of the day there was at last Bageshwar, with its two suspension bridges. The town smelled of bad drains and wood smoke, and it was alive with the sound of

21

rivers. Beyond the first bridge was a cobbled alley with open booths. In one shop there was a collection of old iron. A bent, rusty nail was displayed with care. In another were rolls of cheap cloth; and in a third, lumps of sticky brown sugar tied up in leaves and covered with flies—cholera food! There were baskets of shriveled red chilies and bottles corked with paper, containing some horrible unmentionable compounds that looked as if they came from the cauldron of some Kumaoni witches. It was difficult to drop into the minds of people to whom this was a metropolis.

The resthouse, called in India a Dak bungalow, was beside the fast-flowing river I should be following the next day. Once more I reckoned that it looked clear and fast enough to drink without boiling, but the gravel at its edge was fouled with human excreta, and I decided not to take the chance. So I flopped in a chair on the veranda, and waited impatiently for the water to boil, feeling both exhausted and ill. When I had swallowed a little bully beef and some biscuits, I sat quietly outside until it was dark. A forest fire was raging up a ridge on the other side of the valley. The smell of wood smoke was heavy in the air, and somewhere in the town a drum was beating and people were chanting. As always when I am alone in the evening, I felt miserable and depressed. I went to bed.

I spent a feverish night, and woke in a vile temper the next morning. I got up at dawn, intending to be well on my way before the day became hot, but after stumbling around in the half-light, banging my toes against the furniture, I discovered that my coolies were temporarily lost in town. When my men at last showed up, I shouted angrily at them to hurry. My ill humor caused me to make an embarrassing mistake.

In the midst of the scurry an old man appeared with a handful of moth-eaten vegetables and a rose. He bowed and placed the offerings in front of me. I picked them up, handed them back, and shouted "Go" in my rudest Hindustani. Then I threw him a small coin. "Clear off. Can't you see . . . I am in no mood for beggars."

When I had at last got the coolies off on the road, my headman came up to me, the old fellow with him again. He pushed into my hands a book open at a page signed by Hugh Rutledge, former district commissioner and leader of the 1936 Everest expedition. It was a note praising the Rawal of Bageshwar and his services to the government.

This was the man I had been throwing coins to, the local aristocrat. I blushed at my boner, and moreover, I was ashamed of my churlishness. I set about repairing my lack of manners and wasted another hour in polite talk. I accepted the moth-eaten vegetables, and the rose, giving a few aspirins in exchange, which was what the old man was most in need of. The start was very late indeed.

It was a beautiful morning, and the path lay through a shady wood beside the river. At a wide bend, logs were being collected and made ready for sawing. Paradise flycatchers, with tails streaming behind like white ribbons, were chasing about with their more sober orange-brown wives. I smelled the rose, and the sweet smell took me back to other gardens. To dreaming . . .

Suddenly I was aroused by the twittering of a host of birds. The noise came from a stack of rocks that looked like a stage setting for a robbers' lair. I guessed from the sound that some animal was being mobbed and, leaving the path, I climbed quietly up to investigate. It could be almost anything—owl, snake . . . I reached rather gingerly over a rock and pulled myself up. I was looking right at a huge lizard.

It was about four feet long, with vicious claws and the most evil, sinister eyes. Egg dripped out of its mouth.

23

Frantic birds fluttered, squawking, around it. It had not seen me but went on robbing the nest. I quickly dropped back out of sight and began to climb around to come at it from behind. I had an ice ax as a weapon and thought I would like the skin.

Once more I quietly approached from around a rock. The lizard was still there. But this time it heard me, looked up, and hissed. Instead of running away, it stood its ground. I struck at its back with all my strength, but to my astonishment the ax bounced off as if I had whacked an old boot. The lizard spun around and rushed into a hole under the rocks. I poked around for some time, but I had lost my chance.

Next the path entered a gorge; between it and the river was a sheer drop of about a hundred feet. The rock was clean and white, the water jade blue, and the whole was shaded by a tangle of tropical trees and creepers. It was a cool, beautiful place, and I lingered to admire a pair of giant kingfishers hunting down the water. A small tributary stream came in opposite, and in the corner between the two rivers was the most perfect camping ground, a spit of close green grass, shaded by great trees.

I was aroused by the sound of a bell from higher up, and curiosity led me on once more.

For a hundred-yard stretch the path had been cut out of the rock and was very narrow, so narrow that ponies would not be able to pass. There was a blind corner in the middle, and the bell was hung over the path so that caravans entering the narrow section could give warning. Since there were strong rapids below and the cliff dropped straight down, anyone falling off the path at this point would certainly be killed.

Just around the corner sat a woman with a young girl about eight years old. They sat side by side on the parapet of the path at its narrowest point, and when I approached they stood and barred the way. I saw to my horror that the woman was in the advanced stages of leprosy, nodular, fingerless. It was a terrible thing to be reminded of in such a beautiful place. But worse, I could not get by without touching her.

Of course I knew that leprosy is not easily caught, and to prove it there was the young daughter, her arm around her mother, and not a sign of the disease—yet. Nevertheless I was horrified at the thought of being touched.

There was only one thing to do. The path widened beyond and, taking a handful of coins, I threw them over their heads to this broader section. While they rushed to pick up the coins, I dodged past. The coolies of course went by without taking any notice.

It seemed to be my day for horrors, because an hour later, as I was passing through a village, I heard conch shells blowing downriver. The path had temporarily left the riverbank to pass through the little street, and I turned off through a grove of bananas. A half-burned corpse was being launched on its journey down to the Ganges. What upset me was not the corpse but the fact that I had been drinking that river water the night before and had nearly fallen for drinking it unboiled.

Outside the resthouse at Kapkot, where I intended to spend the night, grew a wild fig tree, the haunt of many birds. There were minivets like coals of fire and verditer flycatchers of a lovely sky blue. I lay on some stones, once more too tired even to get a chair. The last part of the day's journey in the heat had been sheer hell, and my liver was again growling at me. Moreover, the village headman had added to my depression by telling me that it was quite impossible to go more than another day's journey up the track. The route from here, he said, began to climb and was blocked by snow. "Why do you come so early in the year? No sahibs ever . . ." He echoed what everyone had told me in Almora.

I paid no heed, of course—how could I? Indeed, what

25

is the fun in life if you allow yourself to be stopped by the misgivings of every Tom, Dick, and Harry. At the very least you can see for yourself and, if necessary, come back.

On the following morning I managed for the first time to get the coolies off to an early start, probably because they themselves wanted to. And I heard my first whistling thrush, known usually as a "whistling schoolboy." "Milkman" would be nearer the mark, because this bird goes its rounds in the early morning, and you hear its song traveling up the valleys, like that rare milkman who does whistle melodiously on his early-morning rounds.

Again spirits rose with the sun. The path entered a narrow defile which was dark with pine trees, the kind of mysterious place that makes a mountain journey tense. Here the route divided, one track crossing a bridge and climbing toward a little col, the other following the river. That path led to the wilder parts to the north, to Tibet, to Kailas and Lake Manasarowar, to the forbidden lands. I would have taken it if I had had time to spare, but I had none. Instead, I crossed the bridge, keeping to the beaten track.

Above the bridge two men were resting near their loads. I thought one of them was mad until I noticed that he was injured. His close-cropped hair was matted with blood which had streaked his face and clothes. He was grunting and shaking his head as he walked bowed under a towering load.

The hillmen think—or perhaps just hope—that every European is a doctor. They have no doctors or hospitals of their own, except at a few hill stations, so I was expected to play my part. It was explained to me that a stone had fallen onto this poor fellow's head the previous day. That his condition was steadily becoming worse as he carried his load in the hot sun. Now he was thoroughly puggled—

an Indian word meaning ga-ga. Looking at that massive load, I was not surprised.

I set my rucksack down under a tree and examined him. The bleeding had stopped and his skull did not appear fractured—there was nothing I could do about it if it was—the only thing to suggest was that he lie down in the shade for a day or two until the concussion was better. When I mentioned this, I was told that the man could not afford to drop his work. The best medicine I could give was a few rupees to subsidize a rest.

I settled him in the shade of a tree and went on my way, feeling that I had done my kind deed for the day. Half an hour later, I was depressed to look back from the top of the col and see that my patient was up, once more bent under his heavy load and staggering along the path. "These damned stupid . . ." Then I wondered if I was a better patient myself. I too was supposed to be taking a rest.

chapter 3

THE PATH left the river and began to zigzag up the mountainside. By evening, when I dragged into the next bungalow, I had reached an altitude where it was cool—around 8000 feet.

At the head of the valley towered the ax head of Nanda Kot; at its foot lay my destination, the Pindar Glacier. But a maze of rocky ridges with snow-filled gullies lay between. The usual path by-passed these by crossing the wooded ridge to the west, but the more I looked toward Nanda Kot, the more fascinated I became with the idea of reaching it direct. I longed to leave the known route, so far quite devoid of the difficulties I had been led to expect, and push straight on through virgin country.

Talking with the villagers, I found a man who knew the last village in the valley, near a place they called the Cow's Mouth. He agreed to come with me as guide, but since he was a man with a pony—a Gorawalla—he insisted he could not be hired without his beast. I didn't want the pony, but as the extra cost was very small I engaged him.

The next morning the Gorawalla appeared on time. His pony was a thickset creature with a shaggy white coat and a wooden saddle, over which had been spread a yellow and blue Bhotian carpet. I did not intend to ride, partly because I wanted to walk, partly because it would have been cruel to expect such a small beast to carry me, and partly because I don't like riding anyway.

29

"Gorawalla," I said, "you may put some of the coolie's loads on the pony's back."

"But, Sahib, horse is for you to ride."

"I prefer to walk."

"But, Sahib," the coolies also joined in, "the horse is only for you to ride."

I could not understand this at all. I had thought that the coolies, who had complained of their loads every moment of the way, would be overjoyed to have a horse at their disposal. But I had no intention of riding, and after some further argument they all grumblingly set off up the valley. I was already a little bored with the fuss and regretted my arrangement.

After going only a hundred yards across some terraced fields we came to a vertical earthbank some twelve feet high, which we had to jump down. There was no way around, and I thought, not without some malice, that this was where the wretched horse would stay behind. Feeling that the Gorawalla was certain to demand backsheesh in lieu of his day's wages and that I should lose face if I did not give him some, I waited at the obstacle but was astonished to see that the horse plunged down the bank without any hesitation. I could at least congratulate myself on my foresight in not being on it's back.

"You have a good horse, Gorawalla," I said.

"Very good horse, Sahib. Sahib will ride now."

"No!"

We soon left the terraced fields behind and took to a rocky path. It was a wonderful morning and I pushed forward at a pace that I knew would soon leave my coolies far behind. I wanted to be alone. I wanted to fill my lungs with the fresh air, to walk in silence so that I should surprise any wild creatures along the path.

The coolies soon dropped below, but the Gorawalla would not be shaken off, and his horse remained fast on my heels. I decided to lose him and put on speed. Panting

and sweating, I tore up the hillside, but always the effortless pad-pad of the Gorawalla's bare feet and the clip-clop
of the hoofs on rock were close behind.

After an hour of this competition we came out at a small
settlement, a few terraces and a threshing floor, where I
stopped for a rest. Above, the valley swept in spur after
spur toward the snow-covered ranges. Behind all towered
Nanda Kot, a magnificent peak, as sharp as a broken flint.
The ice glittered like a blue gem. Below, in the bottom I
could see the river, a white thread among the boulders.
It was now so far away that it had no sound.

"The Cow's Mouth," said a village boy, pointing up the
gorge. "Bad road, Sahib."

"Yes, bad road, Sahib, can't go there," chorused my
coolies, who had just arrived.

"Why is it a bad road? Do you mean because this
wretched horse can't go there?"

"Yes, horse very good horse, Sahib. Horse can go there.
Sahib will ride horse now."

"No. Sahib will *not* ride horse, Gorawalla, take your
beastly horse on ahead—and start now!"

Reluctantly Gorawalla led the horse away up the track.
I rested in the shade of an apricot tree, watching some
stonechats building in a terrace wall. The coolies had got
their clay pipe bowl alight and were passing it from one
to another, squatting on their hunkers and coughing violently after each drag. I could see they were set for the
afternoon.

Gorawalla now had a good ten-minute start, so I started
to follow. A bird burst from a cliff beside a stream, and
I found its nest with four speckled eggs under a tuft of
dry grass. A little farther on, in a clump of dead cedars,
a party of minivets were playing from branch to branch
like red and yellow butterflies. One could not wish for
anything better than this in heaven.

When I came up toward the crest of the spur I heard

31

the jingle of a horse's bridle, and there was Gorawalla again. He was sitting on a rock waiting for me and contemplating a breakneck flight of rough steps that led several hundred feet down to a village.

"Sahib wants to get on horse now?"

"No. Are you crazy?"

"Sahib, you do not understand. All coolies very sad; when entering a village they like to be servants of Barra Sahib—Bit Sahib—who rides a horse."

So that was it. How little I had understood the minds of these people. They did not want the horse to help with their loads but only to increase their importance in the eyes of the other villagers. Keeping up with the Joneses.

"All right, Gorawalla, I ride—but only into villages—and *not* down those steps."

At that moment my coolies arrived. A chorus of "Sahib ride," echoed on the path.

It now became a challenge to my nerve—dare I ride down those steps? I am the world's worst horseman, and it did not look as if the horse could go down them alone, and certainly not with me on its back.

"Sahib," said Gorawalla, sensing the reason for my hesitation, "we will hold you on. Horse very strong horse."

I now had no excuse. The pony was brought into position on the path and stood there hanging its head, as if it knew what was in store for it. I felt a very brotherly sympathy.

I examined the saddle with a sinking heart. As I have said, it was made of wood, fastened by two rope girths and a bit of string tied under the animal's tail. The stirrups were just loops of rope which would be necessary to keep my feet from trailing on the ground. "Well, here goes!" I thought.

I swung a leg over and lowered my weight carefully onto the creature's back. Its spine went down about six inches, it gave a resigned sigh and broke wind loudly.

"Very fine horse, Sahib," said Gorawalla with pride. He grabbed my feet and thrust them quickly into the string loops. I had no chance to change my mind. He gave the horse a smart slap on the backside, the horse quivered and began to descend the steps.

It was worse than I had imagined. I was at the pony's mercy. If it slipped, I would never be able to disentangle myself and we should both roll down to the bottom. The flight was so steep that my feet were already opposite the horse's nose, and between them I could see the up-turned faces of the villagers who had come out to witness the arrival of this important sahib.

For about a dozen steps all went well, the horse lowering itself down each step with a horrified grunt. Then the tail string snapped. In a moment the saddle slid over the horse's head. I grabbed its tail and yelled for Gorawalla.

As my retinue came running, I managed to get one foot out of the string loop and slid off the horse's neck, but before I could get my other foot free he started on down the steps again. The only thing I could do was hop. This made it a somewhat unorthodox entry into the village. The strange technique of the important sahib was watched with grave interest, and it did not seem to surprise anyone in the least.

Throughout the day we pressed on toward the shining mountain. Much of the reason for climbing is in looking at such a fabulous cathedral, which carries the eye upward and upward. It towers above the clouds, promising sunlight when the rest of the world is dark if only you can reach its top.

By evening, after negotiating some awe-inspiring cliffs and mile-long flights of steps—down which I did not ride—we had come to a village in the shadow of the Cow's Mouth. There were a few ragged terraces and some very dirty and poor homes. I do not know how the pony came

33

over some of the places, but it did, although even today I have seen no Himalayan path to equal this one.

This was a high village, with a singing wind, and to a man the people had a most extraordinary cast of feature, the same heavy faces as some sort of Balkan brigand. They looked morose and untrustworthy. Moreover, these men gave the impression of being wider than they were tall. The village smelled like a very dirty stable.

I was invited to sleep in the village but preferred cleaner air and camped on a terrace about a quarter of a mile away. After the coolies had built a large fire and collected a reserve of wood, I sent them away into the village so that I might enjoy the evening stillness alone. They seemed reluctant to leave me and together with the headman, made repeated efforts to persuade me to sleep in the houses. However, I could not understand them or the reason for their concern. They kept repeating certain dialect words I did not know and pointing into the shadows of the Cow's Mouth. It was a dark crevice from which came the full-throated roar of a waterfall. Maybe they feared a ghost.

I cooked and ate my supper of beans. Darkness came; the stars were bright and the ice on Nanda Kot shone white in the moon. The fire crackled and the river roared and everything was filled with the peace of a mountain night. As usual, I had an attack of the blues. My liver still ached like a dull coal and morbidly told me that decay was the end to all our hopes. That partings and old age were waiting for us all. In such a mood it was best to sleep and to remember that, though spirits always droop with the night, they rise next day with the sun.

It was my first bed on the hard ground; it was cold, the silent cold of slow freezing, and I did not have enough blankets. I lay and listened to the waterfall, while the fire died down to red embers.

Then I heard it, a peculiar cough from the direction

34

of the Cow's Mouth. For a moment I accepted it as normal, as one accepts the soft foot on the stair at midnight. Then I was wide awake, ears straining. *One should be alone in the house!*

And again that hard cough, but nearer. I wanted to pull the blankets over my head, only this was no child's nightmare but a nightmare come true. Now I knew what the village people had been trying to tell me. A tiger was making its way up from the river.

It is a good thing that this episode occurred before I had read the late Colonel Corbett's thrilling book, *Maneaters of Kumaon*, because this *was* Kumaon. I should have learned that tigers are not afraid of a fire, and I should no doubt have beaten all records into the village. As it was, I got up and threw a great pile of wood onto the embers. Then I returned to my bed.

Although my mind now told me (wrongly) that I was safe because of the blaze at the tent door, for the next half hour I suffered every imaginable fright. The coughing approached and circled my camp twice. Occasionally there would be a quiet growl, leaving me in no doubt that my identification had been correct. But this tiger could not have been a man-eater, for at length its coughs began to recede into the distance until the world of sound was again dominated only by the roar of the waterfall.

Shortly after this a party of villagers and some of my coolies came up from the village. They carried blazing torches. An arm thrust back the tent flap.

"Sahib is all right?"

"Yes."

"We sleep by your fire, Sahib. Not good here . . ."

In spite of their appearance these villagers were good fellows after all, and just how good I was not to know till next morning.

The thought of the rocks and snow-filled gullies ahead was not so attractive to my coolies as it was to me. There was no established route, and the villagers had been filling them with terrifying stories of the conditions they would meet higher up and so early in the year. Half of them were determined to go home, even though it meant losing their return pay. Perhaps they were right.

The problem, however, was soon solved by the villagers, who offered to replace the wet spirits among my own men and to guide me into the next valley, where I could regain the usual route. But they absolutely refused to cross the country above the Cow's Mouth, and I had to give way on that.

The ridge I crossed in company with these "Balkan brigands" was memorable for the enormous horseflies that bit them till the blood ran down their legs. Strangely enough, they let me alone, perhaps because I did not smell quite so much like a horse.

It was a long day, but when we reached the gorge all fatigue was forgotten in wonder. Huge walls of mustard-colored rock rose on either side, with here and there waterfalls descending in a fine spray. The wet rocks were covered with thick moss. On both sides of the stream the floor of the gorge was blocked with snow, yet the rhododendron bushes were covered with scarlet flowers, startling against the white background. Here at last I found the birds of my imagination, the birds of blue and gold which darted up as we disturbed them and sailed away over the river. It was only afterward I learned that they were the famous Monaul pheasants, beautiful as any peacock.

I was surprised to find that the hut was occupied. My men told me a yogi was up here, spending the winter in meditation. I could not imagine a more perfect place for the purpose, and I was thrilled because this at last must be the real thing. Perhaps I should see and learn some of the wonders of the East that I had read about. How to stop my heart. How to swallow a bandage and clean my inside out like a rifle with a pull-through. How to sit naked in the snow.

To my disappointment the coolies told me that the yogi was meditating and could not be disturbed, so I turned my immediate attention to making arrangements for a visit to the glacier. Once more the men would not come with me, and neither would the chokidar, the official guide and caretaker of the hut. Indeed, this man was voluble in his efforts to dissuade me from going any farther. The path, he said, was impassable because of snow and ice; it was dangerous and quite out of the question. He was furious when I did not take his advice, but found a shepherd from the district who was not so prudent and who agreed to come at least as far as he could.

This shepherd was a gay young fellow wearing a rather nice felt blanket, white and bound with green wool. The blanket was looped up with a giant safety pin in a special way to make a coat. It was his only garment, but it looked warm. What was not so good was that his feet were bare. However, he assured me that bare feet on snow were nothing to him, and indeed, his feet looked as leathery as the pads of a huskie.

It was a long, hard day to the glacier. In places the debris of old avalanches lay across the track, and we had to clamber over them, but there were no serious difficulties and we neither saw nor heard anything fall. All was silent and in the grip of winter. There was no sound but the crunch of our feet in the snow.

We had reached the moraine by lunch time and, leaving my guide with the packs, I continued up onto the glacier. It was a steep glacier, what a mountaineer would call an icefall, which led up to Trail's Pass, a difficult climber's pass that had been crossed once or twice. Above towered Nanda Kot. I sat down and for half an hour enjoyed the success of my first pilgrimage. It is a wonderful feeling to achieve something, however modest, that you have

37

wanted all your life, especially when you have nobody there to say, "This is nothing," or "Wait until . . ." but just a quiet triumph on your own.

When we got back to the hut, my poor shepherd complained that the soles of his feet were sore. How can a man walk barefoot on snow and ice for seven hours and have any feet left at all? I gave him some ointment and put my supper on to boil. Then one of my coolies came in.

I was thrilled by his bringing a message from the mysterious yogi. He would be glad if I would pay a visit. Now at last I would see? It would be a fitting climax to my journey.

By the time I had had a plateful of stew and warmed my feet it was dark, and I could peep in at the holy man through the window. He was an impressive sight, seated cross-legged on his bed, his long hair hanging loose over his shoulders, but I was disappointed to see he was wrapped in a blanket. I was about to retire again, as I did not wish to disturb his meditations, but his door was a little ajar and he must have heard me.

"Come in, old chap," he shouted in a too-too perfect Oxford accent. "You haven't by any chance got some aspirin, have you? I've got the most frightful cold . . ."

There was of course no logical reason why a yogi should not have either an Oxford accent or a cold, yet it was like expecting a letter and finding a bill. It was even more disillusioning when this obviously well-educated man started trying to peddle lucky charms. I should have suspected him of being a phony if I could have comprehended why, if this were so, he was here at all, away from a gullible public and in a hut where it was the merest chance that he had seen anyone except local shepherds during the whole winter.

I spent the rest of the evening talking to him. If I could not understand his motives for being here, neither could he understand mine. He had, he explained, spiritual reasons for braving the rigors and dangers of this *dreadful* Himalayan winter, but I . . . ?

"Why didn't you spend your leave in the club at Ranikhet, old chap?" To him it was obviously the height of decadent amusement—what he himself would have enjoyed most if he had been a sinful man. He did not understand that for me two hours in a gymkhana club would be the most dreadful penance, while on the contrary this journey into the mountains had been the greatest fun imaginable, as well as being a kind of pilgrimage to satisfy one of my boyhood dreams.

I returned to this area twice more, and on the last occasion I again visited the hut and looked up my old note in the visitor's book.

"Major Stobart is a liar," said the entry under mine in only slightly more polite terms. "He could *not* have reached the Pindar Glacier so early in the year. The chokidar of the hut himself told us he never got near it. He says it is quite impossible at this season."

Still? I felt like Galileo chucking bricks off a tower.

chapter 4

ROY WAS a Yorkshireman, with a grip like a pipe wrench, of which he was very proud. He entered for the Delhi point to point without ever having been over a jump in his life—and finished third. We used to climb on the ruins of the old forts and dream of something bigger.

When the war ended and we were due to go home, we wanted to leave but we wanted an expedition even more. At last it seemed possible, though the equipment was makeshift and poor.

Roy had once glimpsed a ferocious 23,000-foot peak in Ladakh, the province next to Kashmir. It was called Nun Kun and was the highest in the province and still unclimbed. We decided to go for it for a last fling. It was also to be my first attempt with a mountain film, and for the first time it was to be in color.

Nun Kun was a ten-day walk from the nearest road, and in some pretty wild country, so of course we had to take everything with us. It was not easy to get stores, but we managed to chisel assistance from both the Indian and U.S. armies. This was a Godsend, because at first I had tried to make dried food by putting it in the sun, with disastrous effects on my stomach.

Medical supplies were also provided by the Army through a doctor friend, and I even spent three days at the hospital learning how to use them.

One evening when I was going over the medicine chest

shortly before our departure, Roy suddenly introduced the subject of teeth.

"Whatever else we take," he said, "we must have a pair of dental forceps. The hill people have bad teeth, and I think I shall be good at pulling them out." He flexed his bone-breaking fingers, and I had visions of cracking jaws and snapped-off roots. I decided then and there that on no account would we take dental forceps. We would all get our teeth checked before we left.

Unfortunately, the third member of our party, a friend of Roy's, came down with paratyphoid a few weeks before we were to leave. We hastily advertised for a substitute through the Himalayan Club and were put in touch with a major somewhere up on the North-West Frontier. His name was Ralph. On paper, he seemed just right, a tough ski instructor from the Middle East school of mountain warfare, but there was no chance to meet him. We signed him on unseen, a rash thing to do, as human relations are notoriously tricky at high altitudes, but we had no choice.

As I was being demobilized and had indefinite leave, I went off in advance to Srinagar to complete the arrangements. Ladakh, though politically part of Kashmir, was geographically more similar to Tibet, and mountaineering expeditions were not allowed to operate in the province without special permission. We had applied for this some months ago and, having had no reply, we had assumed it was granted. One of my first tasks was to check this. To my horror, I found that the permission had been refused, but no one had bothered to tell us. We had already organized the Army trucks to take our stores to the road-head, and our three Sherpas had started from Darjeeling. It was impossible to change the plans at such short notice, and we were in a spot. After walking up and down the edge of the lake, looking longingly at the mountains and cursing the administration, I decided we should have to take a chance. With luck nobody would discover our destination until it was too late. True, the first few days of our journey would lie along the telegraph line, but once we had cleared the main trade route to Leh we could ignore all but the most determined efforts to bring us back.

On the fourth evening I went up to the expedition rendezvous and was relieved to find that our months of planning had actually borne fruit. There were the trucks piled high with our boxes. Everything had arrived, including the cans of bully beef which we had had to smuggle through the customs—Kashmir was a Hindu state in which the eating of beef was forbidden. It is a great moment on any expedition when you enjoy anticipation without yet feeling impatient.

Ralph, the unknown quantity, had arrived. He turned out to be a brawny redheaded Devonian. I liked him very much, but I could see that he was a fiery character and not given to compromise. I wondered how he would get on with Roy. It was curious that I never worried how *I* would get on with them.

There was another newcomer, but I cast a doubtful eye on him. Roy's colonel had gone back to England and had asked him to look after a black Labrador. This dog's name was Bob, and he was bounding excitedly around the truck. I like dogs but was not sure it was wise to take one on our expedition. It seemed likely he would come to a sticky end.

The three Sherpas from Darjeeling (at the other end of the Himalayas) had also arrived, and since it was the first time I had ever seen them, I was goggle-eyed with admiration. They looked so strong and cheerful, and they radiated confidence. The first one's name was Tenzing, not the Tenzing who reached the top of Everest, but an earlier Tenzing whose feats on Everest were almost as remarkable. He was also an expert skier, a very unusual accomplishment for a Sherpa. Ralph immediately grabbed

43

him for his *personal* Sherpa. Tenzing was a fine man, and it is sad that a few years later he died of dysentery when on a very simple treck in Sikim, but that is so often the way.

Our second Sherpa was Gyaljen, nowadays a well-known sirdar. He had been on many expeditions—including Everest; he was exceptionally intelligent and spoke some English. I took him to act as my camera assistant, leaving Roy to manage with Saki, who was then on his first expedition and an unknown quantity. This Saki, brother of the Everest cook Thondup, later greatly distinguished himself on Annapurna. He was the strongest Sherpa I have ever met, and his grip was even stronger than Roy Berry's. Perhaps that is why Roy liked having him as his personal batman.

The following morning we drove up to the end of the road, unloaded our gear onto the grass, and collected pony men for the next day. It had begun.

The valley was like a valley in Switzerland, with short green turf, pine forests, and sunlit ice peaks rising up beyond. The houses were of wood, and there was some new building going on. We used a half-finished house as our shelter for the night.

Although the laden pony train moved at a leisurely pace along the valley floor, from the very moment of starting I had begun to experience the strain of filming an expedition. Gyaljen and I would walk fast for half an hour to get well ahead of the main party. We would select a viewpoint, unpack the rucksack, set up the tripod and camera, then wait for the train to come in sight. There was usually not long to wait; in fact, we often had to rush to be ready in time. As soon as the caravan had passed, we would pack up at frantic speed and then race on to get ahead once more. The whole process was repeated over and over again all day, and it was awfully hard work. After the

44

first hour I did not see how I should possibly manage on the mountain.

The river ran beside the path, wonderful milky-green glacier water. Spur after spur of pines curved down into the valley, and it was around one of these, while rushing to catch up, that I came upon our first mishap.

The dog Bob had been particularly happy, barking around the ponies' legs and fetching sticks and stones; but unknown to us, Bob was a sheep killer and had got in among a flock with lambs. Before anyone could stop him he had committed murder several times over. Roy was now beating him furiously with an ice ax. "I'll teach you to kill sheep . . ." But when he let go, Bob, not in the least penitent, raced off up the mountainside and disappeared into the forest. We dipped heavily into our small purse to pay for the damage. Then we hung around calling Bob for hours, but he did not come back. At length we sadly had to continue without him, instructing a local shepherd to catch and feed him. We never saw the poor dog again, and if he did come back, perhaps they killed him. We were not yet in Bhuddist country.

Our first pass was the Zoji La, 13,000 feet and dangerous under winter snow. It was melting, and the riverbanks of ice had collapsed in many places and dammed the torrent. The ponies slipped and rolled on their backs. The stocky drivers shouted and fought with the wildly plunging animals, and loads fell off and had to be tied on again. Being a pony man here was not a career to encourage a placid temperament.

The telegraph poles straggled over this barren pass, the only sign left of the civilized world, and they made the place seem even more desolate by their easily severed link with the outside, just as at home the wires singing on a moorland road do not diminish but add to the loneliness. But that telegraph and its wires had another significance for us. Even now a message might be flashing past with

45

an order to turn us back, and we should not feel secure until we left this main trade route.

Below us as we came down the far side, lay Ladakh, called "Little Tibet," and the landscape was barren and bitter, the mountains being desert mountains like those on the moon. It was no longer pines and meadows as in Kashmir, but harsh and ugly. A party of little men, outriders of Genghis Khan for sure, were resting by the track. Their ponies cropped the short brown grass. They had come from God knows where to the north. Nobody understood their speech. They smiled under their thin Chinese mustaches, and that was all the contact we ever had. But it made us turn and look with excitement at the yellow rocks and terraces of the river Indus, because it was a strange land and we had the traveler's itch.

The sun came out and beat down on our bare arms and burned them fiery red. We felt feverish, and huge blisters came up, which we plastered with gentian violet cream till we looked like ancient Britons in woad. If we were bright blue for the next month, what matter? There was nobody to mind what we wore or how we looked— not a care in the world.

Dras consisted of a few houses and terraces in the bottom of the valley. It had a post office and telegraph, so it was a danger point. We wanted to break away over the Umba La to the south, and the sooner the better. The headman had other ideas. He said it was too early in the year to cross the pass. We said people had already done it that year and produced a man who had. But what he really wanted was a cut, and he said it would cost us a lot of money. We said we didn't have a lot of money. We were at a deadlock.

Several times Roy, who was a good negotiator, took the headman aside and nearly reached agreement, but redheaded Ralph would always wander up and, in his best Urdu, call the headman an obstructive bastard, which was quite true. Then he would poke him in the stomach with his ice ax. This would shift the squabble to one between Roy and Ralph, while the headman would fly off in a huff. In order to resume negotiations, we had to raise the bidding. I realized I'd have my work cut out for me, keeping peace between these two fire-eaters.

While this aggravating delay was in progress, the local headmaster invited us to inspect his school. He said proudly that he held classes in agriculture, a new thing, and showed us a hovel containing one moth-eaten chicken in a box. We could not laugh because it was really tragic, but we did laugh at the mass drill of the physical training class. The children had been taught to stand on their heads, but since their clothing consisted of a belted felt coat, felt boots, and no pants, the effect was rather surprising.

The Umba La was a 15,000-foot pass leading south out of the valley. We set off in high spirits, clambering up the hillside above the river. It was hot, and the coolies moved slowly, stopping frequently to rest and smoke their clay pipes. Nobody seemed in any hurry except ourselves. We were relieved to be leaving the dangerous telegraph at last. We had defeated the headman, but we could imagine with what joy he would have fetched us back, and we wanted to be well away.

The first warning of a change in the weather came as we rested beside some twisted rock pinnacles, a breath of cold wind which turned our sweating into shivers. It was followed by a cloud streaming over the ridge. Only an hour later we were in a blinding snowstorm. We came out beside a snow cornice on the top of the ridge and could see nothing at all, only a wilderness of white. Maps were not accurate and therefore the compass was useless. We waited for the coolies to catch up. Meanwhile I wanted

47

to take some shots, but the camera was covered with snow. I had not yet learned how to handle such a situation.

The head coolie came staggering through the mesh of whirling flakes and said he knew the ground blindfold, so we put him in the lead. For two hours we plodded on, seeing only the back of the man ahead of us. Then we descended a steep slope into a hollow. We had apparently reached the camping site, but it did not look any different from anyplace else in this storm—just snow and more snow.

Our Sherpas pitched the tents, every tent we had, yet it was quite obvious that not *all* our coolies could get into them. It seemed impossible that anyone could remain outside all night in this blizzard and survive, even though hillmen must often be faced by similar situations in their daily lives; but there was nothing we could do—not even go back.

We asked Tenzing to investigate, and presently he poked an ice-plastered head through the flap. "Sahibs, there are eight in the two-man tent, and twenty in the big tent. The rest have crawled into cracks in the cliff."

"They'll be dead by morning in this, poor fellows."

All night long the wind scratched and worried the canvas. It was bitterly cold, and my teeth chattered in spite of a good sleeping bag. I could not sleep, but lay worrying about the coolies, crouched in the rocks, without even a blanket, no protection except their clothes to keep them alive. It was one of those few occasions when there is something to be said for a comfortable villa and a warm-blooded wife.

By morning all was silent, as silent as the world can be only when damped by new snow. Looking through the tent door, I could see only mounds of white where the other tents were supposed to be, and the walls of the little corrie which had protected the campsite were smothered in ice flowers.

"Ahoy," and the startled echo came back from the cliffs,

48

"Ahoy." The mound of our Sherpas' tent stirred, and Saki stumbled out. Saki being the youngest, the older hands had thrown him out to do the chores. He got his own back though, rousing the coolies by bashing the outside of their tents with an ice ax. Since they were so tightly crowded, each thump was bound to hit someone, and their tents began to writhe like a pantomime horse with a wasp inside. The tents contained no dead or suffocated, but what of those who had spent the night in the crevices? There was still no sign of them.

Our head coolie went off to search. The sun had come up, and we were anxious either to get away or to know if they were dead. We watched as he moved round the crag, poking at the snow in the deeper gullies. They disgorged slow-moving, stupefied men, as torpid from the cold as hedgehogs in winter but, amazingly, still alive and quite unharmed. It was an astonishing exhibition of the toughness of men who had never in all their lives had enough to eat, yet could humble any prime-steak-fed American when it came to sheer physical hardness and endurance.

In front was a wide snow-filled valley leading up to the final col of the Umba La. Before each pile of boulders was a space stamped in the new snow, and on this sat a marmot, sunning himself and waiting for the heat to melt the cloth that was covering his breakfast.

Marmots are a good armful in size, with an expression that must have been designed by a cartoonist, rabbit teeth like a dentist's nightmare, and a bottom really designed for comfortable sitting. They are without doubt the most annoying animals in the world.

Going up a valley of marmots is like walking a pretty girl perpetually past U. S. Army barracks. Each marmot, with an expression of fatuous surprise on its face, comments in turn by a wolf's whistle. Then he shouts to the next marmot up the valley. "Hey, fellahs, come and see what's passing the door. Never saw nothin' like that before," and his friend answers, "Whew! Whew! You and me both."

We reached the top of the pass in the late afternoon. It was about the height of Mount Blanc, and we were beginning to slow up from the altitude and the hot sun; but we eagerly pushed up the last slope, for we hoped to get our first glimpse of Nun Kun. All we saw was a steep slope covered with loose shale and a maze of rock, snow, and barren valleys beyond, but still no sign of our goal.

chapter 5

I HAD never seen a mountain that looked so awe-inspiring as Nun Kun. We finally saw it as we came around a corner in the valley, and as more and more of the ridge came in sight we expected every moment that it must stop. Surely that mass of ice running upward must reach a point and start coming down again? But no; as we came farther and farther around the corner, it continued to soar upward and upward to a height that outstepped imagination. It looked so big and so dwarfed its neighbors that suddenly all the mountains we had been admiring became mere hills. Nun Kun gathered its own clouds around it which blew with jagged edges among the spikes of rock. It looked about as comfortable as a fakir's bed of nails, and these cold northern precipices, the ones with the least sun and the most ice, looked quite impossible to climb. We prayed the southern side would be more accommodating. So this was the chosen antagonist that we had come so far to meet.

Roy was especially delighted that night when he saw a flock of pigeons on the rocks above our camp. We had been on the march for eight days, long enough to get bored with our canned food.

"Go and get the gun, Tom," he called down to me. "We'll have pigeon pie tonight—I can almost taste it already."

"You bloody cannibal," I shouted back. However, I

51

got the gun and crept quietly up. "Shall I have a go or will you?" I whispered.

"You," said Roy, "if you are quite certain you won't miss."

"I certainly won't."

We needed at least two pigeons for a stew, and at that moment one flew down and joined a friend on top of a a boulder well within range. With any luck I could get two in one shot.

Just as I drew a bead, Ralph came walking back from a wash in the stream.

"What are you doing?" he shouted.

We both turned around, putting our fingers to our lips. "Hush," Roy pointed at the pigeons.

"You can't shoot a sitting bird, old boy," said Ralph, putting down his towel and coming toward us.

"Can't we?" said Roy. "This isn't sport, it's supper."

"You still can't shoot a sitting bird—it isn't done."

"Stop arguing, you'll scare the birds, and then . . ."

I understood both points of view, but with supper in the balance it was no time for argument. I once saw two friends stop to argue whether the place they were in was dangerous instead of first getting the hell out of it. On that occasion the argument was stopped (and settled) by a falling stone.

"If you can be sure of hitting the birds, you take the gun. I'll clap to put them up."

Ralph took the gun and tried the aim several times. "All right," he said.

I clapped. At first they took no notice, but then they rose with a clatter like carrier pigeons released from a station platform.

Bang, went the first barrel, *bang* the second. A few feathers drifted down to earth, but the pigeons flew on and away up the mountainside. There was a pregnant silence.

Over our bully beef that night Roy and Ralph were

almost at blows once more, now on the question of sporting conventions. "The moral is that either you shoot for fun or you shoot for the pot, unless you are good enough to . . ."

"The moral's here," said Roy, "bloody bully beef again in the pot."

"Well, anyway, it just isn't done," said Ralph, "so that's that!"

We reached Suru and took a day to pay off our coolies and recruit a gang of local men for the mountain. We camped near the lonely grave of a British officer who had been murdered there many years before. A little stream ran across the meadow, and we could hear the creaking of the looms of the weavers at work in a nearby house. The cloth was put in the stream to make the beautiful felt the people used for boots and coats. The weaver was paid in food, but everybody spun his own yarn, using a simple spindle and spinning as he walked or rested, as unconscious as a public-library addict at her knitting. There was usually a group watching us and spinning at the same time.

Our new coolies were as wild as brigands, tall men with black or hennaed beards, and ungainly in their long felt robes and turbans. They did not look the type for a mountain, but the few people who had passed spoke highly of their loyalty and toughness.

The first explorer of this range seems to have been an American woman, Fanny Bullock Workman, whose *Peaks and Glaciers of Nun Kun* is a classic. Followed by her husband and a bevy of Swiss and Italian guides, this incredible woman had climbed to over 21,000 feet in a long tweed skirt and a motoring veil. Local men spoke of her with awe and hinted that when the coolies flagged, she beat them with her ice ax. They still referred to her as "The Memsahib." I do not know whether all the stories

53

they told about her were true or not, but she had certainly become a legend in the district. It conjured up a wonderful picture of a more robust age when Aunt Agatha busted policemen with her umbrella and my mother hit a cabby in the streets for mistreating a horse.

Our head coolie, who had been one of Fanny's porters as a boy, agreed to see that we at least reached her old base camp in the Shafat Nalla. This was a large glacier trench that curved around the east side of Nun Kun and gave access to the south face. From here it was possible to reach the strange ice plateau, on the rim of which the mountain stands. It was not sure that the local men would go farther than that. We hoped that at least some of them would, although they were not properly equipped for high altitudes and we had little extra equipment to spare.

Beyond Suru the track crossed the river by a wickerwork suspension bridge. In Himalayan travel such bridges are commonplace but this was something special. The river was quite wide, making two dry stone towers necessary to carry the cables. Each cable was a foot thick and was composed entirely of twisted willow branches. Making these cables at all was a major piece of engineering, let alone getting them into place across the rapids.

The bridge creaked like a dirty clothes basket. We felt that such a structure would not be replaced until it actually fell down, and it was possible—nay, probable—that this moment had been reached. Perhaps the extra weight of a six-footer would prove the final straw. . . . And I had reason to be allergic to bridges.

I once took a girl for a walk in Switzerland and came on a derelict bridge above a waterfall.

"ACHTUNG. Einsturzgefahr. Ubergang verboten," said a notice. I ignored it and nipped smartly across.

"How rude you are," said the girl when she had joined me, "going first and not waiting for me; you might have helped me over."

"I went first to test it—and I didn't want two on at once. The notice said . . ."

"I know what the notice said—but you are just making excuses . . . selfish, inconsiderate . . ."

There are few times that we can settle an argument with a woman by proving it—and how can you *prove* a bridge is dangerous? Far easier a dishonest kiss! But in this case we were both due a lesson, for when we came back an hour later the bridge was no longer there. We looked down the hundred-foot face and then at each other. We had been the last across.

Roy had complained of a toothache for the last two days, now he was in agony; his face was swelling and he obviously had an abscess. By the time we got into camp that night his face was so swollen that we all knew he would have to go back. He had stuck it out longer than most men would have, and only the most terrible pain could have forced him to give up without even setting foot on the mountain. It was such a bitter disappointment that both Ralph and I could not have stomached going on without him, even if we could have allowed him to return alone. The whole expedition appeared to have foundered. There was a certain irony in the fact that I had not brought dental forceps because of Roy's sadistic urge to pull teeth.

"Look, Roy," I said at length, "if I can raise some pincers from the village, are you willing for me to have a go at getting it out?"

"Yes, for God's sake try anything," he moaned.

We sent Tenzing to the nearest village to see what he could find in the way of implements. In the meantime, seeking refuge in ordinary chores, I went to see about our supper and how Abdul the cook was organized. Abdul had been with the Germans on Nanga Parbat and was a character; a large, weather-beaten old fellow, his white beard red with henna. His passion in life was a most revolting tea, which was like blood and made by boiling the leaves in washing soda. It is a drink comparable to the one the Australian tramps drink, which is made with methylated spirits, Brasso and Brown boot polish—one can only remove one's hat reverently to the man who thought of it.

"Abdul," I said, "I am going to try to pull Berry Sahib's tooth out. We need plenty of boiling water."

"*Hazoor*," said Abdul, as if it were an everyday event.

The only gadget that Tenzing could find in the village was a fearsome pair of pincers, which he had borrowed from the local blacksmith. They were hand-forged, about a foot long, and covered with filth. The very sight of them gave Roy a fit, and me too, but we had nothing else. We scraped them with a rough stone and then thrust them into the fire to roast the bacteria out of their holes. With Roy leaning against a boulder and groaning, myself holding the red-hot pincers, the scene was reminiscent of a medieval torture tableau in Tussaud's chamber of horrors.

Before leaving on the expedition I had learned how to treat such things as frostbite and pneumonia, and I had a few tubes of morphine, the kind that resembled toothpaste tubes with a spike on one end and were issued to tank crews. I knew that these contained a knockout dose and that morphine slowed the breathing. I knew that Roy would need something to stand the pain, but we were at over 16,000 feet, and what was morphine's effect up here? I doubted if even the doctors would know. Roy was a strong fellow, so I decided that half a tube would probably help him and not kill him, so with a short prayer I shot the dose into his arm and waited for the drug to take effect.

It was a tense moment, with all eyes on the patient. Ralph stood ready with his camera. The cook stood ready with the boiled water. The Sherpas and some of the village watched.

56

I expected that the morphine would take effect in about fifteen minutes, but Ralph was of another opinion.

"You shoot that stuff into people, and they pass out immediately," he said. "That's how you get the wounded out of tanks. Your stuff can't be any good. Must be old."

"All right, come on, let's get it over with," mumbled Roy, whose face was by now as big as a pumpkin.

I lit a cigarette to steady my nerves and held the pincers up to cool. "Forget Roy's yells," I said to myself; "just take your time and don't break the tooth. Loosen it first and then pull."

At the first touch Roy shrank away with a cry, but stalwart Abdul was standing behind. He seized Roy's head and held it in place against a stone so he couldn't move. I got the pincers gripping the tooth, wiggled, wiggled, twisted, and pulled. It came out suddenly like a cork out of a bottle and in one piece. The next moment Roy, white as a sheet, was spitting out blood on the grass.

After he had drunk a cup of tea, we helped him toward his tent to lie down. On the way the morphine took effect and he passed out. "So we should have waited after all," I said to Ralph. Roy is really going to love you when he comes to."

But Roy was too thankful when he woke up two hours later. The swelling was going down, he had no more pain, and he was happy. We retrieved his tooth from the grass. "I'm keeping this as a souvenir of the expedition," he said. "I'll show it to my dentist when I get home."

chapter 6

T H E river had cut across the snout of the glacier, sec-
tioning it in a great ice cliff. Farther on there was a patch of
winter snow forming a bridge. We decided to cross this
in case the river was unfordable higher up. But now,
having left the path, we found traversing the slopes along
the north side of the mountain was tough going. There
was no sign of a track, and we had to find our own way
over a maze of boulders. Occasionally in the mist we saw
above us the openings of ice-plastered corries—wicked
places dropping from the edge of the plateau.

In the middle of this aggravating country it began to
rain. Sometimes one can enjoy plodding on, dog-tired and
soaked, enjoy the smell of wet clothes and the memories
they bring back of other wet days, even enjoy the dogged-
ness and the thought of a fire and supper at the end (if
you can get a fire to light)—but this was not one of those
times. It was infuriating, soaking steadily all day, and it
was poor consolation when it stopped before supper. We
had dried our gear the day before, but now everything
was mortally damp again. We made a blaze of juniper
that lit the mountainside—when fuel is wet a fire must be
big—and restored reasonable cheerfulness. Ralph, who
was a determined photographer, even managed to take a
picture by its light as we sat around drinking our nightcap
of cocoa. I only wished that motion pictures were as little
trouble, or even feasible at all under such conditions.

The glacier in the Shafat Nalla which we turned into

59

the following day was terrible. In a thick mist in which everyone got separated and lost we probed carefully into it. Gyaljen and I were completely at sea, and half the time we couldn't even keep contact by shouting, but the only thing was to flounder on. The ice was broken and split into towers and crevasses, the whole covered with stones which skidded about and sent us crashing on our backs at every other step. At last, after the mist cleared a little, we found a campsite on a patch of sand left by the receding ice. The coolies were late, and we had to sit around waiting for them, shivering, shouting at intervals to give direction, like a lighthouse in a fog. It is days like this that one ought to film if one intends giving a true picture of an expedition, but all one's energy is taken up just in coping with it. There is no spare strength for work. It was not until the next day that I steeled myself to photograph the others pitching camp and even drinking tea before I had some myself—the first of many such occasions in my life as an expedition cameraman, only I didn't know it then.

The Memsahib's base camp, still marked by cairns built over thirty years ago, was too far from the mountain, so we moved to a campsite below the peak itself. Here a natural cave had formed between a rock ridge and some ice, and we improved it with blocks of snow to make a sheltered cookhouse for Abdul. During the day there was even a trickle of water running down the wall, which saved us having to melt the ice on a stove, and stoves were our weak point—because of the war we hadn't been able to buy any and had only a few borrowed ones. We further improved things by putting snowballs on the rock where they could be melted by the sun. Having enough water to drink is always a problem where all water is frozen.

We could not see much of the mountain from where we were tucked in below, but from the top of the ridge we could look up at our first objective, a point of ice known as White Needle on the edge of the plateau. This was connected with the main body of Nun Kun by a narrow ridge interrupted by three rock pinnacles known to mountaineers as "gendarmes." Could these be passed? From here they looked just big enough to put your foot on—but they were actually several hundred feet of sheer rock.

On the opposite side of our glacier was an unnamed peak, a spectacular mass of ice cliffs, but much lower than Nun—only 20,000 feet. Behind it stretched a limitless sea of mountains—a hundred miles of country still unexplored and unmapped. Only mountaineers perhaps can know the excitement we felt at being able to start at last.

The way to our second camp turned out to be a weary plod with heavy loads, and the sun was hot. This, combined with the effect of the altitude, now over 18,000 feet, produced a lassitude which required every ounce of guts to beat. Each rest became more welcome; we panted like hounds and sucked snow, but this only gave us a more burning thirst. Each time we started it was like getting up on Monday morning—the disinclination to make a move, the lack of will power, exactly as one had read it in the books.

At the same time I began to experience the completely unenjoyable grind of taking motion pictures at high altitudes. It is not as if you could keep the camera in readiness and hold it in your hands. There are times when the camera can be held; it is the normal for newsreel work, and in more serious films you can get away with it when the action is so violent that the slight shaking is not noticed, or when there is a passage of such tension that defects in photography are overlooked. But mostly the camera has to be steady on a tripod, particularly when the view is important, as in mountains. Moreover, when you are racked with the struggle for air and your body is trembling with effort, you cannot hold it even passably still. You must use a tripod, a clumsy, awkward load, a beast of a contraption that breaks the rhythm when you are trying to conserve strength, spoils the fun, and wastes precious time.

Also at such times each climber is concerned with his own problems and his own body: with the aches in his own legs, his thirst, his dry sore throat, his fight for oxygen. He is unco-operative and in no mood to be kind to a photographer, delayed, directed, or messed about in any way.

Yet you need minutes to get ready for each shot, however fast you are, and this time had to be stolen from the rest periods. I would get away before the others and, with bursting lungs, rush ahead to look for a view. Pull the tripod from the rucksack, open it—I would work feverishly to brush some snow off the lens, check and re-check the settings. And then they would come, plodding and panting past. "Don't look at the camera," I would shout, but someone nearly always did, or the tripod would slip in the snow and I would know I had to try again. Then once more I would have to pack up hurriedly, wrapping the camera, teaching my Sherpa Gyaljen to shut the tripod and stow it securely. By this time the others would be well ahead and I would have to flog myself to catch up; and so it went all day, until we became careless of looking for good viewpoints any more, and finally careless of doing anything more than climb.

We pitched camp on a terrace of snow which we gained after a tussle with a nasty wall of ice-plastered rock that exhausted us. I envied Ralph and Tenzing, who were spending the night up here. I had to escort the other Sherpas back to base.

If I had not been so done up with the filming, I would not have been tempted to make the mistake. It was late and I did not relish that wall. Since no previous explorers of the mountain had remarked on any difficulties on the lower slopes, and coolies would certainly need a fixed rope on it, I thought perhaps there must be another and better route. In fact, the terrace we were camped on sloped temptingly down in the direction we wanted to go, and I recalled a photograph of the Bullock Workman guides moving up what looked like this selfsame terrace. I decided to follow it down instead of returning the way we had come up. Surely there would be some way to get down off this terrace and onto the glacier below. This was all an excuse. It was of course stupid to look for a new route so late in the day, and I knew it.

Everything went well to begin with; the terrace was a natural road and it was simple, just a nicely graded walk on snow. But after following it for an hour I noticed with some concern that it was not taking us as far down the mountain as I should have liked, while clouds were gathering at the foot of the glacier and beginning to move up between Nun Kun and the unnamed peak across the way. If the clouds should cover us at the critical moment when we were looking for a way off the terrace . . .

Bad weather arrived on Nun Kun as unexpectedly as an accident to a child. You could not watch it all the time. Standing high above the surrounding peaks, it seemed to suck the bad weather up in sudden vindictive breaths. Within moments the outlook became dour, black and white like a bad photograph, and a great mushroom of vapor came shooting up the mountain and blotted out everything with a malignant will. At such moments one had no doubt that the mountain was a beast alive.

We groped along the outer edge of the terrace for half an hour. Occasional breaks showed an impossible cliff below. The unnamed sometimes cleared for a second, giving us our bearings, and then silently melted away; but as time went on its appearances became less and less fre-

63

quent, till we were wrapped incessantly in a damp gray shroud.

The terrace ended abruptly. One moment the gently sloping highway was comfortingly ahead, the next there was nothing but a gulf with clammy vapor rising up its ice walls, a nightmare for any man with the least touch of vertigo.

There was nothing to do but to turn aside and begin to probe a way over the edge. The ground steepened, and a ghostly tower loomed up. Then a crack like the man of hell which we had to jump. I guessed we were in an icefall which we had passed beneath earlier in the day and which had looked as unstable as the boxes in Granny's lumber cupboard.

Every time we tried a new line we came to the top of nothing. Part of me was thinking, "This is an adventure, this is what you came for." The other half was paralyzed with anxiety from this white blindness, from the slippery pale green slopes with which we were surrounded—slopes like an upended skating rink one knew went down a long way by the feel of the cold mist rising steadily out of the depths.

After an hour of groping, having made no real progress, my Sherpas had had enough. It was getting late, and a night out would mean severe frostbite, possibly death. To these men, whose living depended on an active body, the first was almost the worst. It was not to be thought about.

"Sahib," said Gyaljen, "we must go back."

"I know," but with sinking spirits I realized that I was too exhausted. I should never make it. Moreover, we could only be a few hundred feet above base. The weary hours of struggle back and up were more than I could face.

In such a crisis ten minutes' rest, a piece of chocolate, and a cigarette make all the difference. We sank down in the snow, wasting the last precious hours of daylight, and yet not wasting them.

64

"Just one more try," I told Gyaljen, "then we go back."

We went over the edge once more at a steeper point and began to work our way down, but once more we came up against an impassable crevasse, yet instead of a drop, the slope on the far side seemed to go on downwards into the mist. We followed its edge for a few yards and there found a small ice bridge by which we could cross. Down, farther down we went, farther than we had managed before. As each new problem was solved, our hopes increased, and also our fears. If we were stopped, even the strong Sherpas would find it hard to return to the camp above.

Then again we were brought up by the edge of an abyss and again the mist rose in our faces out of nowhere. I almost cried with frustration. It was *impossible* for the camp to be far below. Or had we come right past it? We shouted and shouted all together, but were only answered by silence and the cold tingling in the ears.

We looked at each other, and it was not necessary to speak. The Sherpas knew I had got them into a mess, but they did not blame me. "We must get back," said Gyaljen again.

At this moment a miracle happened. The clouds suddenly thinned and rolled away, leaving us bathed in the yellow evening light. The cliffs of the unnamed appeared breathlessly beautiful, powdered with chilly evening diamonds of new snow, but more beautiful to us was the sight of our cookhouse with the rock ridge rising above, and Roy Berry standing there with Abdul gazing up the mountain. They had heard our shouts. Now, with the bandages off our eyes, we could see a clear way down and were soon sucking noisily at bowls of hot soup.

For the remainder of the expedition we used this back-stairs route, and the strange thing was that we used our *exact* route. By chance in the mist we had stumbled on the *only* bridges and the *only* way through the maze.

There was just the one line of weakness in the ice cliffs where it was possible to get down.

The overriding problem of any Himalayan expedition is to get enough material up the mountain, gradually building up to stocking a final camp from which a bid for the summit can be made. These eternal ferrying operations can become very boring. Only the reconnaissances up the mountain ahead of the growing line of camps can be called real fun, and of course the final attempt on the summit.

A few days after my adventure in the mist we again made a leap forward and established Camp III. This was in a hollow at the side of an ice ridge, and level with the edge of the great plateau. Chunks of ice as big as houses kept falling off and crashing down onto the glacier below with a thunder that shook the ground. The altitude was something over 20,000 feet, and already we were level with the top of the unnamed and looking away over the unexplored ridges to the south. We looked triumphantly out like a baby from its mother's neck.

I had been going well up to this, perhaps had been fittest of all, but now it was my turn to get a tearing cough; I felt sick and dizzy, and I could not eat or sleep. At night, hip on the doubtful insulation of a felt pad, I could feel the bitter cold striking upward from the ice. Every spare stitch of clothing had to be packed underneath, then I lay on my arms to keep my body away from the ice. It was like trying to sleep on the marble slab of a morgue. Worst of all, my pulse thumped at the rate of 140 all night, racing with the throttle stuck, and every time a man turned he had to fight with the clinging bag until he lay panting and beat. We had not had enough time to acclimatize.

It seemed clear, moreover, that I had strained myself in trying both to climb and take the film. I came to the conclusion that doing both was hardly possible. I was certainly not strong enough, and I wondered if anyone was.

We did not know it, but our expedition was already in its death throes, and the immediate cause of disaster was the terrible strength of Sherpa Saki. Sherpa Saki was by no stretch of imagination a mechanic, but he made up for it by being willing. When tightening screws, he would go on tightening them with commendable patience until he had stripped the threads. We had taken the precaution of keeping the spanner. We did not guess he could strip threads with his fingers. He now appeared apologetically with the pieces of our last primus stove, looking sheepish. "It came apart in me hands."

Crouched in the tent, I attempted to make repairs by melting lead film containers over a tin of methylated spirit and using it as solder. I knew as I did it that such a make-shift would not possibly work. In the end we had to S.O.S. for wood, which our tough Suru men now brought up three days' journey from the valley. We were reduced to cooking on a biscuit-tin brazier outside the tents, and the fact that the criminal Saki was working out his own punishment by doing this cold job was poor consolation, since most of the time it was impossible even to melt snow for a drink, let alone a hot drink, which is about the only home comfort at 20,000 feet.

I think we all realized at heart that we had failed, but we decided to force our way on as far and as quickly as possible. In our next bound we hoped to establish a camp in the gap between White Needle (which was now directly above us) and the rock pinnacles that guarded the summit ridge. From there a long day *might*, if we could by-pass these pinnacles, take us to the top. It was a slender chance because probably we should need several days to find and prepare a route, but it was our only chance. We did not have the resources or the time for long siege tactics.

Loaded heavily with stores, we set out to find a place for our Camp IV. An ice wall led us onto the ridge. On the far side of this an awe-inspiring couloir funneled down between Nun and White Needle. The fragments of ice we dislodged slithered away into this funnel, accelerating sickeningly and ending up on the glacier several thousand feet below. A serious slip would be fatal, and Saki was getting tangled up in the rope, which he had not yet learned to handle.

Above us were the open slopes of White Needle under new snow and likely to avalanche. Moreover, we were near 21,000 feet, not well acclimatized, and our reserves of strength for an emergency were nil.

In the afternoon the bad weather appeared as usual. One of the mushroom-shaped clouds came wopping up out of the couloir with a growl of wind, and in a moment we were gasping in a blizzard, faces stung with blowing ice crystals. We continued for some time, but we could see nothing, so we were at length forced to camp just where we were on the exposed slopes of the Needle.

I had once been caught in an avalanche and ever since have had a wholesome fear of them. To be overwhelmed in a tent and carried in suffocating folds of sleeping bag down the couloir was a nasty idea. All that night I started up from my sleep whenever there was the roar and tremble of an avalanche, wondering if this was the one with our number on it. Nun felt alive and hostile, determined to drive us back.

It was stupid to feel that a mountain was a living personality, but it was not an idea one could escape. Next morning we retreated back into the abyss from which the clouds still roared up at us without ceasing. Not being one of the rich expeditions that can leave things behind, we staggered under backbreaking loads, pulling everything out in case we should not be able to return.

The fixed rope on the icewall was frozen in, as secure to

68

grip as a slippery snake. My load swung and broke open. The camera fell out, bounding off and coming to rest at the edge of a crevasse a hundred feet below. I looked down at it, hanging on, waiting for help, because I could not move without losing the other gear as well. Roy was coming back up to the rescue, but ever so slowly, panting, cursing. All I could do was wonder what the Army would say about my having smashed their Bell & Howell—it was not a new camera, but costly enough.

Half an hour later we reached the camera and recovered it. It was undamaged, thanks to both stout workmanship and incredible luck. But otherwise we were not happy, for we knew we were beaten. Ralph's leave was nearly up, cooking on wood was impracticable higher up, and the mountain's most formidable defense was still to be overcome. Sadder and certainly wiser men, we decided to throw in our hand. There is only a thing one can say; the sadness does not last, but the wisdom does. For me the foundations had been laid, and in a way Nun was the turning point of my life.

Nun was climbed for the first time the same year as Everest, 1953.

chapter 7

ON THE troopship going home there was ample, boring, overcrowded time to take stock. I had made a number of successful films for the Army—one had been so successful that it had been banned: I had learned about how to make films and something about looking after myself, roughing it, climbing, and travel in foreign lands. Now the job was to unite the two.

I was going back to Dartington Hall to reopen the film unit as producer. I had been away for over six years, and I was looking forward to picking up where I had left off. I realized it was a mistake as soon as I got there, I was grateful for their kindness—it is wonderful to be welcomed and remembered—but the place was full of ghosts. Now it was just sadness to walk through those beautiful gardens. Bill was dead, like so many friends. Others were scattered, others no longer full of fun. The war was no sleep, no gap in life continuing on the other side. It was six years of life gone by, and everything had changed. Even I myself was a different man.

Life nevertheless remains fine so long as you keep some fixed ideas and have things left you want to do—and I wanted above all to make some films about exploration. That was my fixed idea. At Dartington I was making films about agriculture—a subject that for some reason dogs me through life—but that did not mean I could not go on working toward other ends. At least if the chance came, I must be ready.

When I looked at the films I had taken on Nun Kun, I was depressed. Frankly, they were awful. Exposures were all over the place—well, that could be corrected—but worse, the coverage was so incomplete. Hardly any important event had been covered—I had been too tired or too involved. Other times I had regarded the conditions too bad to shoot. And as the final straw, the overheating and damp on the way home had taken the edge off the colors, even on those shots which should otherwise have been good. Reluctantly I came to the conclusion that filming a *real* expedition was probably impossible after all. One would have to organize an expedition especially for a film.

There was one thing I could do at Dartington, and that was study 16-mm. technique. Most professional films were shot on standard 35-mm. cameras, but they were big and heavy. If you could not cover an expedition on 16-mm. film, then certainly you could not with 35-mm. But toward the end of the war some outstanding films had been made in America by enlarging, or "blowing up," 16-mm. color film onto 35-mm. Naturally, to do this the original had to be of impeccable quality, something that most people were not prepared to bother about unless they had a special reason, as I had. Ever since the time I had started with Bill Hunter I had felt this urge to capture things on film as they really are—not staged—and there was this parable, for example between the *candid* photography of the great masters of the Leica miniature camera, and what could be done with a little Hmm! machine. The Leica had also demanded super-careful standards of work to compete in quality with its big brothers. Of course it never could be *quite* as good, but it could be good enough to fool most people, and certainly it scored heavily when it came to catching stuff in a rough-and-tumble. It was the same with 16-mm. Not a dignified medium, but a good one for a peeping Tom.

72

RIGHT: Balu the Bear, cheerful and very hard-working, was one of the bare-footed hillmen of Kumaon. BELOW: On the way to the Pindar Glacier, looking toward the Cow's Mouth and the hills I hoped to cross. Nanda Kot itself is hidden by cloud. Gorawalla, my guide, stands beside his pony, on which I came to grief. See chapter 3.

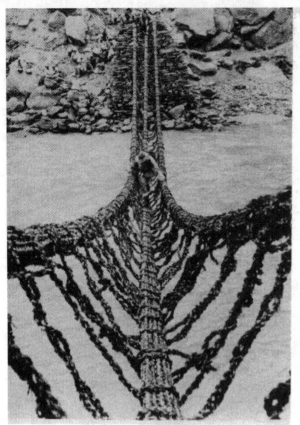

Beyond Suru the track crossed the river by a wickerwork suspension bridge. Each of the three main cables was composed entirely of willow branches and a foot thick; the river's width required two dry stone towers to carry the cables across. The bridge creaked like an old clothes basket. It surely would not be replaced until it fell: perhaps my weight would prove the last straw?

Saki was the strongest Sherpa I have ever met. He was to distinguish himself greatly on Annapurna but when this photograph was taken he was a novice and we were tackling Nun Kun. He wrecked our expedition by stripping, with his strong fingers, the screw threads of our oil stoves.

We had plodded all day in soaking rain. At night, using juniper wood, we got a fire going. With wet fuel we had to have a large fire—and by its light Ralph took this photograph as we drank our cocoa nightcap.

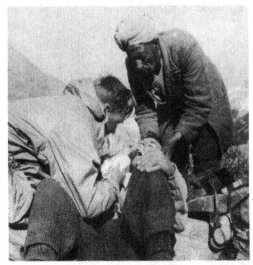

Abdul, the cook, seized Roy's head and held it in place against a stone. I got the blacksmith's pincers gripping the tooth, wiggled, waggled, twisted, and pulled. The tooth came out suddenly in one piece, like a cork from a bottle. Then we found the morphia had not had time to take effect. . . .

In 1946, amid the barren mountains of Ladakh and in that bitter wind, we were not happy. It was stupid to feel that a mountain was a living personality, but here it was an idea one could not escape. The mountain's most formidable defense we had yet to meet. We knew we were beaten.

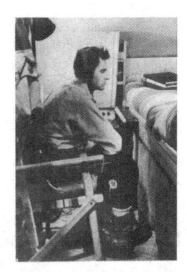

Our Swedish doctor, Ove Wilson, was small and quick, speaking fluent English with an American accent. He was a man I had taken to at sight because he had that speculative intelligence and sense of wonder that make a good companion on an expedition.

John Giaever, our leader, and Captain Guttorm Jakobsen, commanding the *Norsel*. I had met neither previously. Jakobsen is one of Norway's most famous ice pilots, but at our first encounter I took him for the supercargo.

We sighted Bouvet Island, one of the most isolated places in the world, a desolate volcanic cone plastered with ice and sticking out of miles and miles of stormy seas. The spirit of the place was the ever-present albatross, questing endlessly just above the waves, living out life in a world of gray waters and storm.

The islets and caves of this tabular ice bay proclaim it old and eroded.

The 25,000-ton whaling factory ship *Thorshovdi*, on which some of our heavier equipment was brought through the region of storms. The vessel coming toward us is a catcher bringing a whale which will act as a fender when we go alongside the factory ship. You can see the whale's tail but you cannot smell the stench.

The weasels were landed as cold, inanimate metal but, after some heating with blowtorches, started up. To drive in one over the barrier was an experience; it seemed out of place to speed at thirty miles an hour in such a wild region—and at speed the wind bit cruelly. *(Scott Polar Research Institute)*

Norsel in pack ice, which is formed of frozen sea pushed and pulled together by the winds, broken up again by storms, melted and sculptured into a thousand strange shapes.

Picking up S/Ldr. Walford after a reconaissance flight. The plane, fitted either with floats for use on open water or skis to enable it to land on ice, was of very great value for locating "leads" in pack ice and for survey of badly crevassed areas. *(Scott Polar Research Institute)*

The lop of the sea, even in calm weather, caused the rowing boat to pitch appreciably and so made filming difficult. Ice rides deep in the water and so is far more steady at the surface. I got myself landed on a floe and prepared to take pictures.

Under the sheer ice cliffs of the Antarctic Continent we searched for a landing place. Long before we had found one even the huskies were bored. Huskies behave toward human beings as sloppily as lap dogs, but when they pile into a fight their intention is that somebody shall get killed. Fights start easily.

At last, a way ashore: this picture of the *Norsel* was taken from our landing place.

In the African game reserves most of the wild animals are so accustomed to man that even close approach spells little danger. With the rhinoceros it is different; his sight is poor, his power of scent keen, and his temper touchy. If a strange smell annoys him he charges it. I hoped sincerely that I shouldn't be compelled to climb the sheltering thorn tree.

With Armand and Michaela Denis I filmed animals in Africa. I had some very good fun filming Michaela's leopard, and while I did so Duncan B. Whitfield took the picture above. The picture below was taken in Kenya. In African game reserves the lions are lazy; they have long since learned that for them there is no danger in a car; they will look *through* it but won't move from it, even if it drives alongside.

On islands off the Cape of Good Hope penguins and sea lions breed. The island I visited was so crowded it resembled the beach of a holiday resort in a heat wave. The smell of the island was horrid, and the noise, like the bleating of thousands of sheep, continuous. We found that sea lions were more engaging animals than seals; both are intelligent, but the sea lion, with those attractive "Old Bill" whiskers, has a little extra style and personality.

Breakfast halt at Karikola on the approach march to Everest. For once I am in action before the meal is ready. More often I arrived and worked while others ate. *(The Mount Everest Foundation)*

Om mani padme om, decorative Tibetan prayers, cover the boulders. Now you must pass them on the left. ... *(The Mount Everest Foundation)*

Gateway to the Sherpa country: the chortens above Chyangma. *Chortens* are pagodalike towers of stone, often whitened and with eyes painted on them to watch you. As one stands beside them the steady wind rustles in the grass and one's untidy hair; the prayer flags flap like the discarded rags of some tramp caught in the roadside thornbushes. *(The Mount Everest Foundation)*

My Sherpa assistants, Gyaljen (ABOVE) and Sherap (BELOW), without whose help the Everest film could not have been made. (*The Mount Everest Foundation*)

Everest and Lhotse photographed from Thyangboche Monastery. The great mountain appears as a pyramid of rock peeping over the top of the Lhotse-Nuptse wall. The white plumes from the mountaintops are caused by ice dust torn from the mountainside by the roaring, tearing wind. These plumes may extend for twenty miles. *(The Mount Everest Foundation)*

The gateway to Thyangboche. The monastery is claimed to have "the most beautiful situation in the world." *(The Mount Everest Foundation)*

In between my work I often dreamed of the Himalayas and of expeditions in other far-off places, but it all seemed impossible to achieve. Getting selected for expeditions is a highly competitive business, and there are not many of them. Yet I still cherished an ambition to make a climbing film somehow, and I hoped I might do this on a Himalayan scale one day with an expedition tailored for the special purpose. If only I had got a passable film on Nun Kun to show, I might have found a backer—there is tremendous advantage in having something to show—but one cannot get far by saying, "This is lousy but I can do better next time."

However, I stretched out a script and toted it around. "Excellent," they said, although it wasn't, "but you don't have to go to the Himalayas for that. We could do it so much easier in a studio."

I was horrified. In vain I tried to explain—*cardboard mountains are not quite the same thing.*

"Ah, but you are a climber—other people would not know the difference." It was stubborn of me, but I still thought they would.

"Even if you are right"—they always had the final word—"who will risk cameras in the mountains? It's too dangerous. The insurance alone . . ."

After two years at Dartington Hall, I moved up to London to make scientific films on my own. I loved this work, it is almost a hobby, but I could never get out of my mind that it was really a better occupation for old age than for the precious remaining years of youth. If I did not make an expedition film soon, I never should, yet it all seemed an impossible dream, and I felt I had espoused what was probably a hopeless cause. Well, they had told me that a long time back.

Then suddenly the chain began to form again. It was one of those close summer days when you know that what you really ought to be doing is swimming or climbing or poking around some foreign bazaar—anything but working indoors. Looking at the free birds and rabbits along the hedge, a man could not feel that Homo sapiens was quite so smart after all.

The work I was doing that afternoon just would not come right. My assistant and I had waited since daylight to catch a butterfly hatching, only to find we were sitting over a chrysalis that was already dead. So we packed up and drove over to see Joe. Joe was *the* expert on cinebiology and might tell us what we were doing wrong.

We had tea in his garden, and there I learned that an international expedition was going to the Antarctic in the fall and that Joe hoped to go as cinematographer. My heart stopped beating with envy as he dreamed aloud about the sunshine in Cape Town and the long voyage south to the ice.

The film was to be made by the Crown Film Unit, as the official government film unit was called. Joe belonged to this famous unit and was highly qualified for the job, but I detected a note of doubt in his voice when he mentioned that he had already started work on a film about agricultural pests. It was just possible that they would refuse to put it off. Knowing civil servants, it seemed to me more than probable—it seemed certain.

So when I got home that night, I called another friend, Gordon Smith, whom I had known in India and who was now something-or-other in government films. The upshot was that I learned categorically that Joe's film could *not* be postponed and that my name could go down on the application list.

"I don't know why I didn't think of you before," said Gordon. "You should be just right. Of course the final selection is not ours. It is being made by the Royal Geographical Society from those we recommend."

I began to have sleepless nights, wondering if I would get the job, not daring to hope too much, yet hoping nonetheless. Then I wondered whether I could *do* the job if I managed to get it. Technically I was a director, not a cameraman. I had done precious little practical handling of a camera since my apprentice days before the war, unless one could count the fiasco on Nun Kun. I had taken no color since then, and I had never used a 35-mm. camera. I was sticking my neck out an awfully long way in spite of my good general knowledge.

In due course I was short-listed and called for an interview. I was very nervous. The first thing I did at the Royal Geographical Society was to step into thin air and go headfirst down some steps, a booby trap placed by some thoughtful architect just inside the door.

"They won't want a clumsy oaf like me," I thought.

Gordon Robin, leader of the British party, stopped stuffing woolen socks into a box and looked mildly surprised. The huskie pup went on chewing straps in a corner.

Gordon seemed more like a cherub than the tough I had expected. He had dark hair, cheeks like a rosy apple, and a casual, friendly air. He was a physicist in the modern style of polar men.

"Do you mind if I go on with my work?" he asked after we had shaken hands. "Ask any questions you want."

Having come screwed up for a formal interview, I was completely put off my stroke. I walked around, looking at the maps and photographs asking some stupid questions, all the time thinking self-consciously what the books would have told me to do. "Capture your audience's attention. Talk authoratively about your subject. Let them see they are dealing with a man who really knows his business."

But all I could do was mumble, "I can see you are busy . . . I'd better go."

Of course after I had left, I could imagine my two rivals, full of self-confidence and with years of experience. My only hope was that they did not want a man who was too

75

forceful and shouted the odds. They would have to live with him.

There followed weeks of agonized waiting, so long I became quite certain I had failed. At last I could bear the suspense no longer and rang up Crown.

"When are you coming around to discuss your kit?" I was asked. "It's only six weeks before you sail. Of course you've been chosen."

"Of course? Well, you might have told me."

I rushed out of the phone booth and down the street, skipping like a lamb in spring. At last it had come.

Our sailing day, November 23, 1949, was a cold winter's day with a drizzle. I was not feeling too good on account of a farewell party the night before. I seemed to remember that some strange characters had joined in. I am afraid I was to blame for introducing some of the thirteen stowaways the police rounded up in the morning. They were young fellows like me, bank clerks, perhaps, at a desk, but dreaming of the adventurous life. They had my sympathy. I was ashamed of my good fortune.

When I first saw the ship, I did not like the look of her at all. Only 700 tons and 125 feet long, she was already overloaded and rolled softly, although it was dead calm in the Shadwell Basin. She seemed top-heavy. Her name was *Norsel*, which means North Seal, registered in Tromsö, Norway, and she had a black seal painted on a buff funnel. She smelled more than ordinarily of new paint and varnish because she was a brand-new ship on her maiden voyage.

Just now they were trying to pack two huge crates of airplane on her decks. A figure in an old British battle dress stood leaning on the bridge rail, looking thoroughly fed up. It was our skipper, Captain Guttorm Jakobsen, one of Norway's most famous ice pilots; but to me, not having met him, he looked like the supercargo. However, any captain watching his beautiful ship being messed up may be excused for looking sour. I wondered what he would say when he saw the amount of gear I had. I had said all I needed to take were a couple of small boxes and a kit bag, but the film alone was twice as much as that. "You'll be able to squeeze it in somewhere," everybody said. Somehow one doesn't believe a ship can really be full, but this one was.

I found my cabin was in the stern of the ship, between the motor room and the steering engine. The passage was blocked by piles of Oslo flat bread and cases of condensed milk. It looked like a grocer's nightmare. Inside the cabin was an Air Force kitbag, the property of my unknown cabinmate. All my gear was thrown inside, and I was left to sort it out. Not an inch of floor space remained, and it was stacked level with the bottom bunk. I hoped this unknown fellow was tolerant.

On deck it was bedlam. Friends, relations, ambassadors and officials, press and newsreel boys fought with the crew for room to pass. It looked as if we should never get off, but at three o'clock the visitors began to clear and line the quayside. Cameras were clicking. People began kissing good-by. Someone threw a last-minute parcel on board, but it was no use worrying now about all the things that were forgotten or left behind.

At last I looked at the expedition and the crew. Presumably they were the people left standing on the ship. I knew very few of them. Some of those I had seen in the last few days and had thought were members of the expedition now lined the quay; others who looked like relations were on the ship. I was feeling lonely, I was going off in the company of strangers. It was one of the penalties of my work that I was a supernumerary, added at the last moment and not a party to the expedition's plans, its growth, or knowing its members. I was only a privileged visitor and observer.

"Get your gangway aboard," shouted the pilot, indifferent to the general excitement as he climbed on to the ship. An old dockman casually threw off the mooring lines; this was no special moment for him either. Then the diesel engines started with a cough, the ship began to vibrate, and we slowly moved out into the basin.

There was a ragged cheer, led by the Norwegian ambassador. Handkerchiefs were waved. A frantic wife ran alongside on the wet mole, blowing kisses. The newsreel boys, perched on top of a wall, shouted, "Wave, please, come on, wave." Then it was all left behind, we slipped under the swing bridge, past the waiting cars on the road to a blare of horns, and began to head downriver.

The last word came from a bargeman. He stood on his barge looking at us and solemnly beat his arms and stamped his feet, saying in derisive mime, "It'll be cold, chums, it'll be cold where you're going. Rather you than me." But somehow his good wishes were more moving than any we had had.

This was the moment of anticlimax, when we cast off the shackles of our homes and turned to look at each other.

"Don't look so sad," said Gordon, catching my expression. "We shall be back one day."

Inside the cabin, looking hopelessly at the mountain of gear, was Sergeant Weston, my cabinmate. He was a serious-looking fellow, still in spotless R.A.F. uniform. "What about stowing some of the gear in these drawers under the bunk?" I asked.

He looked disgusted. "Some hope. All the drawers are stuck. They must have been made with unseasoned wood."

We took the bunks out, and managed to prize the drawers out. Then with a penknife we attacked the new ship, hacking away at the wood until the drawers were more or less movable. We filled them up, and when we had stacked the remaining baggage we had a space on the floor just big enough for one man to stand. However, the camera gear had to remain in the passage.

"One begins to see why sailors are always so neat," I observed.

Across the way, Corporals Quar and Gilbey had been battling the same problem. These three made up the Air Force team who were going to service the aircraft. Now we all set to work and achieved some order in the passage.

"What's this funny cardboard," asked Weston, holding a package of Oslo flat bread that had broken open. "That bloody stuff's to eat, chum," said Quar. "Try a bit."

We did. It tasted like brown paper.

"Which reminds me that it must be time for supper. Where *do* we eat anyway? And is there any beer on board?"

"I'm told there's more liquor on board this ship than on any expedition in history. All the big companies have given us some."

"Well, I could do with a beer now," said Gilbey. "It's as hot as hell in here. Have you got your porthole open?"

"You know the ventilators are blocked with packing cases up top. If we're sick . . ."

"It's going to be murder in the tropics. I'm going to sleep on deck."

"Oh, yeah," said Quar. "Where's the deck? There ain't no such thing as any mucking deck, not on this ship."

I went out through the iron storm door. The drizzle continued, and you could see the lights along the shore and some of the floodlit ships still discharging cargo. Buoy lights flashed in the channel, all the mysterious signals that enable the pilot to navigate at night. They all added to that supreme feeling of going somewhere, the exciting, wonderful certainty that something was going to happen.

Forward, beyond the engine skylight and the black airplane crates, was another door leading to the heart of the ship. This door was propped open and a light shone through. Inside I passed the entrance to the officer's mess next to the galley. Captain Giaever, our leader, whom I had scarcely met, was seated at the table with glaciologist

Valter Schytt, a big, handsome, blond fellow, the head of the Swedish contingent, and some other members of the expedition. Giaever shouted to me to come inside.

"Do you like aquavit?" he asked, indicating a bottle.

"I've never tried."

He poured me out a glass. "This is the best Swedish brand. You just drink it straight down. Skoal."

"Skoal."

It nearly choked me. Everyone laughed. Obviously the English were the butt of the joke.

Supper was prophetic. It consisted of large and sturdy sausages floating in whale oil. There was also a brown cheese that looked like soap and tasted like rice pudding. The goat hairs it contained spoke of its origin in some Norwegian sealer. One must not forget the Oslo flat bread, which still tasted like brown paper—a gastronome's nightmare.

We turned in early, and I settled in my bunk. It was about six inches shorter than I was, not good to stretch. I picked out a detective story. There was a juicy blonde called Aphrodite; that was something that wouldn't trouble us for a long time at any rate. All was quiet except for the rumble of the diesels and the clank-clank of the steering engine.

"By God, it's stifling in here," I said to Weston, laying down the book.

"Well, we've got the porthole open," he replied, also putting down his book and switching off the light. "It's that blocked ventilator."

We had hardly gone to sleep when we were awoken again by a thunderous crash. The ship had come alive with violent rolls and dives. The carefully stacked gear had fallen in a heap and was crashing about the floor.

Swearing, we switched the lights on and got up. We jammed it more tightly and got back to bed.

"Don't feel too good," mumbled Weston.

A moment later the door was pushed open and Felix came in. Felix was one of the Norwegian crew who played the guitar and spoke a little English, one of the brighter lads.

"Shut porthole," he said.

"Hell, we're nearly suffocating already."

"Captain's orders, water."

As if to prove it, a wave thundered on the deck and water poured into the cabin and ran down the wall. We shut the porthole and screwed it tight. Whereupon Sergeant Weston gave a strangled cry and rushed out to be sick. Five minutes later he came back, looking thoughtful. He got back into his bunk without a word.

When the baggage came loose a second time, I wasn't feeling too good myself, so I just let it crash. But we were not to rest yet.

"Water's coming down the steps into the passage," said Quar a few minutes later, putting his head in at the door. "Are your cameras all right Tom?" I got up and took a look. They were not. I moved them to a dryer spot on top of the Oslo bread, which could get washed away as far as I was concerned. Then I too went on deck to be sick.

Waves were coming over the bulwarks and the deck was awash. As I hung miserably over the side, cursing that oily supper, a wave took me in the middle and soaked my pajamas. It was freezing cold after the stuffy heat of the cabin, and looking out over the estuary toward the shore lights, I could see that *it was still only a slight chop.*

When I was a child, there had been a water color by Dr. Wilson over the nursery mantelpiece. Wilson, who died with Scott. It showed the midnight sun shining over the ice, with small, lonely figures and a sledge. It had the aura and holiness of the real thing, like the hair of a dead sweetheart in a locket.

My father had shared my feelings about exploration; he had been to Spitzbergen with the Oxford University expedition, and I often recalled the smell of his blubber-soaked clothes as we unpacked them on the lawn, or the fun of pitching the great Arctic "octopus" tent, of being allowed to sleep in it, and of brewing soup from old pemmican over a primus stove. This had a dent in it where he had kicked it over the hedge once when he thought it was going to blow up.

Along with Tibet, the Gobi Desert, Everest, and the Amazon jungles, the far south had seemed one of the ultimate adventures, too wonderful and rare to hope it could ever come true. It had a fascination that was not just from reading Scott or Shackleton. The names came out of any Anarctic page charged with that electric romance.

"*The Great Wandering Albatross, wingspan up to 14 ft. Distribution; Southern oceans between latitude 60° and 30° south. Breeds, Tristan da Cuna, South Georgia, Gough Is. Marion Is. Prince Edward Is. The Crozet Is. . . .*" the scene would dissolve into lonely, desolate and stormy seas.

But there is nothing like seasickness to destroy romance.

"Do you realize, Rog," I said, "that it will take us a month even to reach Cape Town."

"Oh God!" Rog groaned. He was a cheerful fellow, with a mouth like comedian Joe E. Brown's, so that the joke around the ship was that he ate his bananas sideways. During the war he had reached Canada via Siberia and Japan, was one of Norway's ski champions and a very tough fellow indeed, but now he was sitting beside me, with no fight left, his face as livid and sickly as a slug's belly. We were leaning with our backs to the funnel to keep a little warm. Since it was amidships, there was less motion here, and we could not face the oily fug of the cabins.

"I wish we could stop this bloody ship and get off," he said. "Even for five minutes."

82

Captain Jakobsen passed, making his way aft. Even he was holding on, though not much.

"Are you boys comfortable? Going in for lunch?" he asked, chuckling like a pantomime wolf in "Red Riding Hood." I thought at that moment he looked dark and remarkably like the devil, but there was no blunt weapon handy.

"Always eat your grub, Tommy lad," the skipper of an Aberdeen trawler I had once sailed on told me. I thought I had better try.

I staggered through to the mess. Lunch today was fat pork stew which I was sure the cook had made as a joke, but if so, there were not many people left to play it on.

"Isn't there any fresh fruit?"

"No, there isn't," said Quar, "I've already asked. The grub is exactly the same as for sealing in the Arctic—bags of fat. *Think what it'll be like in the tropics!*"

As a last resort I went round to beg pills from our Swedish doctor, Ove Wilson. Small and quick, speaking fluent English with an American accent, he was a man I had taken to at sight because he had that speculative intelligence and sense of wonder that makes a good companion on an expedition, and this is a rare bird.

While I waited for the pills I glanced around the Doc's cabin with envy. It was amidships, quiet, and with enough air. Most astonishing, he had the cabin to himself, and though a huge black box of medical kit filled the floor, compared to our hell hole in the stern, he lived in spacious luxury.

"The other bunk is in case someone gets sick," he explained when he saw my eye on it. I decided then and there that I would have it if I could. But now was not the moment to ask, so I returned to the sweathouse in the stern.

At 3 A.M. on the second night we passed Ushant and entered the Bay of Biscay. It lived up to its reputation,

83

but when we picked up the coast of Spain, the weather was calmer, and most of us began to emerge. With a book on sea birds, I sat upon a pile of rafts and tried to identify the various species. This was more how one had imagined the expedition should be.

As we pushed south it was starting to get hot—the tropics were in the offing. The two inches of stinking black water which was now permanently in the passage began to eat into the coverings of my gear. The leather facings grew green mold. The cabbages stored in the steering compartment had got wet, and stank like sewage; the air was foul and stagnant, but still we could not open a porthole; it was high time to tackle the Doc about moving into his cabin.

The Doc was more than reluctant to have his privacy disturbed, but I reminded him that we had two observers getting on in Cape Town, and he might as well choose the devil he knew. He looked at me as if saying in Swedish, "You bastard, you are an old soldier too." Then he gave way. I promised I would move without trouble if anyone became ill. Here there was blessed air, quiet and less movement. I began to think seriously about the film, for the first time since our departure.

As I have explained, on the question of the film I had cold feet, and I had stuck my neck out badly. The fact that I had done it deliberately, knowing the risk but deciding to take a chance, did not make it any better. The plain fact was that I was not a sufficiently experienced photographer, but had taken on a cameraman's job under the most exacting circumstances there could possibly be; that is, in tough and unknown latitudes with no help and no possibility whatever of checking results. Even if he does not have the best possible film, a cameraman knowing little of direction who works alone will at least have *some* film. But a director knowing a little camera work is in

84

quite another situation. If he messes up his exposures, he can very easily finish with *no film at all.*

During the six weeks before departure I had crammed myself with theory, and even now had included the best books in my kit. But what a gap between theory and practice! It was all very well to talk about it in a London office—but here was where you had to do it—and on a sick stomach too.

Luckily there was no importance to the story as far as Cape Town, where I could get tests developed, so there was still a last chance to try myself. Yet I kept putting off the evil day when I must take the cameras out, because the failure of the film on Nun Kun was still in my mind and I was gambling with all I possessed. Whenever I looked at the camera box I was as scared of it as if it had been a time bomb.

We plowed steadily southward at eleven knots down the western bulge of Africa. I had no idea it was such a long way. We are used to a Mercator's map, which makes the tropics look smaller than they really are. At length we reached the Equator, with mirror seas that did not give even the *Norsel* a chance to roll and pitch. There was no longer any excuse for putting things off. I had to make a start.

The evening life in the saloon was noisy and jolly. Rog had an accordion; others, flutes and clarinets; I had a guitar. Nobody could play very well, but everyone could sing, and we made a sunburst of noise as we dug into the liquor ration. I thought it would make a telling sequence for the film, especially as some of the Scandinavian songs had lively good tunes and the Doc had a tape recorder to record them.

We needed lights to film inside, and I had to manage them all myself. This required calm weather, and I felt that I should seize the opportunity. It was very hot, it would be even hotter with the lights, and the saloon was

85

our only common room; still, I thought I should give it a go, and I asked all the members to spare me half an hour dressed in their Antarctic kit.

It says a great deal for the expedition that they turned up at all. Long-suffering explorers, dressed in heavy sweaters, tried to look jolly and cold, with sweat streaming down their faces. Only Rog, glad to be free of his seasickness, could produce his banana eating smile and play madly on his accordion. It took me an hour to get what I wanted. When I got back to my cabin, the Doc had something to say.

"Not only did you sweat everybody to death," he told me in his most serious manner, "but many of them object to you faking scenes."

"What do you mean faking?" I asked. "I call it reconstruction. I don't take anything that doesn't happen—but in this case I can't take it when the sea is at all rough. What else can I do?"

"I know, Tom. I agree with you. I'm just telling you what other people say for your own good." He began changing his socks. "You have to remember they are scientists, not artists. They have a respect for the truth."

Now it was my turn to be annoyed. I said a rude word. I felt hurt, outside the pale, knowing that I had a difficult job ahead in human relations, that I needed more tact in the future, that I must guard my behavior very carefully. But to accuse me of faking!—it was just silly.

This, however, was not the last of my mistakes. Due to bad weather the ceremony of "Crossing the Line" had to be held several days late. Captain Jakobsen was dressed as Neptune, and I could see by the look in his eye that the party was going to be rough. Preparations for the ceremony had been made in private, and we had no idea what was in store for us.

The first victim was blindfolded. A mop dipped in a mixture of diesel oil and soot from the funnel was slapped right in his face. This was the shaving soap. Then the fire hoses were turned on.

I had my cameras ready. It is the great penalty of being an expedition cinematographer that you so often cannot abandon yourself to the fun, but have to work instead. I asked the Captain to give me the next treatment so that I could be free to do my work. "*And please not too much oil because I want to get back to my cameras. And don't turn the hoses toward my camera, please.*"

I was given the modified treatment with no enthusiasm. I was a wet blanket. I did not have to be very sensitive to see that the restraint I asked for was a bore—to be of an expedition *and yet not of it* was hard.

I changed quickly and got my camera. Within a moment the hose was turned full at me. I had just time to grab my equipment and run.

I tried sneaking pictures from the cover of the bridge, but every time I showed my head, the hose came at me. As I could never obtain an interesting sequence like this, I gave up, put my cameras away, and joined in the battle.

When I got back to my cabin, I was a little subdued. The day's events had given me serious food for thought. It was clear that my film did not mean very much to anyone else. That I must be content with a little co-operation at times, but mostly with none. That somehow I must learn to do my work in spite of adverse conditions, and never get in the way or spoil the fun. I was learning that the expedition photographer walks a tightrope. Temperamental stars require nothing in tact in comparison to a bunch of explorers who have to be lived with amicably for many months. They are not interested in the film in the least until afterward. Then, of course, they expect the best. But at the time they are interested only in the expedition and in getting the maximum results and also the maximum pleasure out of it. Indeed, you have to realize that your aims and the aims of the expedition are often completely antagonistic. "I don't want to wish you ill, Tom, but I hope every disaster imaginable happens to you. If the expedition goes smoothly, you will get a very dull film, won't you?" someone had said to me before I left. He was right.

On December 21, after twenty-eight days at sea, we picked up the low sandy coast of South Africa. At about four in the afternoon, after following the coast all day, what looked like a flat-topped, craggy island came up over the horizon to the south. It was the top of Table Mountain, and there were shouts of joy on all sides. We were days late because of the storms, but this meant Christmas ashore and the discomforts of the past were immediately forgotten.

We entered Table Bay on a fine chilly evening. We sat on the foredeck discussing the orgies of fruit eating we would have on landing. We had missed fruit most of all, and we felt it was the only thing that would put our insides right after our seasickness and prolonged inactivity. There would also be the mail, the letters from girls and wives. It had been accumulating in Cape Town for the last month, but that was nothing to the two years some would have to face afterward.

Now the black outline of the mountain loomed above us. We stood on the wings of the bridge, watching the necklace of lights along the edge of the water. A car's headlights swung around a bend above the town, a small signal lamp mysteriously blinked a message to us from halfway up the mountain face. We tried to signal back, but our own signal light refused to work. As we got closer, the signals from the shore became more insistent, and the Captain decided to use the foghorn. But one blast and it stuck on, making a frightful rumpus in the silent night. There was some explosive cursing in Norwegian, and then the mate climbed the mast and kicked the machine into silence.

We tied up beside some cranes at the floodlit quay, in a strong smell of bad fish from the lobster cannery next door. Officials came on board, among them a bearded figure, Phil Lawes of the Australian Antarctic Expedition, and the Norwegian consul. The press also descended on us, but it was none of my business. I went ashore with the Doc to stretch our legs among the cafés and jukeboxes of the harbor quarter. The ground heaved and swayed, and we could not walk straight. That night I slept peacefully on top of the chart house, looking up at the Southern Cross and the great crag of Table Mountain, longing for daylight, excited as always in my life at the prospect, the sight, of a new land.

chapter 8

We WERE to be in Cape Town only a few days, and most of these would be taken up by Christmas holidays, so we had to rush. It was very hot, and my only tidy suit was thick and blue. The *Norsel* was tied up at a remote mole, as she was lousy with dynamite and high-octane gas. The dynamite had been packed at the bottom of the hold and could not be got at, so there the ship lay, away from the other shipping, flying the red explosives flag. It meant a long walk every morning before we could find a taxi.

There were two vital tasks to be completed. First, to get a report on the film I had shot; second, to get a waterproof box made with a glass front, so that I could get pictures in heavy weather without soaking the cameras, for amid all the complicated gadgets, this simple necessity had been forgotten.

"And you'd better make the most of the girls," said Captain Jakobsen with his devil's grin directed at those who would be staying on the ice. "You won't see any for a very, very long time."

Yet our main preoccupation was shopping, to fill all the omissions we had found in our kit and to lay in a few luxuries. In particular, I had on my list to get a case of oranges and a bottle of Worcestershire sauce to take the edge off the greasy food. Unfortunately the sauce was forgotten in the Christmas celebrations.

On December 28 we were told to be ready to sail at

91

four o'clock. It was a disappointing day, as I learned that in spite of heroic efforts by Kodak, my test films would not arrive in time for me to see them, so that I should have to depend on radio reports.

At six we were once more in the saloon—the mahogany and whitewood veneer, the picture of Flensburg Harbor, the wet circles from our glasses on the brown linoleum table. We sat with friends for a last drink, our minds already on the next stage of the journey. Half an hour later the ship was cleared and we moved out into the harbor, amid cheers and waving handkerchiefs, the kind of occasion on which flags become important. The sun was low over Table Mountain, and photography from the ship, quite impossible. It is one of the difficulties of expeditions that vital events occur at the wrong time of day, so that by force of circumstances there are serious gaps in the story you are trying to tell.

We lay out in the bay, and while the crew made everything fast for sea, I went below to store the boxes of fruit I had bought. I found that everyone else had had the same idea. The passages were now scarcely passable because of the fruit. There were sacks of oranges, crates of pineapples, peaches, apricots, melons, and apples. Great bunches of bananas lay like bodies in the bunks. The ship smelled like a fruiterer's store, stuffed with the luxuries of South African sunshine.

"All those peaches won't keep long," said Doc Wilson, who was changing out of his best clothes. "In fact, we're going to eat peaches until we're so bored with them we shan't want any for the next two years."

I was lying on my bunk reading *War and Peace* for the fifth time when the ship's engines started, but even the beautiful Natasha could not keep me from worrying. This departure was final. What was left behind was left behind, and what was left undone would remain undone. From now on I could only help myself. I would either return with a film or . . . I should never hold my head up again.

Even when someone brought a radio message—"Tests O.K."—I was only a little comforted. The fact was that I did not know enough, so I put down *War and Peace* and picked up another book, *How to Take Colour Films,* and read it till I fell asleep.

We were once more surrounded by green seas. The wind was fresh, and away to starboard an albatross was drifting over the waves, almost touching the crests, then slipping down into the troughs. There was a nip in the air, and already a feel of desolation. We were out of all accustomed sea lanes and would not see a blot on the horizon nor a ship wallowing past for several weeks. That is, unless we happened on a whaler or her catchers.

Duty had driven me out of my bunk, but the decks were deserted, nothing to film, only the mate at the wheel. Everyone must be feeling ill. I was glad to go below again and with a clear conscience resume a book and the struggle with nausea.

"'Full Fahrt's' just taken over the watch," I told the Doc. "We're in for a bashing." "Full Fahrt" was the Norwegian for *"full speed ahead,"* and the name had been given to the mate on account of his driving the ship only at maximum revs, thumping the ship into whatever was coming.

Living on oranges and peaches was not too bad until New Year's Eve, but then it blew up to a full gale. We were in the region of the Roaring Forties and still headed south into the stormiest seas in the world. Our meterologists—Liljequist, Schumacher, and King—spent much time in the chartroom plotting depressions and to see one of these maps was to get a depression oneself. The information they had was coming by radio from isolated stations as far away as Herd Island, on one side, and the Argentine on the other. It is difficult to see how forecasting would

93

be possible at all without radio. The information they had was scanty, but as there is only sea around the Antarctic continent, and no land masses to upset calculations, we were in a perfect weather laboratory, with everything behaving more or less according to the book. I must say that the forecasts of depressions were always right, but since they hit us every few hours, it was, as Doc Wilson pointed out, difficult to be wrong. The value was in knowing exactly where the depressions lay, so we could to some extent avoid the worst. We needed to do this because the airplane now lay assembled on deck, protected only by a canvas jacket, and in danger of being smashed.

In this weather it was difficult to take any pictures without help, and nobody wanted to turn out. I struggled around the ship, dressed in an old U. S. Navy anarack. With one hand clutching the camera wrapped in canvas covers, and only one numbed hand to hold on by, it was the merest luck that I escaped disaster, because it was easy to be washed overboard, and on a deserted ship. . . ! One has a stupid loyalty to the camera, and herein lies the danger. At what point do you abandon it to hold on with both hands? and while you are deciding, all is lost.

Fred Roots, our Canadian geologist, who was always ready to help anyone at any time, agreed to hold my legs so that I should not slip. It seemed sensible to brave seasickness, make one great effort, and get all the storm shots needed. It was a miserable and prolonged battle. The wind snatched at the camera, now bulky in its watertight box, and threatened to tear it out of my hand. I would hold a cloth over the lens to keep it dry till the last moment, then begin the shot, letting the ship roll under me and fighting to keep the horizon level. When the next wave arrived and smothered all in water, I would have to go below, and clean the glass for another attempt. It was difficult not to put it off with the thought that

94

there would probably be an even bigger storm tomorrow and the job did not really *have* to be done today.

Toward evening the violence of the gale increased even more. The measured angle of roll was sometimes over 45 degrees from the vertical on either side. Nothing that was not lashed down stayed in place, and you could not keep your feet for an instant without holding on.

I lay wedged in my bunk, listening to the waves beating the ship like sledge hammers. Something had come loose in the forehold, and it crashed about with every roll.

"New Year's Day," I wrote in my log. "The storm has slacked off, but the Met. boys say we are being chased by another depression and will have a full gale again tomorrow. Have a heart!"

Our first task in Antarctic waters was to find and meet the *Thorshøvdi*, the 25,000-ton whaling factory ship which had the really heavy gear aboard, the weasels, Walter Schytt's special boring machine for making research holes in the ice, and some fifty huskies, along with the expedition members who were looking after them.

One would expect the *Norsel* to have been kept informed of the day to day position of the *Thorshøvdi*, which of course, with her catchers in attendance, would steam slowly about in search of the best whaling grounds. But the position of a whaling team is kept secret. The International Whaling Commission allows a yearly agreed catch. Once this has been reached, whaling must stop, and there are inspectors on board to see that it does. So each outfit is engaged in a race to get the lion's share of the quota, and does not want someone else horning in if it has the good fortune to strike a concentration of whales.

So to add to our troubles, when we established radio contact with the *Thorshøvdi* for the first time that night, she gave her longitude, but did not state whether it was east or west. If it was west, then she was between South

Georgia and the South Orkneys, and miles away from where we expected, in fact quite on the other side of the South Atlantic. In that case probably the airplanes would not last, and I might get some good pictures.

We were now between latitude 45 and 50 degrees south, right in the track of the storms. In the evening we altered course from S. to S.S.W. to avoid a depression to our south—the depressions are always chasing eastward. The R.A.F. men continued working to keep their airplane intact, and it continued to blow. I spent some time up on the bridge. It was frightening. Not so much the power of the seas which came roaring over the bows each time the *Norsel* put her nose down, but the ghastly loneliness of the place, the miles and miles of turbulent waters streaked with wind. The gray storm clouds tearing over, the squalls of icy rain, and the dismal moaning in the rigging.

The spirit of the place was that ever-present albatross which quested endlessly just above the waves, never seeming to alight to catch a fish, but always looking—looking for God knows what—always alone, like the lost soul the bird is supposed to be. What a life! Giant wings that can sleep in the air; always being blown around the globe, living out its life in a world of gray waters and storm, gathering to nest once a year on some remote rocks, creating more lost souls as playmates for the elements, and then returning to this awful solitude, a thousand miles from a perch.

Often the birds would fly close beside the ship. You could almost reach out and touch them. They would look at you, with head turned sideways, a cold eye, and a fierce hooked beak, then sail off once more. "The Great Wandering Albatross. Wingspan 14 ft. Breeds Tristan da Cunha, Gough Is. . . ." There was the book come to life at last.

We contacted the *Thorshøvdi*—a game of hide and seek even with all modern aids. The news came through in the morning that indeed she lay to the west in the Scotia Sea on the other side of the ocean, about two weeks away.

"This means we shall lose those mucking kites," said Quar.

Captain Giaever was worried. One had only to look at his grave face, usually so ready to break into a smile, to see that. Having to go all this extra distance, we could be too late, and not have time to find a landing place on the mainland shelf ice before the short Antarctic summer was gone and the sea froze once more. Surely there were enough hazards already? Nobody had ever landed on the coast for which we were bound, and it was by no means sure that a low enough point would exist in the terrifying ice cliffs of the shelf. We needed all the time we could get to look for one. With all the planning that had gone into the expedition, it was still a gamble, and the shorter the time, the greater the gamble would be.

By January 4 we were beginning to get south of the main belt of the storms. It was a dull overcast day with mist. There was a raw feel about the air; fine moisture covered with clammy breath. We were now covered with bruises from being flung about, and we longed for something calm and solid. I for one was not sorry when heavy weather was replaced by cold, although it meant a new phase to film.

In a film everything has to be illustrated by example. You cannot simply say, "It is cold." You have to suggest cold. Find people that look cold; views with a flurry of snow; people reacting to cold, like blowing on their hands or buttoning up their windbreakers. To get this material you wage a war of attrition, spend hours in chilly and patient waiting for the scene to come along.

When I was not on deck, I lay on my bunk covering a notebook with little sketches of all the things that *might* happen, so that if they *did* happen, I should be ready and know what I must take. In filming an expedition you do not know events in advance and therefore you cannot have a script, so you must think of all the possibilities and how you would treat them.

In the evening I was on the bridge when we passed our first "growler," a fragment of ice the size of a steam roller. We were doing a full 11 knots, and remembering the fate of the *Titanic*, I wondered what would happen to us if we hit one on a dark night. I did not then know how tough the *Norsel* was, or the punishment an icebreaker is designed to take.

The growler was a warning. On the following day we saw our first icebergs. To begin with they looked like white flecks on the horizon, but late in the afternoon we came up with them and passed a tabular berg at less than half a mile. Tabular bergs, occasionally even vast enough to carry the whole of London or New York, are peculiar to the Antarctic. As their name suggests, they are flat on top, with vertical sides. This one was old, eroded, and rotten. It had drifted far north of its place of birth. Its sheer two-hundred-foot cliffs were pale blue, undermined with caves and rounded like the towers of a fairy castle. The sea spouted over the smooth, shining curves and boomed under the arches.

We saw a huge piece break away from another berg. Seconds later we heard the sound, like distant thunder, and the sea boiled for several minutes at the place. The berg was now unstable, and began to turn over, a jagged submerged cutwater arose from the ocean like the bows of a sinking battleship. We hoped it would turn right over, but it ponderously took up a new equilibrium, and had not moved again at the time it dropped astern over the horizon.

Two days more, on January 6, at breakfast time, we sighted Bouvet Island. It was snowing and the island now appeared white against driven clouds; you could hardly tell which was storm and which was the island, a desolate volcanic cone, plastered with ice, and sticking out of miles and miles of stormy seas, in the track of the depressions, the most isolated island in the world.

We passed it respectfully close. Black fangs of rock broke the waves with a continual roar; ice dripped down into clefts like blue cream. A few silent albatrosses wandered disconsolately along the coasts. Then the island dissolved once more into the driving snow as if it had never been. A dot on the map and a name. We rubbed our eyes. Was it a nightmare? Surely the genius of God could think of nothing worse for hell than Bouvet Island.

"A good place for the ladies of the Côte d'Azur—in their bikinis."

As we pushed farther south, we passed the track of the worst gales, and for the next six days we made good progress west under dark, cloudy skies.

I continued with photography in a desultory way, but when today is virtually the same as yesterday or tomorrow as you guess, there is little stimulus to work, so I mostly sat in the saloon and played chess to keep away the growing boredom—and boredom is a very real problem on expeditions. At other times I watched the birds, the various petrels darting over the waves, like swallows, the light-mantled sooty albatross, the cape pigeons, the whale birds, and the other romantically named inhabitants of the southern oceans. But we all began to chafe at the uneventfulness and inactivity.

chapter 9

ON JANUARY 10 we had a celebration, and a giant turtle was dug out of the cold store. The creature was so big that only the strong man of the crew could lift it, and at that only just. It was a gift from some noble company to provide us with some royal turtle soup.

As the only zoologist on board, I was called upon to advise the cook on how to cut it up, which I did remembering its anatomy, but when I was asked how to make turtle soup, I was not so helpful. The undefeatable Doc, however, produced a book. He returned to the galley shaking his head. "It's like 'nail soup,'" he said.

I did not know what nail soup was, and he repeated the fairy story. As far as I remember, the most thrifty girl was to marry the prince, and the test was to make the cheapest soup. Poor Prince.

All failed until the one who was going to get him appeared. She asked for a nail, and put it on to boil.

"It's a pity such good soup should be spoiled for want of a little onion," she said, tasting and smacking her lips.

So she got the onion.

"It's a pity such good soup should be spoiled for want of a little meat."

So she got the meat.

A bit of this and a bit of that—and so she got the prince!

"Is that a story against thrift—or encouraging kids to be smart?" I asked. "It's a Scandinavian thought anyway, I bet."

101

The Doc ignored my baiting.

"We have enough turtle for a mayor's banquet," he said. "But we also need six pheasants, twelve chickens, twenty hams and a case of truffles, not to mention a barrel of sherry and a bouquet garni."

"Not provided?"

"No. But the cook thinks it looks like veal, so he's trying to make it into weiner schnitzel."

The experiment was a doubtful success, though it gave us a welcome break from pork stews. It must have been the most expensive and tasteless schnitzel on record. How I wished I had not forgotten the Worcestershire sauce, which is surely the first priority in any explorer's kit.

Our course was to take us through the South Sandwich Islands, a crescent of volcanoes, some of them active, rising from the rim of a fearsome ocean deep, and we impatiently looked for a sight of them. Saunders Island, Candlemas Island, they came up over the western horizon one afternoon, a line of snowy cones stretching to the south, and stayed with us until night fell. Many of these islands had never been landed on, and I pored over the chart, fascinated as Fred Roots explained their geology.

The charts of this part of the world were not very reliable. We had two charts, one issued by a Norwegian insurance company, a plain outline with just soundings and large blanks in the coastline where it was unexplored —it was the chart used by the whaling fleet—and we had also a chart by the U. S. Navy Hydrographic Department, a beautiful affair printed in colors and with plenty of detail. Both charts were continually compared, and they differed a great deal. If appearance was all that counted, there is no doubt which you would choose, the American; but the American chart had been filled in from aerial survey, while the whaling chart rested only on accurate observations made from ships. Some people prefer to have a map marking everything that is reported, even if it is not known accurately. Others to have only what is known accurately. Having used maps in the Himalayas that may mark nonexistent villages or whole valleys and leave out distances of a day's journey, I think I personally prefer the former. Once a map is printed, it is difficult not to think that it has some basis in fact.

One evening the Doc came down to the cabin, laughing.

"A very interesting experiment is going on tonight," he said. "The American maps show our course goes right over an island. The Norwegian maps don't mark the island."

"I hope we go by the Americans'."

"Oh no, the Captain swears the Norwegian map is the more likely to be right, so if we feel a bump in the night, we'll know he is wrong."

"That seems to be carrying national pride a bit *too* far."

"If it's the mate's watch we shall go 'full fahrt' right over the top."

We all slept soundly. There was no bump in the night and no island. Indeed, we all had such confidence in the wonderful seamanship of the captain and his Norwegian crew that it never occurred to us that they ever had problems or anxiety in navigating or finding the way.

In the morning of the twelfth a slight odor of bad glue could be detected in the pure Antarctic air. This increased unpleasantly for some time until we sighted smoke over the horizon, and then the *Thorshøvdi* gradually came up, side-by-side funnels amidships spewing a black cloud downwind. We came to within about a mile of her and then stopped. Through glasses we could see several whales trailed astern, surrounded by Cape pigeons. Unlike the gulls in the Northern Hemisphere, the Cape pigeons mobbed around in utter silence.

Occasionally a catcher would come up fast with one

or two whales lashed tail first alongside. The whole operation had the silence, speed and purposefulness of a naval operation in wartime. A whaling outfit works against time, and every man has a stake, a bonus on the catch.

We were beginning to get tired of leaning over the rail, nothing happening, when a catcher headed toward us, powerful and fast, a little rusty, and with the harpoon gun prominent in the bows. As she came close, we could see that there was a barrel lashed to the mast as a crow's-nest, and a catwalk from the bridge to the gun. The skipper is the harpoon gunner and must be able to reach his gun quickly.

A line was flung over, and we sent across the sack of mail we had brought from Cape Town. There were shouted exchanges in Norwegian. A cook, to my astonishment in a white cap and apron, came from the catcher's galley, and with scarcely a look at us, emptied a pail of slops into the sea. Then the little ship headed back to its vast mother. It seemed almost indecent, the casual meeting in this lonely place, not even stopping work to say, "Hello," so little fuss and formality.

For some time we waited expectantly, smelling the barbaric smell of burning flesh. There was something monstrous about this slowly steaming death factory—a sort of floating Belsen—but nothing happened, and interest flagged, although occasionally we heard the howling of our dogs blown down the wind to remind us of our business.

"We're going on to the *Thorshøvdi* tonight," announced Captain Jakobsen, who could for once relax and was having one of his rare drinks with us in the saloon. "A good feed, a dance or a movie. How would you like that?"

"Stop kidding us," we said.

"I'm not kidding you, am I, John?" He turned to Captain Giaever for support.

"Of course not," said John. "We've been keeping it as

104

a surprise. There are even women on board, Doc," he added. "We'd better all get cleaned up a bit."

Everyone laughed.

"I can believe they have a movie, but women—down here?"

"Certainly. You don't imagine the whalers these days spend six months in the Antarctic without their comforts. They have found that it makes for peace on board for the men to take their wives."

"Sure. The *Thorshøvdi* is the most modern factory ship afloat. The living quarters are like a liner—she's as big as a liner anyway—bigger than some. Whaling is a hard business, but once you pass through the baths, it's as near civilized as is possible. Like miners coming out of the pits. The days when they went home dirty are over."

"Exactly," said the Captain. "Now you boys go and get a shave."

At dinner that night there was some unusual cleanliness.

"When are we going on the *Thorshøvdi?*" someone asked. Captain Jakobsen gave us one of the wolf grins he reserved for such occasions and further comment was unnecessary.

During the night the *Thorshøvdi* changed her grounds, steaming first southeast and then southwest. We followed, holding contact by radio. Next day only the catchers were in sight, and we continued southward, keeping a sharp lookout for whales. Occasionally we could see one. First a spout, and then a shadow with a fin, sliding up and over. From such flimsy evidence, a harpoon gunner would have known the kind of whale, its age and its size, but to us it was a mystery, just a blast of hot fishy air, a back and then silence. As the minutes passed, one imagined the whale holding its breath and sounding to some incredible black depth.

There was now an "ice blink" to the south, a lightening of the sky due to reflection. A snowy petrel of the purest white went past, flying silently. It too was a sign that the pack ice was not far away.

An hour later a shining white line appeared and grew along the horizon. Everyone was on deck. John Giaever stood a little apart in the bows of the ship. I photographed him, wondering what his thoughts were. For a man who had spent so much of his life within the Arctic Circle, did he sniff the air like a wolf at the approach of spring or did he again dread the lonely years ahead?

As for me, I was sniffing the spring. To a dweller in the Northern Hemisphere, looking south means sun, so illogically, even in the Southern Hemisphere one's mind retains this primitive instinct. South means sun, and here it was, shining broadly and kindly on a white world of silence and peace. Even the sea seemed suddenly to be stilled.

We bumped gently into a line of floes, white lambs and lumps of sugar in a turquoise sea. A group of ringed penguins passed, progressing in a series of dives like comic porpoises. They quacked like ducks, and the crew quacked back, shouting with laughter. Penguins, which only inhabit the Southern Hemispere, were as new to these professional sealers as they were to me.

All day long we followed the edge of the pack, a day with daylight already stretching far into the night. We were looking for a bay in the ice with mirror-calm water where the transhipment could take place, but we did not find one.

Early next morning, however, we awoke to find ourselves in the lee of a huge tabular berg blocking the horizon to the northeast. Captain Jakobsen hoped that here, although the operation would be tricky, it might be calm enough to make the attempt. No one but a crack Norwegian seaman would even have considered it.

The *Thorshøvdi* was lying about half a mile abeam of us, black smoke rising densely from her funnels. Presently a catcher came over, towing two fin whales which she passed over to us. We lashed them alongside to serve as fenders. They lay floating with their ribbed bellies uppermost, just awash; the tail flukes had been trimmed off and steel hausers passed through. One could see the spigots where they had been inflated with air. They looked like large rubber toys.

When all was ready, we closed the *Thorshøvdi*. Her grease-smeared sides began to tower above us. The sinister smell became overpowering. It was like burned feathers or singed hair. Lines of faces stared down at us from the rail, from portholes and from blood-stained doors. There were friezes of fat driblets and a scorched patch on the plates like the mess from a toy firework. Clouds of steam and foul-smelling brown gravy pumped slowly from a pipe in her side and spread as a discoloration on the sea. Bits of intestine were snagged on a hook. It would have made a good backdrop for hell.

Ropes came flying down on us from above, and the fender whales went squelch between the two ships. But whales are tough, and they showed not a mark as they began a prolonged roly-poly between the opposing plates. Whales make splendid fenders—if you have whales!

As if to make the picture complete, a bedlam of dogs' voices broke out from the deck above, and the sound of shots. Soon the bodies of several huskies came drifting past, yellow hair sifting like fine seaweed in the water. There could be no more nursing. The sick and the weaklings had to go.

Mandus Hansen, the tough-looking mate of the *Thorshøvdi*, was leaning over the rail and shouting to our captain in Norwegian. Presently the first weasel appeared, hanging dangerously above us, tracks sagging and turning slowly on the end of the derrick cable.

The *Norsel* rolled and heaved up and down sometimes as much as forty feet, and only seamen with the confidence of the devil would have persisted. The weasel had to be lowered without damage and dropped in exactly the right place. It was a spectacular operation, and I filled my pockets with film, prepared for action.

I went up into our crow's-nest to get a good view. This was level with the *Thorshøvdi's* bridge. It was reached from the top of the wheelhouse by a narrow iron ladder running up the mast. Cold to the hands, difficult to grip, and with a nasty fall onto the winches below, I did not relish the climb with the camera gear. I tied it all inside my anarak and began to ascend without looking down! Every roll of the ship tried to tear one off. The ladder ended halfway up, and you had to step sideways over the crosstreds onto another ladder, and finally climb over the edge of the barrel. I had watched our mate go up in a gale, with heavy sea boots and oilskins, so really it had to be all right, but it did not feel it.

Even when one had arrived, it did not feel safe. Every time the *Norsel* rolled, the barrel shuddered in the iron clamps that bound it to the mast. The bridge of the *Thorshøvdi* zoomed up and away with bewildering jerks, like a gadget in a fun fair. One moment I could see the whole of the flensing deck with its sumps of blood and whale guts, the next I was almost kissing the agent who was standing rather smartly dressed with a camera on the wing of the *Thorshøvdi's* bridge.

After taking several shots I became careless, fumbled, and dropped my filter into the barrel. It would not have mattered except that the barrel was so narrow, I could not bend to get it out. A stupid situation. After much cursing I had to climb out and go into the barrel head first. Being upside down immediately made me sick, and being sick while standing on your head in a barrel is no joke. Feeling ill and cold I had once more to cling my way back down the ladder.

I now asked the Captain if he would send me to the *Thorshøvdi*, and transhipment was interrupted while they sent over a basket. It was an alarming ride crouched in the basket, creaking, dangling and swinging over the sea. Then I was dumped onto the Thorshøvdi's deck forty feet above.

"Have you got any film to spare?" I was asked as soon as I had shaken hands with our expedition members aboard. "Film and photographic chemicals. The Thorshøvdi has run out."

Bartering with government property was an excellent idea.

"I've got stacks of film and chemicals," I said. "I'll trade with pleasure for some Worcestershire sauce, if you've got any."

The decks of the Thorshøvdi were a disgusting sight. The vast flensing deck led to a stern ramp, which sloped steeply into the water. The whole of this deck was laid with splintered planks soaked in blood. A partly dismembered whale lay there, looking quite small in the vast open space. Above were winding drums with steel cables as thick as those on a pithead. They were splashed with horrible black slime and grease. Drains in the deck were mirrors of red. Steam came gently from around the edges of the iron covers of the blubber boilers. It was so slippery, it was almost impossible to stand without the spiked boots that the whalers were wearing, and I had to edge along like an old lady on a skating rink.

Since I also had to hold on whenever I could, my hands became covered with evil-smelling black fat, which soon got maddeningly onto clothes, everywhere, even into the camera.

The Norsel was taking on seventeen tons of whale meat for the dogs as well as the heavy gear. When I got back to the side, a game had started. The men on the Thorshøvdi were trying to drop chunks of meat on the heads of those stacking it on the decks of the Norsel below. Although whale meat is soft, even squelchy, the chunks, as big as a prime sirloin, were falling forty feet. There were shouts of laughter when someone got a bull's-eye.

It would not be fair to the *Thorshøvdi* to describe only the scenes outside, for below decks the scene was quite different. There was of course the same smell, and some suggestion of being in Sweeney Todd's kitchen, but otherwise it was a clean modern factory, a mass of lagged pipes, mixers and tanks. The purified whale oil that came out of the taps was as clear and odorless as spring water. There were also the spotless cabins and showers that Captain Jakobsen had talked about. Even so, nobody would come south with the whaling fleet except to make money, and lots of it.

Back on deck, the dogs were being lowered in cages, and it was soon our turn to follow them down. To save time I was to share the basket with Alan, and it was a tight squeeze to get the two of us in, especially as I was now the proud possessor of six bottles of Worcestershire sauce, which I held as well as my cameras.

The technique of dropping onto the deck of the *Norsel* was to hold the basket on the derrick just above the highest point to which the *Norsel* rose, and to deposit it on deck as she fell. This required very nice timing. Unfortunately, as the *Norsel* heaved up beneath us, we were a little too low, and the tracks of a weasel caught the edge of our basket. Next moment we were tipped out upside down. I clutched my camera, which was now a reflex action, but had to let the sauce go. There was a crash of broken glass, a gurgling sound, and a strong, piquant smell. I did not laugh quite as unreservedly as everyone else, but thankfully two bottles remained intact.

We finished at suppertime. It began to snow. I put the camera away and had just entered the shower when I saw through the porthole the quintessence of a whaling picture. A catcher had come to collect the fender whales. In the blowing snow, which blotted out the background, a muffled figure was standing by the harpoon gun waiting to catch the rope. A photographer's work is never done. I dashed out, collected my camera and went on deck, but by that time the catcher was almost lost in the storm. Sadly, having missed the picture of the day, I went once more below to wash off the smell of whale.

We had whale steaks for supper, best back of cachalot, and in spite of having to forget where it had come from, it was delicious. It even passed muster with Phil, our Australian observer, who had not eaten a full meal for weeks because of a delicate stomach.

chapter 10

I N T H E long Antarctic twilight we entered light pack and headed southeast. There began a procession of ice floes past the cabin porthole that was almost continuous for the next six weeks. Occasionally we would bump one and it would grate past like icing sugar on a sieve. The continuous roar of heavy pack which we later became used to had not yet begun, and a bump was still an event.

Pack ice is formed of frozen sea, pushed and piled together by the winds, broken up again by the storms, melted and sculptured into a thousand strange shapes.

When the pack is open, it wallows gently in calm seas, seas that are sometimes blue and sometimes black and clear like volcanic glass. The ice under water is green, a wonderful shining green, bright with moving reflections. Above water it is alabaster white, and carved in a million shapes, as ever-changing as the scenes in a fire. There are castles, strange animals and birds, human faces, gods and devils, all moving past in endless procession; as if this is not enough, the pack is as stuffed with life as a garden with spiders.

Crack went a rifle from the bridge, disturbing the Antarctic peace, and a seal rolled over on the floe, spouting blood that spread like wine on a tablecloth. The telegraph rang and the engines went violently astern. We ground against a floe, a long drawn out scraping as ice scored off the paint all along the ship's side. There was confused shouting. I grabbed my camera and ran on deck.

The seal lay dying on the floe, twisting about in pain and surprise. The dogs began to howl. A burly seaman jumped overboard and gaffed it expertly in the head. The body became shapeless and heavy on the ice.

And then, attracted perhaps by the noise, a snowy petrel darted across the scene, more white than the ice itself, quite silently, as if it were a snow angel, the poor seal's departing spirit taking wing, away across the frozen desert.

On deck, a little man sharpened a curved knife to a razor with professional skill. The skin, with two inches of yellow fat, was pared away from the meat as easily as the peel from a Jaffa orange. They spread it on deck, blubber upward like a slippery mat. The body, the meat almost black, lay steaming in the frosty air. The meat was for the dogs; the kidneys and liver, for our supper. Phil brought an ax and chopped out the brains, a special tidbit for his delicate stomach.

It was the beginning of a trail of carnage that followed us south. Whenever man is with animals—many animals —there is *always* blood, but this was the first time I had seen it so violent, and I was shocked.

To the Norwegian sealers a seal was a cabbage and nothing more. They were wonderful fellows, but their callousness made me sick; they butchered with gaffs and knives and guns—and a deft flick of the wrist.

I knew that what I took of such scenes would never be shown.

There was one seal, however, that I illogically did not object to killing, and that was the leopard seal. It is described in the *Antarctic Pilot* as a "carnivore of the most ferocious and bloodthirsty kind." It is a great slug-headed brute, thirteen feet long, with jaws like a reptile and a set of teeth that would make a tiger look silly. On the ice these great seals will certainly attack a man who is stupid enough to venture close, and they have been known to snap off an arm in one bite; but they are ponderous on land, and it is in the sea that they are supreme. Along with the killer whales, they are the great predators of the Antarctic. There is hardly a seal without scars on its body from their attacks. It also accounts for the fact that the Antartic seals, unlike seals elsewhere, are reluctant to take to the water.

The seals in the Antarctic have no natural enemies on the ice, there are no polar bears. So when man comes along, they are easy prey, having no fear and not understanding what it is all about. So day after day as we forced our way south, whenever a seal lay sunning itself near our course, it would be shot.

One afternoon I was sitting on the bunk with my guitar, watching the procession of pack through the portholes. The loneliness of the place had put me in a mood, and I was composing a piece of music to fit the occasion. The Doc was sitting at his tape recorder dictating a long letter in Swedish to his mother. There was one of the usual rifle shots from the bridge. The ship stopped to pick up the seal, but by now it was so commonplace that we took no notice.

Suddenly Walter put his head in at the door. "Tom, would like you to go up to the saloon."

Most of the expedition had already assembled there when we arrived, and they looked excited.

"We have just shot a Ross seal," our leader announced. "This is an achievement. You know that it is very rare. There are hardly any specimens in existence, and even if the expedition does nothing else . . ."

Ross seals, we had read, were peculiar creatures, ugly like a bulldog, with a small, almost decadent mouth and enormous double chins.

"You are the only zoologist on board, Tom. Will you take care of it?"

"Certainly, John. The most important thing to preserve is the skull, but there may be other parts that require study. It would be best to radio back for someone to check with the museum. In the meantime we can keep the whole animal on ice."

"Good," he said. "Well let's go down and see it."

He led the way and we trooped along to the after deck. Our precious specimen, the first important discovery of the expedition, lay in the cuppers, surrounded by an interested group of the crew. Phil Lawes was chopping its brains out for his supper with a large **ax**; his delicate stomach.

"Phil. . . !"

"The most expensive dish ever eaten," someone remarked at dinner that night. Fortunately, next day *two* more Ross seals were shot, so Phil's error ceased to matter.

However, the most wonderful creatures of this white desert were not the seals but the penguins. The fact that one had seen them in zoos and in pictures, had read about them ad nauseam, did not detract in any way from the thrill of actually seeing them, because nobody had ever done them justice.

A rather amusing incident in connection with penguins had occurred shortly before I left London. I had attended a briefing at which, since there could be no script, I was to be told just what sort of film was required and what the government angle should be. In order to have something to work on practically, every Antarctic film—from Ponting's film of Scott onward—had been collected for projection.

John Grierson, the father of documentary and a great character, was to give the briefing, but he was caught up in a meeting, and we had to start without him; later on he arrived, but after watching only five minutes he impatiently stopped the show and the lights were put on.

"Stobart, that's not what we want at all. Everyone makes these goddam subjective films. What we want is an *objective* film—not a film from the point of view of the expedition, but a film of the invasion of the Antarctic *as seen through the eyes of the people who live there.*"

There was a startled silence. Then an anonymous voice at the back said quietly, "There ain't nobody there but penguins."

"Oh, we don't want any ruddy penguins in the film," shouted the great man jumping up. "O.K., that's all," and he dashed out.

"Well," I told the Doc as we leaned over the rail watching a group on a floe, "at least such a surrealist briefing makes you *think!*"

If John was certainly (and thank God) not a typical civil servant it was equally certain the penguins were. They were all little men from the Treasury—town and country planning—enjoying endless conferences. Their view would surely express the official government view of the *Norsel* invasion, if only one had been making a satire.

We had pushed southeast for some days, now following the ice edge, now forcing our way through the pack, and now getting stuck and just drifting. It was during the first of these periods when the ship was stopped that we caught the first penguin. It came trudging toward the ship purposefully, like a keeper come to tell us off for trespassing.

Felix, the comedian of the crew, and I, went over the side after it. To begin with the penguin clearly regarded us as just two more penguins. He maybe thought us a bit big, but what of it? Nobody on the ice did each other harm. We each took a flipper and began to walk toward the ship. He came with us, not unwillingly, waddling between us like a fat child between its parents. But very soon, also like a child, he got bored and refused to come. He began working himself into a rage exactly like Donald Duck does when he is frustrated. He got so mad he gave Felix a sharp peck. Felix let go. Then he pecked me and I let go. Then he took off over the ice.

He was not very fast, but expert at dodging. A hilarious chase ensued, which became more and more hectic as we were encouraged both by yells of laughter from the ship and by the irate quackings of the penguin.

At length Felix brought him down with a Rugby tackle and held on. I took off my sweater and dressed him in it. There was not much he could do then because he was in a strait jacket, and we carried him triumphantly back. Once on the ship, he quieted down and simply stood about looking puzzled; finally the crew got bored and, having no fresh fish to feed him, we let him go.

There were many different species of penguin, and some had never been kept in a zoo, so it was inevitable that we should discuss whether we could take them back. They could have survived the tropics in the refrigerated room, but there was the insuperable problem of what to feed them, so the idea had to be dismissed. Personally, I was glad, because I do not like to see penguins in a zoo. My objection is not because the penguin minds, because I don't think he does. It is the surroundings we give them! Painted concrete spirals, even if objects of architectural beauty, are no setting for a creature that lives in the most white and virgin land in the world. Far from giving pleasure to any sensitive person, it hurts to look at them. It is a truth that when we move things from their natural surroundings, they usually cease to be beautiful. For instance, nobody who has hated everlasting flowers as dusty relics on their landlady's mantelpiece can realize how beautiful they look growing on the dry Cape mountains. On the other hand, it is reasonable for a man to want to satisfy his curiosity, even though he cannot travel. What is the solution? Well, it is at least one of the rewards of my work that through film I can show things in their natural settings and perhaps help to plant a nail in the coffin of concrete penguin pools, which will one day be as surely out of fashion as stuffed foxes in glass cases.

Whenever the ship was stopped by heavy ice, I tried to get shots of the penguins but there were difficulties. The huge emperor penguins were fabulous birds standing as high as a child, with glossy silver breasts and a shade of yellow on their necks. Unfortunately the seamen thought their feet would make good purses; others, that the skins would make good capes for their girls at home. So as I was filming, a ring of men waited around to kill my actor as soon as I had finished. I found it hard to keep my temper, not only because I wanted to work quietly and undisturbed, but because it went so strongly against the grain to kill such beautiful and confiding creatures. However, for the sake of peace you must keep your mouth shut on an expedition, and for a cameraman especially that is a golden rule.

Ever since we had taken the dogs and whale meat on board, the deck of the *Norsel* had become an evil, slippery surface, a mixture of dog ordure and whale grease which had even been trampled down the passages inside the living quarters. In fact Peter, our little Norwegian dog expert who had joined us off the *Thorshøvdi*, stank so badly of blubber and dog that I could not bear to sit next to him at meals. Working almost without ceasing, looking after forty dogs, he had no time to change. Peter had an almost brotherly understanding of dogs, and even used to mix in their fights. Huskies behave as soppily as an actress's lap dog toward human beings, but when they pile into a fight, their intention is that somebody should get killed. And a fight is easily started. It may be set off by a bully, by a dispute over a bone, or by sheer jealousy. Patting one dog and ignoring the rest is a sure way of starting a bloody battle.

The fights would break out at least once a day, especially in the fore part of the ship where the dogs were loose. Lips would be drawn back to show wolflike fangs, and unlike the Irish, nobody *asked* if it was a private fight—everyone joined in. This included Peter, who would come running from whatever he happened to be doing, and dive among them, literally head first.

A moment later the dogs would scatter, yelping, in all directions. It was impossible to see what actually happened, but I gathered that the technique was to seize the ring-leader—who, like any agitator, is always the same one —and bite his nose, a much more effective and personal punishment than using a whip.

By alternately forcing our way through the pack and drifting, we reached a point off the ice tongue on the Queen Maud Land coast. This could be seen as vague shadows from the crow's-nest, although some said it was a mirage and others, a cloud. In any case the argument was academic, since we could go no farther. The pack was impassable unless bad weather came and broke it up. Occasionally we would move the ship to keep it free, occasionally, enticed by the glimpse of a lead from the crow's-nest, we would batter our way for a mile—but mostly we were just stopped.

We were stopped for so many days that many of us began to wonder if we should ever reach the Antarctic coast before the short summer was over. We became really bored, and one symptom was a ring of empty bottles that littered the ice around the ship. This, with the sewage that spilled onto the ice, made stopping for long periods even more unattractive. Yet all around us was this peerless desert, and when you walked half a mile over the pack and turned around, it looked quite ridiculous, as if a ship had somehow got into the middle of snow-covered land where it had no business being.

To me these prolonged halts were a godsend, as I was able to move about at leisure with the camera. The safest way to do this was on skis, but I was not expert enough to manage without sticks and also carry the gear, so I had to go on foot.

Mishaps occurred to many of us, and mine happened one day when I was crossing a patch of unstable ice. A floe suddenly turned over under my boot, and I went straight through up to my armpits in the icy sea. I had just enough time to sling my camera to safety before I submerged.

Shouting for help, I wondered how long it would take a leopard seal to find my legs and bite them off. I doubt if I should have felt much, as after the first shock my body began to numb. Someone came running and took the camera but they could not approach close enough to drag me out. However, I could catch hold of a ski stick and managed to pull myself flat and so crawl out. Although I had been in for only a minute, already my legs were growing useless from the cold. It was a warning that the Antarctic is not such a safe playground as one might think.

After some days it became clear that we should never make the coast at this point, so we pulled out and headed back toward open sea. The idea was to find calm open water from which the airplane could take off. From the air the pilot might see an opening.

The first take-off must have been a nervous business for S/Ldr. Watford, the senior R.A.F officer with the flight. The machine had been transported through weeks of storms, drenched in corrosive sea water, and was certainly not as good as when it left the factory. Then the floats were a new design, never tested. The open space in the ice was calm but not all that big and bits of ice the size of footballs drifted about, quite enough to smash the floats. Whales were likely to pop up at any moment (and later did), and in spite of the special radio compass, once airborne it was not going to be easy to find the ship again in this wilderness—and if you didn't?—well, everyone talked of rescue, but were the chances all that good?

One must always have the camera ready to catch a

possible disaster. The little machine streaked over the water but seemed reluctant to part company. The run cannot have taken more than thirty seconds, because I caught it all on one winding of the camera, but it seemed far longer before the machine was pulled clear of the sea. It had to be jerked off to hop some ice fragments, then it settled almost back again before gaining height and turning away out of sight.

That first flight did not discover open water, but after further reconnaissance the airplane spotted a lead running south, and once more we made progress.

The days went on and we always found open water. Sometimes, of course, we had to stop, back up, and charge at a heavy floe, sometimes the route was tortuous and we had to corner sharply in narrow channels between miniature bergs too large to break; but now, short of very bad luck, we felt sure we should get through to the coast. Then the problem would be—could we land?

chapter 11

WH E N we first saw the continent it looked like a dome
of pink sugar rising over the pack, but as we got nearer,
we could see it for what it was, a vast cliff of ice, broken
in capes and bays, but everywhere as sheer and clean
as a precipice of white marble. There was a strip of open
water between the pack and this cliff, and when the
weather was sunny, it looked as blue as the Mediterranean
in spring, dead calm, and with little icebergs floating in
it. In the red of midnight it was wine dark with pale
pink castles. Only when there were sudden snow squalls
or overcast and all gray with a bitter wind flicking the
water did the Antarctic hold any menace or the promise
of the black winter to come.

It was urgent that we find a place to land, but in most
places the cliffs were some two hundred feet high, and
the few places they were lower, the ice was broken and
torn by crevasses. Even now we could be turned back.

We hunted for several days, first one way along the
barrier edge and then the other. We would stop, lower the
airplane, and watch it go skimming away on its search,
sometimes with Captain Giaever as passenger and sometimes with Captain Jakobsen. We listened to them over the
radio, recording the conversations on Doc's tape machine
so that if they crashed, we should have a record of all
changes of course and *perhaps* be able to find them.

"There seems to be some sort of a bay here," said

Flight Lieutenant Tudor, the second pilot, one day. "We are just going down to see. Hold on."

This proved at last to be *it*, a real harbor with an ice quay just high enough for unloading. It might have been made for us, and we christened it "Norsel bukta"—North Seal Bay.

We landed at night in a twilight too dark to film— a disaster because it was a climax to our story, but otherwise lucky because when I jumped off the boat, I was so excited I left my spare film behind. While crowbars were driven into the ice to make the ship fast, a ski patrol was organized to reconnoiter the route inland. Some hours later it returned to tell us that the way was clear onto the barrier. We had arrived.

It was good to get off the boat, but when the dogs came ashore, they went wild, rolling in the snow and biting chunks of ice. They tried to fight, barked, wagged their tails, and showed their delight to be alive. It was sad to think, as they were tethered out in lines (out of reach of their neighbors), that these dogs would never go back. That when their two years' work was done, they would have to be shot.

At the moment the dogs were useless, they had to be trained before they could work, but we had the weasels to haul the sledges. They were landed as cold inanimate metal, but after some heating up with blowtorches one by one they were started up and driven off to be got ready for the job ahead. This job was to haul a hundred tons or more of gear and stores up to the top of the barrier and to the site of the base.

The barrier ice is a feature of the Antarctic. There is this vast continent, so big that if you put it down in the north, it would fill the Arctic Ocean from Norway to Alaska. Ice accumulates here, and being plastic, eventually flows outward from the middle—since it floats—riding out over the sea. From time to time the edge breaks away in icebergs. This is the shelf, or barrier, with its clear-cut edge, and it may be floating or grounded on the arms of a bay. You do not know, and you can only hope the bit you land on is not destined to break off as the next iceberg. Like so many things, it *looks* all right, but then so does the earth—until you have been in an earthquake.

Because of the shortage of time, it was not possible to site the base in from the edge of the ice a sufficient distance to make entirely sure that it would not go floating out on top of an iceberg one night. It was only too clear that this was a distinct possibility. The quay on which we landed felt quite definitely as if it was floating. Looking down crevasses even farther inland, one could clearly hear the sound of water in the depths. Yet the bare two-mile margin eventually given to the base was the result of other considerations. It was now getting late. Once the sea began to freeze, the *Norsel* could not get back. So the ferrying of the stores from the quay to the base site—"Maudheim"—would become a race against time. It must not be too far.

At first it was the ship that was the center of activity. All day long there was the rattle of the winches as crates, boxes, and the sides of timber houses came out of the holds and onto the ice. And the sound of motor engines as the weasels ground up the hill to the top of the barrier with one or two heavily laden sledges in tow. The R.A.F. men were assembling a second airplane and fitting it with skis instead of floats. I was prancing around, covering all this activity and occasionally venturing to the top of the cliffs for a distance shot, but even on skis the number of crevasses made moving about alone a little risky. I could have done much more with a companion and a rope, but everyone was working.

The weather blew up into a blizzard and slowed down the building. The wind was more raw than I had ever felt, burning the face like fire. It was not cold for the body— that is something you mostly feel in the city, where you dress for fashion rather than warmth—but it was wicked for the fingers doing any delicate job. One would go out with hands buried in large gloves hung around the neck in a lampwick harness, but when it came to operating the camera, one had to strip to a thin pair of silk ones. The fingers were white and numb in a trice, so now they must be warmed in the pockets, dancing with the pain as the blood returned. Then once more, over and over again in agonizingly slow progress.

It was poor comfort to watch Weston and Quar on the airplane, fumbling clumsily with nuts and pliers in the same sort of misery.

Only the huskies did not seem to mind. Soon they were drifted up and covered beneath the snow, just mounds marking their position. But when I set the camera up near them, a tail would push up at one end of the mound and bump up and down in welcome, then a nose would appear, and the mound would get up and shake itself into an animal. This was maddening, because I wanted to catch those incredible mounds of snow before they moved, but they always jumped the gun.

Driving over the barrier in a weasel was an experience. It seemed out of place to be speeding at thirty miles an hour in such a wild region. The wind bit cruelly as one headed along the well-beaten track toward the distant black dots where the stores were piling up in the middle of nowhere. All around was *sastrugi*—ice formed into sharp ridges by the wind—and over toward the sea were huge icebergs in the sky, although you knew there were no icebergs there. They were mirages of icebergs many miles out of sight, yet so absolutely clear in the sky that one rubbed one's eyes and just refused to believe it all.

There were occasional accidents between the ship and the base. On one occasion I fell off the weasel with my camera, but managed to roll on the ice like a parachutist, clutching the precious camera to my bosom.

Then boxes were always dropping off the sledges, and if unnoticed, they had to be retrieved by the next convoy. One day this led to a more alarming incident.

Charles was driving, and I was perched up on the back.

"There's a box fallen off over there," he said, pointing to a black shadow on the white some hundred yards off the track. He swung the weasel around and we headed toward it.

As we came near, from my better vantage point I suddenly realized it was not a box but a great hole in the ice.

"Stop, Charles. For God's sake stop."

We halted with ten yards to spare. The hole was at a point where the canopy of snow had just failed to cover a large crevasse. From the depths came the sound of the sea, although we were already a mile inland from the barrier edge. It was not pleasant to think that perhaps this great crack ran under our *road*, perhaps even under the base itself, like a hidden well under the old kitchen and dry rot in the floor—perhaps! One could never tell.

As the stores began to pile up at the base, we began to work there instead of at the ship. Foundations had to be dug for the huts, through the softer snow and down to hard ice. The huts, double walled and lined with silver foil, like a thermos, had to be erected and tied down with cables anchored in the ice. It was quite easy to make concrete. All one did was melt water and mix it with ice chips. The whole conglomerate froze solid in a few minutes.

Meals had to be cooked in the open. The potatoes in the crates were iron hard and you could scrape the skin off in flakes of dirty ice. All the water for coffee had to be melted, and yet working when the sun shone was thirsty work, so coffee was always being brewed.

I don't know why I got the idea that iced coffee would be a welcome drink—partly thirst and partly seeing so much cold coffee poured away. So one day I added some tins of condensed milk and stirred in snow to produce a delicious drink.

"What, iced coffee here?" people shouted at me. "Don't be silly." But by the time a few had tasted it and found it good, I was to mix a bucketful. Then we all drank so much we made ourselves ill.

"You have to be careful about cold drinks," said the Doc. "You know what happens in Arctic Sweden? Alcohol reaches a very low temperature before it will freeze, and people come back to their hut having left the aquavit bottle out. *Skoal,* they knock it back and down goes liquid ice. Every winter someone gets killed that way."

We had got a hut completed, and stacked all the boxes in double lines, with their lids inward. If you have ever tried to dig a box out of one night's snowdrift, you will know why. But if boxes are stacked properly, the top of the channel between the rows can be covered by a tarpaulin. Then the whole thing can get drifted in—as it will—and you have a passage lined with cupboards full of stores.

It was now time to say good-by. With one hut completed and another nearly done, there was nothing the wintering party could not do for itself, and we all repaired to the boat for the last time. It seemed slightly unreal that we, who were going back, were already looking forward to seeing our friends again, while the others were busy scribbling their last letters, as they then believed the last and only letters they would send before they in turn pulled out in two years' time.

It was a sad thought that we were now going to leave the party behind. It was bad enough for us, but clearly the strain told heavily on those who were to remain. Like many things, it is one thing to decide something and another to do it. Corporal Quar was asked to stay—he was a radio technician—and he did (after urgent cables to the Air Force in London). I too was asked to stay—which I regarded as a great honor—and I was awfully tempted, but I had made no arrangements, and it was impossible at such short notice, so reluctantly I let the question drop. Moreover, I had my film to finish. It is an experience missed that I have regretted ever since—and yet if I had stayed, I should have missed other things, so perhaps imagination must supply the rest, as it must for many things.

The sun was shining. Killer whales were breaking surface in the bay, but it was not that side of the ship we were looking over. We were watching the men on the ice. We had searched the ship high and low for things that might have been forgotten and had given, sold, or swopped everything we could spare and some we could not, such as most of the ship's food. Doc had my dry shaver, and we had shaken hands, really meaning it. It was going to be lonely in the cabin without him. Now they all lined the ice as the moorings were cast off and the ship, going slow astern, pulled out to show the frieze of icicles that edged the quay. Waving, waving madly, we gathered speed, and the little figures of our friends became small and passed out of sight behind a bluff of ice. So great was the tension of parting that it seemed silly to do it at all—or why *now*— why not go back for just one more chat, like the man who must always have one more for the road.

My cabin felt deserted now that Doc was not there endlessly dictating into his tape machine the long incomprehensible letters in Swedish to his mother. To recall old Doc and his tape machine made me laugh. It was partly there because John Giaever had forbidden a record player.

The Doc used to pull everyone's leg by listening through earphones to some music he had recorded on his tape machine, bouncing up and down to the rythmn, which was disconcerting to watch since we could not hear the music he was bouncing to. It had seemed an odd thing for a leader to forbid a record player, which one would think a sensible comfort. But I wondered now if a situ-

ation would arise such as the one John had experienced—
which had made him forbid it. Well, one did not know.
Repetition gets on human nerves. The same habits, the
same personal foibles, the same dirty stories for months—
and then years—with no relief. Can there be any greater
strain imposed on man than wintering in the polar night?
So maybe John was right.

John had been a long time alone in the Arctic with
another fellow, and this other fellow had a record player.
One by one the records got broken until there were only a
few left. The other fellow still liked them, but John did
not. He hated them, he hated them like poison, and they
began to drive him mad.

"Well, you can't go on telling another man, 'For goodness' sake, stop playing that damn record player,' without
causing trouble," said John. "I couldn't break the last few
records, but there was the record player. I fixed it by
breaking the spring.

"But that other fellow was not so easily beaten. The
bastard could twiddle the record around with his fingers
and still get a caricature of the music."

It was interesting to speculate on how many of my
friends would still be friends when they got back.

We were pounding north through pancake ice, which
is ice like pancakes with their edges curled up, floating
on the sea. It meant it was freezing, winter was coming,
and we were cutting it close. I was reading in my bunk
when I was surprised by Captain Jakobsen. He burst in,
his face as black as thunder.

"I've just had a radio message. Has Doc left a box
here?"

"No, we searched the whole place."

"Then what's this?" He pointed dramatically to the
huge black box which filled the cabin floor. It was so
large and so much a part of the furniture that we had
forgotten it.

130

"That contains all that bloody Doc's medical stores. We shall have to go back." He lapsed into Norwegian cussing. "How could you have missed it?"

"It was like looking for the spectacles on your own nose, that's all I can say. To us it had become the cabin table."

So some hours later we were back at the quay. As a contrast to our touching good-by there was now not a soul there to see us. In silence we dumped the box on the ice and put straight back to sea, headed at full speed through the fast-freezing lanes and toward the open ocean.

chapter 12

We EXPECTED to be in Cape Town for break-
fast, but we were still at sea. At dawn there was a thick mist
all around and the engines were going dead slow. It gave
us a little more time to spruce ourselves up, but I did
not see how I was ever going to get the creases out of my
tidy suit. I was not looking forward to the difficult hours
ahead when I should gradually have to convert myself
from an aboriginal man to all the nonsense of our civilization. Because of course it is nonsense. For one hour or
more on returning from an expedition you can still imagine
man as he really is, with beard and hair down to the
waist. It is an amusing experience when you are closeted
with your bank manager. He, of course, does not know how
he appears to you, and while he unearths bits of paper
that will enable you to beat up the town, he is no doubt
thinking that man's natural state is a smooth, pink face,
powdered and scented discreetly with synthetic flowers,
and that you, you scruffy object, smelling of dead whales,
are the eccentric because you did not really have to be
that way unless you liked it. You may comfort yourself
with the thought that he is the one with ulcers.

Just now I was not looking forward to landing because
I was in the halfway house. I was clean, yes. My suit
was clean enough though crumpled, yes. But what made
it all the more incongruous was that I had a mop of hair like
a basin cut below the ears and a sackful of stinking seals'
skulls to dispose of somewhere in the town. No doubt the

museum would help in due course, but the skulls had first to be got there in a taxi.

I had been a bit silly about these skulls. Making our way out of the ice, we had lived in a refrigerator and there had been no particular reason to clean them properly. There had been other and more important things to see to.

We had run slap into heavy ice not long after leaving the Antarctic coast, and for several days we had made more ground drifting toward the treacherous Weddell Sea than we had north to open water. Continuously over two days we had to use dynamite to break the ice, and in the empty ship the explosions had sounded alarming, *whang*, like a sledge hammer on a boiler. Each time we made a little progress, but there was always the Captain or mate in the crow's-nest, peering out with an anxious face over the desert of ice, searching for the dark reflection of a water sky, for an opening running north toward deliverance. And every day it got colder, more dismal and cloudy, with snowstorms, so that one knew that winter was closing in.

Nobody had really dared to think much what would happen if we did get stuck. The ship would drift into the Weddell Sea, where the ice jambs up against Graham Land. There she would be squashed as flat as a sardine tin under a steam roller. We had little reserve food because we had left everything for the expedition in a fit of last-minute pity and generosity; we should have to exist on seals and penguins if we lived at all. The only hope would be to make our way over the ice—back to our own expedition or west toward the Graham Land bases—not much hope really, and for me, as far as I could see, none. Because I did not have the clothes. The only kit allowance the Government had been able to find a precedent for was one designed for the tropics, a quite inadequate sum for the Antarctic, and I had only managed on it by combing war-surplus stores for parachutists windbreakers and discarded U. S. Navy gear. The government would spend thousands to save me, but not to give me an extra vest.

We got out, of course, but we had a damaged rudder which made the ship difficult to steer. We had also been treated to an awe-inspiring sight which, next to an earthquake, is about the most frightening display of natural power I have ever seen.

It had been a tense morning. We were approaching the open sea and had just begun to feel the ice move slightly with the swell of water beneath. The ice was dirty, and there was an odd yellow light which filtered through storm clouds and made everything look like brimstone, the color of a river in flood. The ship was forcing its way through the floes very slowly, and there was a bitter wind from the west.

There were two icebergs in sight, standing up from the level of the pack like ghostly aircraft carriers. At first this did not seem anything unusual, but I could see by the faces around when I went onto the bridge that there was some worry nagging in the air. There was a faint booming sound which I put down to the floes grinding against each other in the swell. I thought there must be a walloping storm out to sea, perhaps fifty or a hundred miles.

But when, standing there and shivering in the cold, I borrowed some fieldglasses, what a murderous sight! The icebergs, with their million tons of momentum, were plowing through the heavy pack as easily as if it were tissue paper. Indeed, watching the point of impact, from which came the thunder of tumbling ice, seeing the whole floe structure crumbling and pushing up, one could only shudder at the terrifying forces of these nightmare polar seas. It was man's skill, and his skill alone, that would bring him through, because it was Captain Jakobsen and not our steel hull that would save us. We hoped devoutly that our ship was not in the way.

135

"Icebergs move with the current, the pack moves with the wind, and when they are in opposition . . ."

But our captain knew his business. The nearest berg passed astern and went roaring on toward the horizon. When the danger was past, we drifted below to eat and get warm.

Our relief was soon forgotten once more in the misery of the sea. The outwash of the storm increased, loose floes rose and fell in the waves, as oily as our sausages. That seals skulls might stink in the heat was forgotten, only nausea occupied our minds as we limped with our damaged rudder across the south Alantic.

And now we were nearly home. The fog began to shift and swirl. Sometimes there were clear holes like islands, then an increase in speed, but always followed by a dead crawl and incessant blowing of the foghorn. "Come on, Captain, come on Full Fahrt, our luck will hold, you won't hit anything on the last day and we want to get in." But when the fog broke, streaming upward in the sunlight there had been good reason for going slow, for the towering cliffs of the Cape of Good Hope lay close on our starboard hand.

"I need assistance, my rudder is damaged," went the message proudly to the signal station. The wounded ship had returned, moving dead slow into Table Bay, with the sound of welcoming hooters and a tug guiding us alongside.

I flung my film and the sack of skulls in the taxi, jumped after them, and gave directions hurriedly before the smell seeped through. After a moment the driver turned round and gazed at the sack, then his eyes slowly came up to mine. Was I a trunk murderer or was I not?

"Some specimens for the museum . . . scientific! Not too bad with the windows open. Ha, ha!"

The driver said nothing, but meaningfully took a handkerchief from his pocket and held it to his nose.

When I reached the museum and paid off the taxi with a handsome tip, I thought this business of the skulls was all over. But of course it was not. A gray little man behind a desk was unhelpful, and then another, and another, all over the town, until finally, defeated by their lack of interest, I took the bag back to the ship, and asked the crew to deliver it safely to the expedition committee in Oslo. All that embarrassment had been for nothing. And all the work had been for nothing if I had known it, because as soon as my back was turned, someone without a love of science chucked the precious specimens overboard.

It seemed a pity to be in Cape Town and see nothing of South Africa, so I determined to see it if I could. Besides my curiosity, there was another good reason for staying. I was in great anxiety as to the outcome of my months of work. The film would go on ahead by air, and I imagined everyone sitting in a theater in London, fangs bared to criticize my work. I wanted to keep out of the way until I knew the worst. The most wearing aspect of expedition filming is that you see nothing until it is all over, have no possible chance to correct mistakes, and the accumulated worry of this drives you to the breaking point. You fear returning as if it were the end of life.

The snag about touring South Africa was that I had no money—a depressingly recurrent theme—but it occurred to me that perhaps Crown might have use for some South African material. I had film left because I had not used the 35-mm. camera at all, it had frozen solid in the cold, so I cabled London saying that I intended to tour the Union and asking how much was it worth. London thought it as taking a great risk in sending me 200 pounds—this included the first-class boat fare to which I was entitled. I intended to go tourist class and put the money toward the trip, but the tourist class was full. I was lucky to get a first-class cabin at 140 pounds. This left me 60 pounds to see South Africa and to get a list of shots as long as your arm. However, due to people in South Africa being more prepared to take a chance than the civil servants at home, the Tourist Corporation gave me 100 pounds' worth of free travel and introductions to various big interests. The project had become possible.

For six weeks I toured the Union, visiting the diamond fields, the gold mines, and even the new Free State gold-field which was then still getting the first shaft sunk to the reef. I held in my hands uncut diamonds that would have financed all my expeditions for life, and even saw 100,000,000 pounds worth of gold stacked up like so many brass bricks in the reserve bank.

Yet what I was really waiting for was that telegram from London, and when it came I scarcely dared open it.

"ANTARCTIC MATERIAL EXCELLENT. WHEN ARE YOU RE-TURNING?"

Now I could make haste back to the boat, bearing away in my mind a glimpse of the wonderful scenery of Africa and the determination to return one day if it were possible.

chapter 13

"HAVE you seen today's personal column in the *Times?*" John asked over the telephone. "Because there's something that might interest you. Some fellow in Belgium is advertising for a 16-mm. cameraman for work in central Africa."

"It sounds like missionaries," I answered. "Something to do with missionaries in the Congo—in any case I'm not interested, but thanks for calling."

I put the telephone down with annoyance, the sort of annoyance a saint must feel when he is tempted, because although it is fun to be tempted when you may possibly fall, it is a sheer waste of time when you know you will not.

The fact was that I had just turned over a new leaf. For years the wives of friends had been telling me that I really was getting old now and ought to *settle down*, and at last I was going to take their advice, I was going to take an office job.

When I had got back from the Antarctic and the film *The White Continent* was a success, I had hoped for a time to get more expeditions, but nothing came along, and it all seemed to have been an autumn summer because I began to feel I really was getting older, as those depressing women said. I had worked on as a free-lance, turning once more to scientific and biological films but at the same time trying to develop some inventions. Nobody, however, seemed to be in the least interested in financing the work, and I did not have the resources to carry the projects through on my own. Discouraged and with a dwindling bank balance, the prospect of regular employment seemed attractive, although I hated myself for being resigned, for admitting defeat.

Geoffrey Summer, director of a cartoon film unit in London—whom I had known in India during the war—had come down to look over what I' was doing. At that time he was searching for someone who had both artistic and scientific qualifications. He hoped to achieve a better integration between these two sides of his unit. He offered me this job, and I took it.

"Are you quite sure, Tom, that you want to settle down now?" he asked me.

"Yes, I'm quite sure," I answered.

"All right. You can start next week."

But now there was John on the telephone, playing the part of fate and saying, "No, no rest for Stobart," because of course as soon as I got back to my laboratory I began to wonder what this African business was all about, and surely there could be no harm in finding out—not that I would take it any further, of course!

When I telephoned Antwerp and a distant foreign voice asked me to meet his wife at the Dorchester, it was on a Friday night, and my new job began on Monday. However, my curiosity was now thoroughly aroused. What sort of person would advertise for a cameraman in the *Times* personal column?—in England from Belgium?—and then send his wife over to interview candidates in one of the swankiest hotels in London. It did not make sense. It was so odd that I was suspicious, and nothing could have prevented me from going along just for the hell of it.

"It's obvious," said a friend. "Belgian missionaries have never heard of any other hotel in London but the Dorchester, and I'm sure the missionary's wife feels she is the best judge of character. I bet she's a grim hag and runs the whole show."

This seemed the only possible explanation, so when I walked into the lobby of the hotel one afternoon to keep my appointment, I was expecting a formidable religious woman with perpetual disapproval written all over her face.

The few people in the lounge were clearly not what I was looking for. A redhead who looked as if she had stepped out of a beauty ad; an elderly woman with purple hair and hands heavy with diamond rings; obviously the missionary's wife had not yet arrived, so to while away the time my attention went back to the redhead. I wondered from the bit of spotted veil she had over her eyes, whether wearing it seemed like a permanent hangover.

I went over to the desk. "I am expecting to meet a Mrs. Denis here. When she comes in, will you tell her . . ."

"But *that's* Mrs. Denis," said the porter, indicating the redhead.

If you have ever taken a sip at a cup of tea and found it coffee, you will know just how I felt. . . .

"Now," said Mrs. Denis, when I had sat down, somewhat flustered. "Please tell me all you have done . . . your experience."

"Well . . ." I had to collect myself; after all, my main reason for coming to the interview was to satisfy *my* curiosity, not hers. Here she was, questioning me and behaving as if I wanted the job.

"I've been in the Himalayas, the Antarctic—perhaps if you have time to see my work . . ."

"When would you be ready to come to Africa?" she asked at length.

"You haven't told me what the job is yet."

"Oh, you don't know what the job is?" She seemed surprised. "My husband, Armand Denis, is making a big game picture for R.K.O."

141

"Good lord, I expected missionaries."

"What, us missionaries!" She laughed. "I admit the *Times* personal column was an odd place to advertise, but I thought we might find someone who liked exploration as well as being a technician. If my husband agrees, I will see you in Nairobi in a month's time."

Of course it was unthinkable that I should settle down, and the situation was somewhat embarrassing. I had been in my new job for exactly three days and I had to give notice. Geoff, however, took it very well, just looked at me and said, "I thought you told me you'd got it out of your system, y'bastard." Well, I'd thought so too.

A month later I flew to Paris and there boarded a Constellation bound for Africa. Even hearing the announcement on the airport speakers—Rome—Athens—Cairo—made my spirits lift. The lights of Rome looked like an elaborate pattern of jewels; then there was the moonlight on the Greek islands, and all night one great black wing with the red glow and blue fire of the exhaust gasses as we droned south. The dawn came up as we flew up the Nile Delta, and the sky was sandy, as if lit by the reflection from the desert. At last one could again breathe the air of lands that were not crowded, not tamed, and not hedged in with regulations.

I had to spend a week in Cairo on a small job photographing a T.W.A. "Connie" over the pyramids. It was hot, and flying low was very bumpy, though somehow the pictures were taken, the Armenian photographer who came along to help retching on the floor, poor fellow, during the whole flight.

The Ethiopian Airways plane with a huge Technicolor Lion of Judah painted on the fuselage took me down the Red Sea to Asmara. I spent the night in a hotel that was suddenly Italy in Africa—then over green mountains and towering thunder cumulus to Addis Ababa, where it was raining, very green, and with pools of water and mud in the unmetaled streets.

South of Addis the mountainous landscape became brown, with bushes following the endless dry water courses; but we passed over rivers swollen with floods from the highlands, and one had spilled a great patch of red storm water into a blue lake, the edge spreading in feathers like a wet water color. Another huge cloudbank marked the place where Mount Kenya stood, but we had no glimpse of its 17,000-foot crag, and gave it a wide berth.

In Nairobi I could see Michaela Denis waving from the other side of the barrier as I waited for the customs and immigration check. Beside her stood an out-sized man wearing a pith helmet and a loose American-cut suit. This was the redoubtable Armand, with whom I was shaking hands a moment later.

Nairobi was a bigger town than I had expected, ablaze with purple bougainvillaea, but otherwise so much like any other town that I was surprised to learn it was still easy to see lions and giraffes only a few miles outside. The people for the most part looked as people do in a colonial town, not very smart and a bit pasty-faced, but now and then there would be someone with a rugged tan and a battered bush hat, or a car disgorging a party of travelers with a mountain of baggage and veneer of red dust that showed they had come a long way. They suggested the wilder Africa that stretched out beyond this oasis of modern buildings.

For a day or so I enjoyed the rather plush and carefree atmosphere of the Nairobi bars. Armand had a lot to do, and in fact the longer he stayed, the more he had to do. Even when he thought he was free, Michaela always seemed to have an appointment with the hairdresser, so Armand would arrange to see yet another man who claimed he knew a place where the elephants wore pants or something equally improbable. It was all talk, as it

143

always is in Kenya, and it seemed as if we should be stuck in the town for the rest of our lives.

Then one day Armand came storming down to breakfast. "Let's go," he said. "If we don't just get the hell out of here and leave everything, we shall be stuck forever." A lesson that my friends who say it is business that keeps them from enjoying their life might well remember.

As soon as our van stood loaded for departure, I could feel Armand's mood change. I know mine did, because now at last I was going on safari, my first trip in Africa. The pick-up, however, was not large enough for all of us to sit in front, and someone would have to sit shut in the back. I guessed that would be me.

The back of the pick-up was closed in and the only way to see out was through the expanded wire of the rear doors, not a very good first view of any countryside. Moreover, it was filled up with boxes, cages, ropes and axes, cans of gas and camping gear—everything you can imagine that might (or even might not) be needed in the bush. Whoever sat there would be cramped and miserable.

It was then that Michaela showed what kind of woman she was. "You have long legs and you haven't seen the country before," she said. "I will ride in the back."

That the boss's wife should not demand as her right the best and most comfortable seat, as nearly every other woman in those shoes would have done, was a great surprise, and it was a very kind gesture. Of course I pretended I couldn't possibly allow her to travel in discomfort. Equally, of course, I intended that she should. I did not appreciate just how generous she was being until she emerged at the end of the 150-mile drive, bruised, suffocating, and almost unrecognizable under a mask of dust.

The first few miles was on a good tarred road, edged with white posts. There were grassy hills with here and there a clump of banana trees and an African village. The

144

side of the road was bare red earth, with a creeper like convolvulus growing on it.

Presently we came to the lip of the Rift Valley, to a point which must have one of the most wonderful view-points in the world. I was expecting it because it had been described to me in advance by Professor Julian Huxley, with whom I had had dinner just before my departure from London; but even his enthusiasm had not done it justice.

The Rift Valley is, of course, a gigantic line of weakness in the earth's crust which runs from the Dead Sea down the length of Africa. In Kenya it cuts deep, with escarpments and several soda lakes, the haunt of countless flamingoes, so numerous that from a distance they are like an incrustation of pink coral at the edges, always shifting, as if seen through the rising hot air. Opposite us was the extinct volcano of Longanot, and behind it a range of hills rising from a grassy plain.

"That's the Masai country," said Armand.

My ideas of Africa were still a muddled mixture of Rider Haggard, Cherry Kearton and Martin Johnson, so it came as a shock to look down on the Masai territory from the seat of a comfortable vehicle on a smart tar road. I had thought that there should be at least a foot safari of several days to reach it, but I learned with regret that in these days foot journeys in Africa are virtually unknown and that it is unusual to have to walk more than a few miles on foot.

The road dropped in many hairpin bends down to the valley floor. Here it was hot, and while above was forest, down here the grass grew long, was hay dry and rustled, suggesting concealed snakes or leopards. The grass-hoppers sawed a steady chorus. There were euphorbias like branching candlesticks of olive-green, and the flat-topped thorns which above all provide that romantic quality to the African landscape. Some blue bee eaters sat on a bush and watched us, while all the time Armand was throwing off his town worries and becoming a different man; he showed off this country with as much enthusiasm and pride as if he had planned and planted the whole place himself. I understood this because it is one of the reasons for wanting to make films, this urge to pass to others the thrill and excitement you yourself feel.

"Don't you think Africa is wonderful?"

Certainly Africa was wonderful, and I breathed great hot lungfuls of it.

We still had over a hundred miles to go, and soon we had turned off the main road onto unmetaled dirt and were climbing out of the Rift Valley toward the Kenya highlands. Here in the little settlement of Rumuruti was situated Carr Hartley's Big Game Farm, which was to be our destination.

We arrived after dark. To one side of the driveway was the dim outline of huts and pens from which came the sound of soft breathing. Senses pricked at the terrifying smell of large carnivores. Something was banging against the wooden walls of its pen, the wild uneasy at being enclosed.

Our headlights shone on the cluster of thatched round huts which comprised the living quarters, and Carr was standing there to meet us. In his late thirties, red-faced and heavy, my first impression of him was that he looked like an extremely tough proposition. I was right.

After cleaning up, we were sat down to a meal of game stew. I had stupidly expected all Kenya to be hot, as the colony lay right athwart the equator, but it was now bitterly cold. Not having brought any warm clothes, I had an uncomfortable time, as all through dinner the wind whistled in at a broken windowpane behind my back. Carr's children had been on the prowl with catapults.

The following morning I was up at dawn, eager to look round the Big Game Farm. I had imagined stock

146

pens with, instead of bulls and cows, giraffe and rhino, and this was pretty much what it was like, except there were also giant rabbit hutches of leopards, lions, and cheetahs, and a flock of ostriches wandered around instead of barnyard hens.

But there were no fields. Outside the compound was raw Africa with its dry grassland and thorns, patches of rock alive with lizards and a sudden green swamp in which one imagined all sorts of nasty snakes. Far in the distance was a gently sloping cone of blue forest with a white spike on top—Mount Kenya. In the early morning air it had already collected a few fleecy white clouds.

Looking nearer home, within the tumble-down fence of the farm were several battered trucks. Bill Longenecker, Carr's American assistant, was already lying under one, repairing a broken spring. A Turcana tribesman, wearing a gray clay hair-do with dried cow teats holding ostrich feathers, was cutting up a zebra to feed the lions. Wherever you walked in the long grass there were bleached bones to trip over. Skins were drying in an open shelter, and there was a pile of old horns, dry, with the life gone out of them. The atmosphere was that of rough danger, very refreshing after too long a time in a city.

However, the chief hazard to the newcomer in this place was Carr himself. Carr—and his wife, Daphne, were both inveterate practical jokers, and I was very soon caught out.

After a day spent filming tame ostriches and various babies around the pens, in the evening we drove to examine an old compound in which some of the scenes for *King Solomon's Mines* had been made. It was a beautiful place, rocky, with some yellow-trunked fever trees, and as we strolled in the cool of the evening, Daphne pointed out a certain plant, something like a landlady's asphidistra but with spotted leaves.

147

"If ever you run out of sweets, try that," she said. "It's juice tastes like honey—try it."

I picked a leaf, and sure enough a lovely yellow syrup ran out. I took a good lick. *It was bitter aloes.* However, Daphne's jokes were quite subtle compared to Carr's.

I went out with him not far from the farm one day, taking a few shots of his truck plowing through thorn-bushes. The truck was a power wagon and it could go through obstacles like a tank. The only risk was that one of the three-inch thorns which grew on the bushes and were as hard as steel would penetrate the heavy tires, which they could easily do.

When the work was finished, I stood on the running board outside the cab for a ride home, too lazy in the hot sun to climb into the seat. "Mind my legs on the thorns," I told Carr. "Don't drive too close."

No sooner had I said this than he put his foot hard on the accelerator and headed straight for a large clump. I was not unduly alarmed because I knew he was just trying to frighten me. He would swerve away. But he didn't swerve and we went crashing right in. Somehow I managed to hold on until the truck came to a standstill. I had not felt any pain, which was a bad sign because you never do when you get the full works.

Looking down, I could see that my legs were covered with blood from a dozen gashes, my clothes were torn, and there were some nasty purple lumps where thorns had been driven in an inch or more and broken off. These were mostly in my bottom, and would have to be pulled out with pliers.

"I'm sorry," said Carr, tears of laughter streaming down his red face. "I meant to put on the brakes at the last moment, but I forgot that I had torn out the hydraulic cables on a tree stump a way back."

chapter 14

I HAD read several times of Carr Hartley's fabulous animal-catching excursions, and when some days later Armand told me I should go on one of these trips to see what I could pick up, I knew I was in for some really rough stuff. I was already getting hardened up and used to the large animals, which I suspected was Armand's main reason for starting me off at Hartley's farm—a sort of battle inoculation. After all, it is less alarming to meet a wild rhino after you have rubbed noses with a caged one—well, a little.

We started out at dawn, Carr in his battered catching truck, followed by the transport vehicles loaded with crates. There was quite a party, with a dozen Africans and several assistants, which included Nancy, Carr's secretary, and Bill Longenecker, the assistant.

After driving along rough tracks for about two hours, we turned off into a range of low hills covered with the ubiquitous thornbushes and dry grass. Here we stopped to organize ourselves for the catching.

The dispositions were as follows. Carr was driving—the key job. On a seat bolted to the front mudguard, and well strapped in, sat Bill with a long bamboo pole and a rope noose looped around it. One end of the rope was held by the African "boys" in the back of the truck, while on the other end the noose hung from the bamboo as if it was the business end of a fishing line. Bill's job was to fish the noose over the neck of the running animal and then let go of the pole. The animal would be held on the rope by the boys behind.

I was supported in a wooden cage just behind the cab. Here I could stand operating my camera without using my hands to hold on. Unfortunately the planks were not padded.

Nancy, who under a feminine exterior had a body as tough as a lion, stood up beside me like a tank commander. Her job was to warn me if I was going to have my block knocked off by overhanging branches, (looking through a camera, you can only see the small area you are filming) and also to bang urgently on the roof of the cab if from her vantage point she saw any large boulders or hollows ahead. The driver would not see these until the last moment because of the long grass, and as he would be doing 50 miles an hour across country, virtually blind. . . ! The reason for the speed, of course, was that animals have to be outpaced in a short dash. An animal that has been chased to exhaustion dies, and the good catcher ropes his victim in a first desperate rush.

The other trucks were to follow behind, keeping us in sight, and ready with crates to hold the animals we caught.

We drove slowly across the country. Beyond a low ridge we dropped towards a donga, or river course, along which grew a thicket of yellow-trunked fever trees. Suddenly our pace quickened. A large herd of zebras could be seen on the far side of the donga.

The zebras, which had stood watching us for a moment, now wheeled with a flash of stripes and set off up the valley. Not wishing to press them too soon, we followed slowly up our side, looking for a place to cross. After two hundred yards a gap appeared and Carr swung the truck toward it, accelerating at the same time.

Now, with the vehicle bucking and swaying, and with violent swerves to avoid the worst obstacles, we tore across the donga and up the other side of the valley, rapidly

150

closing in on the flying herd until we were driving right alongside.

The zebras were a wonderful sight, straining every nerve to get away, tails flying and a mad light of terror in their eyes. But it did not last long. A young Zebra was singled out, the truck edged toward it, and the noose was expertly dropped around its neck. A moment later the truck stopped and the boys jumped off and pinioned the unhappy animal by sheer weight of numbers. The lasso was loosened. The captive stood there panting, head hung low and froth dripping from its mouth. The excitement I had felt in the chase now gave way to the pity one must always feel for a creature that is defeated.

The zebra was given a drink of water and an injection to stimulate its heart and to calm it. Then it was loaded into a crate and left in the shadow of a tree to be picked up later, and begin its long journey to captivity in some zoo. We got back into our truck and started off in search of our next victim, which was to be an oryx.

The oryx is a tough animal and tricky to catch. He is the size of a small mule, gray, with long horns, straight and sharp like rapiers, which he does not hesitate to use when pressed. Moreover, he is cunning, and doubles suddenly in his tracks when chased, making for rocky or stony ground where pursuit is impossible.

We had not driven far in our search when suddenly, as we were crossing a hollow of particularly long grass, one of the lookout boys behind shouted, "Cheetah." The truck swerved at the same moment and accelerated up the valley.

I saw very little of this chase—I was too busy hanging on. The cheetah was only occasionally visible as a brown streak flying through the dry grass, and I do not know how Carr managed to keep it in sight.

The cheetah is the fastest animal in the world, and even tame ones have clocked 64 miles per hour. My guess is that a wild one in the pink of condition can do considerably better. Therefore, however fast we tore over the ground, there was no hope of our keeping up with the animal during its first burst. But a cheetah tires easily at this pace, and within a mile ours was exhausted. Somehow the place where he sank down was marked and we made a beeline for it. It was wonderful spotting on the part of our boys.

The cheetah crouched, panting, his teeth bared in a snarl, a beautiful spotted creature, looking like a cross between a dog and a leopard.

No sooner had the truck stopped than Carr sprang out and grabbed the animal by its long tail. The cheetah, the dumb blonde of the wild, is better endowed with body than with brains. Instead of turning and tearing the man on its tail to shreds, as of course it could do, it always tries to escape. In this case the tug of war did not last long because the catching team was well trained. One boy had nipped around to the front with a folded sack which he thrust in the cheetah's mouth. The cheetah bit and held on, thinking it was knocking hell out of its enemies. Two more boys had a box open and ready. Carr picked the growling animal up by the tail and the scruff of the neck, and with one heave dropped it neatly inside. Then the lid was slammed shut and tied down.

Before we found our oryx we had captured several more animals, including a baby giraffe. The same technique was used, but in the giraffe's case the mother stood by, and the separation from her baby was tragic. She circled round, not quite daring to attack, and uttering a strange groaning cry which gave the lie to the general belief that the giraffe, which has no vocal chords, must therefore be dumb. The baby stood on its wobbly foal's legs and looked bewildered, not understanding what was going on—only appealing desperately to its frantic mother.

And then my feelings of distaste for this occupation were forgotten because we were once more off in full cry after a herd of oryx, and I had to admit that this was the most exciting sport I have ever taken part in.

To begin with, everything went well. We cut a suitable young animal out of the herd and pressed it hard. But just as the noose was about to go over its neck, it changed direction, swerving right across our front. Carr had to brake hard to avoid running over it. Then it doubled back on its tracks. We swung around after it so fast that I thought we should turn over, passed between two thorn-bushes so that I had to lower my camera and duck. Then we once more accelerated after the fleeing prey.

The oryx was now making for a rocky escarpment, and we had to go flat out to head it off. Once more it doubled back, we dodging between boulders and thorns. It was a superb piece of driving, and our quarry was beginning to tire, but of all animals capable of being caught in this manner, perhaps an oryx is the toughest and can survive the most prolonged effort.

All eyes were now on the chase when suddenly we saw ahead through the long grass a depression in the ground the size of a swimming pool. Nancy hammered frantically on the roof of the cab and Carr crowded on his brakes, but it was too late. There was a violent crash and everything seemed to explode.

The next thing I was helping Nancy up from the truck floor. Splintered wood was all around. We had gone straight through three-by-four timber, which lay about like firewood. Neither of us seemed much hurt, and there was no time to lick our wounds, for although a spring was broken, Carr was already reversing out of the hole. The boys were sorting themselves out of a pile. The only thing that wasn't nice was that we were surrounded by the business ends of nails that had held the photographic cage in place before. But there was no chance to do anything about it now, because Carr was once more going hell-for-leather after his quarry. This time there was no mistake, and the noose went firmly over the oryx's head.

As we came to a standstill I could hear Bill Longenecker from the mudguard seat complaining that the crash had broken a rib. The oryx stood there, half choked by the noose, and yet it still had plenty of fight, for as soon as Carr tried to approach on foot, it put its head down and came straight at him, the two rapier horns in line with his stomach.

Carr coolly stood his ground like a bullfighter and at the last moment parried the horns and threw the animal sideways. Immediately half a dozen boys jumped on top, and the oryx was manhandled into a crate. Even then he did not give up, for before the day was out he had almost kicked that crate to pieces.

The difficulties were not always over after the animals had been caught. On one occasion Carr had roped a fully grown bull buffalo, in many ways the most dangerous animal in Africa. After a sharp fight, the animal had been thrown, and its legs tied for the journey back to the farm.

On arrival, a gang of boys had managed to get poles underneath the huge beast and lift it off the truck, but they could not carry it beyond the door of its pen, as the opening was too narrow. It was deposited with its head inside the entrance but its body outside.

When the ropes were taken off its legs, I expected the buffalo to spring up and charge into the pen. The way it rolled its bloodshot eyes around suggested it was in a perfectly devilish mood.

We were all surprised therefore when the animal refused to budge. Not only would it not budge of its own accord, but took no notice whatever of the thumps, kicks, and whacks we gave it, as we would encourage a refractory cow or pig on a farm. The substantial wallops seemed to pass quite unnoticed on the tough hide.

I had just put my camera down in order to join in

by giving advice and suggesting ways and means when a young Turcana tribesman, recently joined to Carr's circus, jumped down from the truck. Before I realized what he intended, he had knelt down by the buffalo's rear end and sunk his teeth into its tail. That did it. With a bellow of rage the huge beast sprang up and rushed into the pen. The door was hastily barred behind it.

Two nights later it got bored with captivity and charged straight through the back of its sleeping shed, splintering the timber like so much matchwood. That was the last we saw of that buffalo.

chapter 15

I T W O U L D be no exaggeration to say that for sheer unadulterated fun, the year I spent with Armand Denis in Africa was one of the best in my life. Sometimes I worked with him, but as often as not he would hand me a thousand dollars and an air-line ticket, poke his finger somewhere down on a map, and tell me to see what I could find.

"Pick up all you can," he would say, "and cable me if you run into anything really good. I've got to go over to the Congo to see about that gorilla capture." After that it was up to me.

It was the sort of dream assignment that I had always hoped for yet had never believed could come true.

It was after I had been working with him for about two months and had begun to know the ropes that we all flew down from Kenya to South Africa. We wanted to work in the Natal game reserves, which are quite the best for rhinoceros. We hired a car in Durban and drove up into Zululand.

As far as I was selfishly concerned, it was one of the misfortunes of Africa to find that Messrs. Smith, Cohen and Bokie Van Rensburg—complete with wives, kids, radio, and new car—could see just as much game as I could. Game parks are just a glorified zoo, with little Willie throwing oranges at the lions or squirting his water pistol up the elephant's trunk and waiting for it to come back. We used to laugh at a Colonel Armand had met who considered it unsporting to photograph animals with a telephoto lens, but maybe he had something there. It would not have been so bad if one would do better on foot, sticking one's neck out, but one would not: one would do worse. In spite of Willie's oranges, lions had learned that cars were not a danger, and they wouldn't even open an eye when you drove right up alongside. Literally, they would look right through any motor vehicle, and seemed most at home in the middle of a car park. Of course the reason you don't see this in the movies is that every film man wants to show that "Africa is wild and lions are plenty tough," and every audience wants it too. The truth is less attractive.

There are, however, some animals that keep you on your toes when driving even in a game park, and one of these is the rhino. The rhino is dumb, stupid, and does not see very well. He is apt to charge anything he does not understand, from a sparrow to a campfire. He is usually in an evil temper. He hears a suspicious noise, he smells a nasty smell, and comes at it like an express train.

I knew all this, so in spite of the fact that I had been talking to an old lady, a grandmother, the night before, and she had seen the lot, I was still excited to see for *myself*, and when within five minutes' drive of the rest camp we bumped into our first rhino eating thorn by the roadside, I was not disappointed. Under any circumstances a rhino is a most sinister beast.

But Armand was not content with a rhino eating thorns by the road. We had special permission to drive away off the track. The country was hilly, with gullies and dense bushes, so our car was hardly a suitable vehicle; nevertheless we decided to go looking for trouble. Armand was an exceptionally good cross-country driver—he had taken an early Citröen expedition across the Sahara—but today he wanted to do the photography himself, so I had to drive. Michaela was in the back to give us more elbow room.

We drove slowly down into a valley, picking our way carefully between the clumps of thorn. We disturbed various species of antelope and a family of wart hogs, one of Africa's most attractive animals; the latter ran off, daddy in front and babies behind, each tail held stiffly erect like a rampant bottle brush. On a branch a giant lizard turned its cold eyes on us.

Then suddenly Armand was whispering, "Stop, stop, stop," but I had already seen them too. A couple of rhinos were standing together not thirty yards away, and were looking in our direction suspiciously. A car on the road was one thing, but a strange noise here? No, not here.

"Switch off the engine," whispered Armand, who wanted things steady for the camera. I reached over and turned the key. Silence. Grandmothers or no grandmothers, I could hear our hearts beating. I again reached forward and kept my hand near the starter. Then Armand pressed the camera release. The *whiss* broke the silence, and at that instant the rhinos gave a snort and came at us both together. Simultaneously I turned the key of the starter, but the engine did not fire. It was like a Hitchcock thriller.

I was too busy trying to get the engine started to notice much. There was a thunder of feet and the rhinos went shooting across out front. Then I had the engine going, and as they wheeled for a second attack, I crashed the gear home and ripped straight through a clump of thorns in a panic to escape.

"That was a wonderful shot," said Armand winding up the camera, "two at once," and then he was suddenly suspiciously quiet.

"What's the matter?" asked Michaela from the back. She did not seem to have turned a hair.

"I'd run out of film," he said with bitter disappointment, "and we'll never get two charging like that again." We could have cried.

But somehow it was our day; within half an hour we came round a clump and saw *three* rhinos facing us.

"Switch off," whispered Armand as he started his camera, but I was not going to be caught a second time. If the engine made the shot unsteady, it was just too bad.

It was as well. This time the *three* rhinos came at us. I held on till the last moment and then let in the clutch. As we moved forward, they thundered across our back. We had obtained a superb and perhaps unique shot after all.

I said good-by to Armand and Michaela in Durban, I was to go on alone to the Cape to take a look at the bird and seal islands belonging to the South African Guano Administration.

The blue seas around the Cape abound with seals—it is actually the South African sea lion—and you can often see them in the fishing harbors, lying on the surface a stone's throw from the jetty, sunning themselves, rolling over and waving a flipper in the air.

The island I had to visit was a rocky outcrop about a hundred yards wide, with a derelict radar tower, now white with the perching of sea birds, and a ruined hut, a relic of the war. It could only be landed on from a rowboat in the calmest weather. I took an unsuspecting friend named Geoff, from the Shell Company, as a companion. We neither of us quite knew what we were letting ourselves in for.

After brushing noses with seals so closely in the Antarctic, I might have seen enough of them. In fact, I was more interested than ever to visit some breeding grounds because it was something I had not seen in the south and I wanted to complete the picture.

The first surprise was the smell, and the second, the noise. We approached upwind, and the stink was shattering; the smell of guano from the birds, the smell of sea lion droppings, and above all, the smell of dead carcasses under a hot sun. No permanent cold store here, as in the polar regions. Sea lions died ashore, fought and died of wounds, then rotted where they lay. There were no undertakers. The vultures performed this function over most of Africa, but out at sea there were no vultures and seabirds could not cope with that quantity of refuse.

The island was so crowded that it resembled a beach in a heat wave. It looked quite impossible for another animal to get onto the rocks, and the whole mass was in continual movement, making a noise like the bleating of a million sheep.

Before we had time for second thoughts, Geoff and I jumped ashore. The boat was to come back for us on the next day if the sea was not too rough. In the meantime it was all ours. The sea lions made a lane for us to get through, bulls moving into other bulls' territory in the process and starting numerous fights. These bulls were enormous, and we were a little frightened of them, so we made a bee line for the sanctuary of the old radar hut, where we could put our gear and collect our wits. The hut was foul, with Pelicans nesting on the roof.

It was pure joy to work on this island. So often it is a battle to obtain material, but here it crowded in as fast as one could turn the camera onto the subject. Moreover, sea lions are more engaging animals than plain seals. They are both intelligent to a degree, as anyone who has seen them in a circus knows, but a sea lion has a little extra style and personality, with those so attractive Old Bill whiskers and almost a smile.

We slept on the bare boards of the hut, and the sea lions crowded in from the sea until some were using the doorstep as a pillow right alongside us. I suppose sea lions do sleep sometimes, although all night the bleating went on as loudly as before. It was an eerie sight to see them spread around us like black maggots in the moon-

161

light. Their cries were sometimes so human that on several occasions we even looked out to see who was calling us.

Everything went well until the following afternoon when the fishing boat arrived to take us off. The landing place was a rock at the end of a spit. Two large bulls had staked their claim halfway along. They rushed to drive us off, and we stupidly ran back. After that there was no holding them, they knew they were boss.

I suppose an expert would have marched steadily forward with a steely eye and filled with sangfroid. But faced by a roar of fury, backed up by over half a ton of galloping blubber, we were not so brave. We spent half an hour being chivvied about the rocks, eventually outwitting them with man's final answer—superior intelligence. I drew the fire to one side while Geoff sprinted past on the other, and then vice versa. It was not a very dignified exhibition for the waiting boatman.

Even now our troubles were not quite over. We had to get back into the boat. It is one thing jumping from a rocking boat on to solid rock, and quite another jumping from the rock into a boat. The swell had got up and it was very tricky indeed.

First to get the precious cameras to safety. I stood on a rock with my feet awash and waited for the boatman to come within range so that I could hand them in. He had to wait for a lull, and I was watching the somewhat alarming surges when suddenly a larger wave came unseen from behind. The boatman saw it coming and got out, but I did not. It took me into the sea, cameras and all. I had hardly time to gasp before I was washed up again among a pile of terrified sea lions some twenty yards farther down. I looked in dismay at my dripping gear, because I was sure all my work was spoiled. However, the exposed film had been resealed, so the cameras proved the main worry.

Back in the hotel I dumped them into a warm bath.

162

The corrosive sea water had to be got out somehow, and heroic measures were called for. Under more normal circumstances the idea of dumping your photographic apparatus into a bath would be considered a little eccentric —nevertheless, it worked.

chapter 16

My NEXT trip was a longer one, to film, of all things —*penguins*. Somehow one does not associate these birds with Africa, with hot sunny days, but they are there. One of their larger breeding colonies is on Dassen Island, half a day's journey from Table Bay.

I arrived at the dock gates just as it was getting light. The sheer wall of Table Mountain towered over the harbor, with fingers of mist from the tablecloth trailing down the gullies, and throwing into relief the ridges and walls on which the mountaineering club did their sensational climbs.

It was cold, and Antonio, the Italian boatman, was late. I hung around, peering in through the steamed-up windows of the custom's box, wishing, in my thin tropical clothes, that I could get inside. A shunting engine bumped a line of closed trucks across the road and away toward the mail steamer, whose funnels and masts showed above the warehouse. Except for the mountain and the notices in Afrikaans, I might have been on docks anywhere in the world.

Presently Antonio arrived, and picking up my cameras and bag of food, I followed him over to the fishing wharf. It was next to where we had come in on the *Norsel* two years before. I began to think of my friends still down there. When Corporal Quar had agreed to remain, he had made a fateful decision. He had been killed with two

165

other expedition members, drowned when their weasel had fallen over the barrier edge in a fog. Only one of the party had escaped, and he was the Norwegian cameraman who had replaced me down there. I wondered, if I had stayed . . .

Antonio's boat lay bobbing in an inlet behind the main basin. The wharves were already active with the night's catch of crayfish. I passed down my cameras and we set off.

The *Nina II* was a fishing tub, with a diesel engine and a small house enclosing the wheel. She was very slow. I found a place where I could avoid the exhaust fumes to some extent, and jammed myself in. Now this is one of the wonderful things about my work. How else would one pay for such a boat, and how else get permits to see these wonders in the world?

Toward midday the red-ringed lighthouse of Dassen Island came faintly over the horizon, with a sandy smudge that showed it really did stand on land. We put into a lagoon surrounded on three sides with white sand. There was a rusty iron jetty and some low buildings which housed the bird warden and in season the workers who scraped off the yearly guano deposits. This substance is so valuable as a fertilizer that it has proved economical in some places on the coast to construct artificial islands of wood on which the birds can nest.

We were met at the jetty by the bird warden. He examined my pass, and speaking English with a strong Afrikaan's accent, invited me into his house. The boat put off again for fishing.

The warden's cottage was redolent of pebble dash, light, and high winds. There were a few plants growing in pots around the porch and along a thick whitewashed wall that surrounded the yard, but most of the garden was shingle.

After I was shown into the spare room to leave my

166

belongings, I was offered lunch. It consisted of brandy and hard-boiled penguin's eggs—the most indigestible meal I have ever eaten in my life.

"You pay a pound for one single egg in Jo'burg, man," said the warden. "They are a delicacy."

Penguin's eggs are white and chalky, a little bigger than a duck's egg. Nothing striking about the outside. But inside there is, for the "white" is as transparent as glass, with the hardboiled yolk showing yellow in the middle. It looks like an eye on your plate, and you mash it up with Worcestershire sauce.

The penguin I had to film was the jackass penguin, the least attractive in appearance of all the species of penguin; it is the one most commonly kept in zoos. The jackass does not like the cold, he likes warmth, so you do not need to feel sorry for him on a hot summer's day.

Yet *all* penguins are amusing clowns, and the jackass, despite rather dowdy plumage, is no exception. I had only to look over the warden's garden wall to get my first good laugh. Here, on a stretch of level sand, was the breeding ground.

These penguins burrow out of the heat of the sun to lay their eggs, and at first I could not make out more than some dirty beach with a few penguins standing around on it. But then sand suddenly shot into the air. It was a penguin kicking out its burrow. For an hour I tried to film these spouts, but as I never could tell where the next would come, it was a forlorn hope to get good shots in the short time I had. It would take several days' patient work and a lot of film.

My father used to tell me as a boy that when he was in Spitzbergen, he could make the seals come out of the water by playing an accordion. I wanted to try the same thing with penguins. I borrowed a portable radio from the bird warden and took it down to the beach.

Here was a wonderful sight. The beach was swarming

with bathers all dressed in shabby dinner jackets. They swam just outside the surf, they dived into the rushing cream of the wave, and landed ashore with sedate unconcern. They paddled. They played King Canute, running back at the last moment so as not to wet their feet. They stood about in groups discussing the price of fish. They shouted at their children, poked shells about with their beaks, and soon reduced me to helpless laughter. They were not particularly concerned with my presence, and watched with polite interest while I set up the camera. Some landed from the surf to have a closer look, others stood about to pass the time, just as people will crowd round a hole in the road to watch the British workman dig up drains.

When I had got my camera set up, I put the radio down on the beach and tuned in to Springbok radio, turning the volume up loud. They were playing "Sweet Violets," there seemed to be no other tune at that time. The effect on the penguins was immediate. Even from far up the beach, near where the terns flickered over the rocks, the penguins began streaming in to see what was going on. Like a very curious, very serious queue of old men, they shuffled in on the music, with an occasional one coming up at a run and nearly falling over in its anxiety to get a good seat.

At about ten feet from the radio they stopped and formed a ring. The loudspeaker screamed lively jazz at them, but they stood as gravely as a city council at the laying of a foundation stone. They were profoundly interested and puzzled and their respect for toothpaste advertisements was a lesson to cynics like myself. Finally one more enterprising than the rest (and no doubt a future leader), walked hesitatingly toward the magic box, with many a backward glance courting approval. He walked to within a foot of the speaker and with flippers akimbo and head on one side inspected it closely. That penguin now knows as much about how a radio works as does Mrs. Smith of Muswell Hill—in other words—damn all.

Having filmed the general scene, I set about getting close-ups and expressions. To do this, I put my camera and tripod only eighteen inches above the ground and lay down beside it in the sun for a short snooze. The penguins had retreated to a safe distance along the beach or out just beyond the surf, where they washed about like seaweed after a storm. I had hardly lain down before they began to let themselves be thrown up on the beach again by the waves, rapidly running up the sand beyond the wash, as if they were frightened of getting their backsides wet again.

I closed my eyes and kept them shut for ten minutes, enjoying the hot sun and the rhythmic wash of the sea. At the end of this time I began to be worried by the sort of nervousness one gets when standing up to give a lecture and the feeling of being stared at, the focus of a hundred minds. Then something tweeked my foot. I opened my eyes; four feet away all around the penguins stood with solemn faces, peering down at me. I was like a girl who had fainted in a crowd. I felt like shouting, "Stand back and give me air," but very slowly I raised myself on one elbow, and then up till I was sitting and could use the camera. While I filmed them, they took no notice but continued to stand around in solemn and respectful attention.

When I had finished filming I thought I would try an experiment and stretched out my hand to the nearest old gentleman, but a short peck drew blood and made me withdraw my hand hurriedly. These penguins have a small hook at the end of their beak which is very sharp indeed, and they are not so dopey and inoffensive as they seem.

Back in Kenya I was introduced to yet another aspect of making animal films—looking after and handling large pets. It seems to me now that there has been an awful lot of hot air about this, as about most other things—for example, that to a wild animal you smell very nasty if you are scared. I am sure the truth is simply that you must not be jumpy—but that applies to any animal, from the largest to the smallest. You may sweat with fear as much as you like, and provided you behave in an apparently calm manner, don't move quickly, snatch away or run, you will be all right.

But you are full of old wives' tales and do not know this, so it is quite an experience to have a leopard rub its whiskers on your face for the first time.

You are so scared of being scared, when you look into its eyes you feel he can smell your thoughts, as dangerous as if all blondes were mind readers.

Michaela had collected a leopard on her travels since I had been away, and Armand just asked his handyman Bill and I to take the truck and go to collect it.

This leopard was fully grown, a beautiful creature with shiny spotted coat, heavy tail, and big paws. It looked as floppy as a child's toy stuffed with silk, but anyone could see that this cuddly animal would turn into a very mean playmate if it became annoyed. With a leopard you are wise to copy Agag and walk delicately.

The leopard had to be driven through Nairobi and out to the new Spanish style house Armand was building toward the hills. Bill suggested that it would be more comfortable—and more under control—if it sat on my knee. For a time it did this quietly like a dog, enjoying the ride and looking out. I began to gain confidence.

But in the main shopping street, opposite a woman's clothing store, it suddenly decided it would be rather fun to get out of the window (which I had stupidly half opened on account of the heat). There was a dog it wanted to chase. Before I realized what was happening, it was half out, and I had to grab it by the tail, yelling for Bill to stop.

The leopard did not like being held by the tail and began to growl, quietly at first, but with increasing disapproval.

The crowd on the pavement behaved as Etruscans facing Horatius across the bridge. Those behind cried "Forward," but those in front cried "Back."

The crisis was ended by Bill, who rushed around to my side of the car and took the leopard in his arms. With the window up, we quickly bundled it back and drove on.

Armand's new house had a central stairway and there were arches on the second floor which were one day going to be filled with ornamental ironwork. Armand seemed to own a house or a desirable plot in every country in the world, but he never lived in them. I was sure he felt it would be nice to have a home, with all his possessions under one roof for once, but he got restless before the house was completed, wanting to be off somewhere new, a feeling I understood only too well.

At this moment, however, a house project was going strong. Indian painters were standing on scaffolding all over the place, and slapping paint on the upstairs ceilings as fast as they could, no doubt showing Armand—or thinking they did—that it was not *their* fault that the work was getting on so slowly.

We brought the leopard into the hall, where for a time he stood quietly watching the whisking of the brushes on the roof, and gently swishing his tail. The painters had not noticed him.

There was no warning crouch. A ten-foot bound took him onto the sill of an arch, the next onto the scaffolding. The poor fellows were electrified to see a leopard suddenly arrive in their midst. They screamed, dropped their pots and scrambled to safety, leaving a bewildered leopard

171

among spreading pools of paint. The leopard could not understand why nobody would play.

The leopard, which was christened Chewy, proved to be very tame indeed. Even so, with such a potentially dangerous animal it was as well to keep it away from other people—to whom it might take a sudden dislike. Only when you know an animal well can you gauge its mood and learn when to play and when to leave it alone.

The leopard used to play enchantingly with its friends, like a great cat. It was the greatest fun to lie concealed in some long grass and rustle the stems so that he would stalk us. He would finish with a spring, sieze your neck in his mouth, or bat you with a large paw, but he never bit or put his claws out except by accident. Incidentally, the story that if one of these big cats tastes your blood he will eat you is another tale that is quite untrue. Yet the prudent traveler keeps his tame leopard well fed! There are also days when he should not attempt any larks. Like human beings, animals also have their moods. Besides his playful days and his bad-tempered days, Chewy also had naughty days. We had moments of anxiety, as when he suddenly sprang onto our little African boy who was sitting at some distance eating his lunch. On this occasion the leopard made such a rush that I was sure it intended to kill. The two rolled over and over into a bush, but it was only the leopard's game. The leopard and that little boy loved each other like brothers.

On another occasion Bill's girl friend invited me to join them for dinner in her apartment. Bill brought the leopard along too, surely an excellent piece of one-upmanship.

We sat in cane chairs with a whisky and soda while our hostess saw to the cooking of a leg of mutton. The leopard, having explored the house and knocked all the ornaments off the mantelpiece, was lying stretched out on the hearth rug. It was a very peaceful domestic scene until the joint was carried in and placed on the table.

Then the leopard smelled it, and he no longer felt sleepy. With the effortless grace of a ballet dancer, he landed on the table and grabbed our dinner. Then he rushed into the garden with it.

I thought our hostess would now have to open a can of beans, but I had reckoned without her woman's temperament. With a yell of indignation she dashed out after the fleeing animal, seized him, and opening his jaws by pinching his lips as if he were a lap dog, made him drop the joint. She then angrily banged it back on the dish. Chewy was so taken by surprise he did not even growl.

"Bill," she grumbled. "I don't mind you bringing that leopard when you come to dinner, but you might at least train him not to steal off the table."

But perhaps the most scope of all is open to a leopard when he gets loose on a farm.

We had gone to call on Raymond Hook, a farmer who lived under the slopes of Mount Kenya and one of the colony's most famous characters. Hook was an elderly man, tall, bearded, and wore a greasy Australian bush hat with the turned up part of the brim straight across the front instead of at the side, so it gave the impression of a tricorn, and he only needed a steel gaff for a hand to be Captain Hook of *Peter Pan* brought to life.

Among other things, Hook was an expert at training cheetahs, and he also had a collection of other animals of which he was very proud. They included some crested cranes and some odd-looking ducks which looked as if their mother had been shopping out.

Chewy the leopard was now getting cunning. He knew the length of his chain to a *T*, and before we had been in the house five minutes, one of the funny ducks had come within range and been dispatched. Hook was not amused. It was therefore with a certain amount of panic that twenty minutes later Bill and I saw Chewy in action again, but this time he had got completely free from his chain and anything could happen.

The sporting possibilities for a leopard loose in a farm-yard are considerable, but what interested him most was a pig rooting down by the pond. He had never seen a pig before, and approached warily. The pig stopped rooting and turned to face the leopard. He had never seen a leopard, so he did not give an inch. Chewy's advance became slower and slower, until he stopped ten feet from the pig, and the two animals gazed into each other's eyes like two gunmen, each waiting for the other to draw first.

Then the pig gave a defiant grunt.

To our amazement the leopard let out a yowl of terror, turned tail, and rushed headlong back to us. He ended by taking a spring for refuge into Bill's arms. Bill staggered, but managed to hold up.

The leopard, now having a safe vantage point, let loose the most bloodcurdling snarls at the pig, but that worthy, having got the better of it, decided to beat it out of the farmyard as fast as he could go.

A few days later the incident was repeated, but this time the leopard triumphed because the pig's nerve broke at the last moment, and the leopard chased him across two fields scarifying his backside with playful pats.

The disposition of this leopard was, as you may have gathered, almost unique. Tame leopards are usually un-predictable—much more so than lions or tigers—and the fury of a wild one that has just been caught is something one can scarcely believe. I lost a lot of bets one day, trying to keep my face near the wire of a newly trapped leopard's cage without flinching when it sprang. I am told that no-body, however steady their nerves, can do it. The fact that you know you are safe makes little difference. The ears go flat, the eyes look meaner than a maniac's, the lips draw back, snarling, showing the great fangs, and then without warning the whole terrifying fury launches itself at you, for a leopard has the most ungovernable temper of any animal God made, and this temper is never far below the surface, even in a tame one.

Not so a cheetah. Once a cheetah is tame, you can do almost anything with him—in fact, a Cheetah that has been reared on a bottle becomes quite as reliable as a dog. It will purr when it is stroked, give its peculiar bark of pleasure when you come near, and show in many ways that it really likes you; but I am afraid it is otherwise a dull pet. It is dull because it is stupid, and will sit for hours, its beautiful eyes just staring into the distance.

Only once did I see a cheetah bite, and that was a wild one, captured as an adult, that Raymond was training for racing. When you are training a wild animal, there comes a time when you have to handle it for the first time. My impression was that this cheetah was not ready for it —at least, nothing would have induced me to put my hand into its cage. But Raymond was the expert, or maybe he was tough enough not to mind being bitten.

As his hand advanced, the cheetah drew back into a corner, its fangs bared. I was quite sure it was going to bite. The whole thing seemed to take place in slow motion. Hook did not flinch or try to withdraw his hand (the sure way of getting it worse)—and we watched with horror as the cheetah bit in deep.

"Keep still," said Raymond, "keep absolutely quiet."

The cheetah was gently growling, and blood from the injured hand was pouring out and dripping from its lips. Raymond held his hand still and went on talking in a soothing voice. It was a wonderful example of self-control, and this very casualness made it the more horrifying for the onlookers.

The cheetah relaxed its grip several times, but some slight movement and it clamped its jaws together again. The blood flowed more freely, and the teeth sank deeper. For perhaps a minute this dramatic battle of nerves went

175

on, and then the animal gradually let go. Hook was in no hurry to remove his bitten hand, through which the eye teeth had practically met. He poured some water over it to wash off the blood, then he went patiently on with the training, rewarding the creature with pieces of meat as if nothing had happened. I do not think I have seen more icy fortitude in all my life. Hook was certainly a stoic who could have stood having the fox in his shirt.

chapter 17

LABUAN in Borneo was like a greenhouse, with the same smell of watering cans and earthy fiber, but what little one could see from the airport was beautiful.

They had finished refueling our Skymaster for the long leg over the Timor Sea to Darwin. The Air France crew were yammering away as they walked back over the hot tarmac. There was no hostess on this flight, which was perhaps as well. I had somewhat shattered the last one by inquiring the time of the *de coltage*.

"Messieurs . . . there is champagne aboard for fifty passengers. It is in the icebox. If you are thirsty . . ."

There were only five of us on this monthly flight via Brisbane to Nouméa in the Pacific.

I had been clearing up in Africa and was now on my way to join Armand's next expedition in Northern Australia. I was very happy, not only because I was once more bound for a new and exciting country, but because the most exciting of all possibilities was in the air—an Everest expedition.

I suppose of all things I ever wanted to do, going on an Everest expedition was *it*. But I had given up hope long ago. Now, suddenly out of the blue had come news of a fresh attempt scheduled for 1953—and the possibility that a film would be required. I had sent a cable at Christmas, paid a fleeting visit to London in July, and had been provisionally accepted. Everything was hazy—one did not begin to count the chicks—but nevertheless . . .

We were roaring over mysterious jungle-clad islands, balancing our glasses on the arms of our seats. The bubbles winked, the air up here was cool, an intruding comfortable room rushing smoothly over the fever, the crocodiles, the sharks down below.

All you could see of life as the evening drew on was an occasional tiny fire in the mountains of Timor. And then, after eight hours had passed, came the clustered lights of Darwin, with the airport pricked out and a beacon flashing into the dark.

We landed smoothly. The doors opened, letting in a blast of hot air. There was a bump as the steps were pushed up to the opening, and then I was conscious of stepping off the last step and onto the continent of Australia for the first time. To mark the occasion, I bent down and took a handful of soil. It was hot and gritty and very, very dry. Somehow radioactive—and I was not sure it liked me, but that was silly.

"Anyone getting off here?" asked an immigration official hopefully.

He was greeted by derisive laughter. "My oath. Darwin! It's a fair cow."

I bought a map of North Queensland—the part of Australia that sticks up like a horn on the right-hand side of the map—and found Mitchell River. It was a mission. The country was so deserted that the names of individual cattle stations were marked—with plenty of space all around.

"What's there?" I asked the airline stewardess.

"Just a few shacks."

The stewardess's name was Jean, and before I reached Cairns we were all on Christian names—pilot, co-pilot, and the passengers too.

"We'll see you the day after tomorrow to take you to Mitchell River," they told me.

Meanwhile I hired a boat and went out to Green Island on the Barrier Reef. You could walk around it in an hour, a perfect tropical gem, with deep green jungle and white coral sand. I looked down through the crystal water. The floor of the sea was covered with monstrous coral brains, and the fish swam among them like butterflies, while in the little jungle behind, the leaves looked artificial, as if made of wax, and on the overgrown paths there were fat pigeons, all gold and emerald. It was nice to know that some parts of Australia were a paradise, because I gathered that where I was going was not.

The old Dakota touched down in Normanton for an hour or so while we went to a hotel for a meal. We had been hopping from one cattle station to another all morning, landing in rough clearings, and the plane was covered with dust.

"This is your last chance to do some shopping," said Jean. "Burns Phelp store sells everything. Just along the street and . . ."

The street was of red gravel, crystaline and sharp. One had the idea that the soil was brick dust made by the baking of the sun. Corrugated iron houses and hotels with verandas and saloon doors looked as if one had landed in a Western. The few men wore high-heeled boots and were more used to horses than to walking. They were thin, rangy, and bow-legged. They were all making for the bars.

"In the days of the gold rush there were over a hundred hotels here, but now . . ."

A small whirlwind crossed an open space with a twisting column of dust. It picked up several sheets of old corrugated iron and clattered them. Then it went hissing off towards some scabby gum trees. It was all hot and dry as hell.

We landed in a clearing and taxied back to where a group stood by a truck. A bishop who was visiting the mission was dressed like a Boy Scout. Do bishops know how much gaiters and a purple whatnot help them? Armand and Michaela were there too, and I thought they looked a little pale and run-down under the dust and tan.

"How are you . . . What did you get . . . Tell me what you've been doing . . ."

There was also a group of tough browned young Australians standing by the power wagon. Armand's Australian unit.

We drove away to the mission, and at the mission Armand's cameraman Des Bartlett lay in bed, looking like a skeleton. He was suffering from an unknown disease known locally as gulf fever.

Michaela was scratching the backs of her hands. She looked like a case of nodular leprosy. She saw me looking and asked, "Did you bring the insect repellent? The mosquitoes in the estuaries are the worst we've ever seen."

By the mission shacks was a pond of water grown thick with purple flowers and floating leaves. There were aboriginels with faces so black you could not see their expressions until they laughed and showed the whites of their eyes and their teeth. The women were dressed very properly in white mission frocks. Not very beautiful people, downright ugly to our taste, but very nice, friendly, and jolly. Blackfellows!

We slept on camp beds in a grove of mangoes. In the night the fruit bats came and dislodged the ripe fruit in the rain. We could have done with tin hats, picking up the fruit and throwing it back, trying to drive the bats away with pithy Australian curses. But the whispering in the trees went on, and we ended by moving our beds.

To the south of us lay ranching country, the holdings mostly belonging to large companies and being measured by the hundreds of square miles. The land was poor, covered with dry grass and anthills often ten feet high. Unlike the grasslands of Africa, it was very uneven and rough going for the trucks. There were endless gum trees but little undergrowth, which to me made the country dull and monotonous.

Although Australia is mostly famous for its jumping marsupials—kangaroos and wallabies—the wild life of Australia does not begin to compare with Africa's, except in the matter of birds. And Australia's birds are superb.

Through these Queensland woods, especially in the vicinity of water, flew hosts of parrots and cockatoos. Black ones with a splash of red, dove-gray with pink, green with blue and orange, and others as white as snow, and as plentiful as snowflakes, so that when they settled on the trees beside some billabong, it was like a cloud, and the tree at once became clothed in spring blossoms—blossoms that flew away and settled on other trees as casually as if the breeze had wafted them on.

Down on this wonderful scene beat the Queensland sun, and it was so dry that without water a man would die as quickly as in the desert.

"You have to know about this country."

One of the cattlemen took an ax and cut into a bulging gall on a tree. A gallon of liquid flowed out.

"It tastes like mouthwash."

"Yah, that's the gum—but it's safe to drink. . . ."

We wiped the sweat off our faces and got back into a truck that was too hot to touch. Contact with the scorching seat sent shivers down my spine, reminding me that over 100 degrees a man's body must be cooler than his surroundings—or else. If his sweating stops, his temperature will go up—110—120—beyond any conceivable fever—and he dies in the delirium of heat stroke!

I was to go off with a local fisherman—Norm Smith—to the mouth of the Station River on the Gulf of Carpentaria. There in the estuary I was to pick up some sequences of sharks and crocodiles. It was reported that there were some huge crocs there. Armand had already

181

caught one, but he was not satisfied with its size. Although it was a big one, there were reports of monsters, up to thirty feet long, since these estuarine crocodiles are the largest in the world.

"The trouble is the professional crocodile hunters and the high price of hides—all the big ones have been shot out—but see what you can do."

Norm was a little man, serious and shy but experienced at his job. We loaded up a three-ton truck with an iron boat, ropes, barrels of water—gas. We took a quantity of food and some shark hooks. Also a radio transmitter.

"We'll call each other every morning at eight," Armand said as we shook hands good-by. "Just so we know you are all right."

We reached our new location after two days' hard driving, and in all this vast country we saw only one person, a half-caste stockman living in a green-painted corrugated iron shack. His home, like all the homes up here, was very primitive. A giant tropical bean was growing up the veranda, the only vegetable I ever saw growing in this part of North Queensland, where people just live on beef and more beef until they die.

Nearby we discovered the "nest" of a bower bird, an extraordinary tunnel of dried grass with a playground decorated with white stones. It gave the impression of being a child's game, but there were no children here—no women, and few men even for fifty miles, nothing but this desiccated gum forest, and not a sound except the squeaking of the windmill that needed oil and the occasional shriek of a passing cockatoo.

All afternoon we ground along a rough, sandy track, always in low gear, with the radiator boiling. Then we came to open salt flats, we were nearing the home of the crocodiles.

The salt flats looked like dirty snow, and we had to drive over them fast to avoid sinking in. Here and there were pools of water or dark patches of mud and wet quicksand which had to be avoided. Only our truck, a couple of drums of water, and our radio stood between us and an unpleasant death from thirst.

We came to a raised shingle beach and turned right along it. On the other side was the sea, gray and misty with the heat, with patches of muddy surf where it broke on sand bars. One of these was exposed like a low island, and covered with sea birds. There was a pelican nest colony, now deserted, with the desiccated bodies of the failures and unfortunates littering the stones.

"That's our camp," said Norm, pointing to a line of mangrove trees that bordered the river. "My word, it's hot."

When I scouted along the riverbank, keeping in the fringe of trees, I could see through my fieldglasses several large crocodiles on the opposite bank. They were lying on the soft mud. The crocodiles didn't look like logs, but one huge log looked like a crocodile.

The first thing to do was to catch some bait. We had two shark hooks, with steel wire traces, tied to ropes. We had brought with us some bits of meat, just to start off with, and these were lashed onto the hooks.

"Don't forget to tie the rope to a tree before you chuck the hook in," Norm warned me.

I had only just flung my hook into the water when Norm hooked a shark. I knew it was a shark because it flung its head out of the water and I could see its sickle-shaped mouth and teeth, like a torpedo with a grin.

The shark fought like a maniac, twice pulling the two of us to the edge of the bank, but this very fury was the shark's undoing, because it was soon tired, and we dragged it, snapping and thrashing, out onto the mud. Dodging to avoid its vicious teeth, we approached and killed it with an ax. It was eight feet long.

"That's the bait for ''gators'," said Norm.

The Australians always call their crocodiles by this abbreviation of the word *alligator,* although they are not in fact alligators.

We launched the iron boat, and laden with bits of the shark, with axes and ropes, we rowed up the river to set the traps. Occasionally crocodile eyes would break the surface of the muddy water, examine us, and then stealthily submerge.

We rowed in close to the banks, searching for a suitable site for our traps. The mud shelved gently up into the twisted roots of the mangrove thickets. Trees grew on stilts, so that they might have been dead trees stuck upside down in the swamp. It was dark inside. Whatever lay there would be a surprise—an unpleasant surprise.

Inhabiting this nightmare environment were thousands of tiny crabs. They scuttled about, watching us with their nasty little eyes on sticks, or lurked in holes in the mud. There were two kinds. One bright red and the other having a large white claw which was waved like a kind of semaphore. After watching them, I reached the unmistakable conclusion that they were actually signaling to each other, and the fact of their vast numbers and their seeming intelligence brought back memories of Wellsian horror stories—and how helpless man would be if these malicious creatures hit on the signal to attack in unison—for one was quite sure they *were* malicious and that they *were* talking to each other about us. That one day a mutation caused by fallout might spark them off.

Norm found a place for the first trap, a place where there was thick undergrowth and taller trees, flanking a narrow gulley in the mud. A gully just big enough for a crocodile to push up. Here we must land.

Over the side of the boat I stepped knee-deep in mud and, being a heavy man, I kept on going down. It was bottomless. You felt nothing under your feet, as if you

184

were floating—only you were not floating, you were sinking.

"Keep moving," shouted Norm. "My word, Tom, you don't want to stand around in this stuff. Make for the roots."

I did, struggling to pull each leg free. Every time a foot came clear it sounded as if the mud were smacking its lips.

We constructed the trap, climbing about from root to root. It was a simple trap, but ingenious, a log weight over a pulley, a loop over a nail to which we attached the bait, and a wire rope noose to tighten behind the prospective crocodile's front legs.

We made three traps along the river and then rowed back to our camp. As we approached, I noticed that my rope fishing line seemed stretched tight to the tree.

"Probably caught a grouper," said Norm.

We made fast the boat, and springing out, I rushed up the bank. Suddenly, but quite calmly and without any struggle, a huge weight began to move. I had caught a monster. Norm joined me, but we were as powerless to stop it as if it had been a steam roller. The line went steadily out until the strain came on the tree. The rope creaked, the tree bent over and shook, but whatever it was did not fight or break surface—it just sat down on the bottom once more.

"It's a big grouper," said Norm, diagnosing expertly. "Leave it. We'll come back later."

When after an hour we returned, we took in the slack with a hitch around a tree. When the grouper at the other end of the rope started to move, he could no longer pull the rope out—but sometimes he came closer in, and we were able to take up more slack. In this way we gradually got him into shallow water. The first sight was of a spiny dorsal fin, then a great head, and finally a barrel-shaped body. The monster fish did not fight, on the contrary, it was sluggish, but it had a kind of dead weight and stubbornness, like a mule that pulls backward and refuses to be led. Norm reckoned it weighed 400 or 500 pounds.

We had to cut the fish into several chunks to move it, and we carried them up the beach into the mangrove trees. Then we went back to the truck to prepare our supper. There were clouds of mosquitoes, so we moved our beds to the top of the beach, where we got a sea breeze. This kept the insects off.

"Don't forget," said Norm as he spread his blankets, "we've got to be up early. We must look at the traps first thing and be back to call Armand on the radio at eight."

I went off to sleep with difficulty on account of the steady but humid breeze. It seemed that I had only just got off when I was awake again. Some unexpected noise perhaps. It passed through my mind that there was nothing to stop a crocodile from creeping out of the water and grabbing one of us in the dark. Norm's snores proclaimed that he was not worried, but the thought had made me very wide awake.

It was moonlight, and I could see the waves breaking on the sand bar. In the dark shadow of mangroves along the estuary some night bird was calling. It was a strange cry, and since I was so wide awake, I decided to go for a walk and investigate. I got up, trying not to make too much noise on the loose shingle, and putting a flashlight in my pocket, crept down onto the sand. Then I began to walk quietly toward the trees.

The bird stopped as I came to the edge of the mangroves, and there was no sound except for the breeze in the leaves. It was dark in the thicket, and I switched on my light, waving it over the rotting logs and scum-covered pools. Then I cautiously entered. At night the mangroves were a sinister place, and yet the danger was fascinating.

When I came through to the quietly flowing river, I

shone my light out over the muddy water, looking for the red eyes of crocodiles. It was then that I first heard the noise, a ghastly shuffling noise—indescribably stealthy.

For a moment I imagined that a crocodile was stalking me, sliding along on its scales. It did not sound quite right, but it sounded horrid, and the nerves began to tingle at the back of my neck.

Then I realized. The sound was coming from farther along the bank, where I had left the grouper. Something was eating the bait.

I flashed on the light, but at this distance I could not see very much. All I could see was that the place seemed to be covered by a shifting white sheet.

I clicked off the light and began to edge closer.

Sometimes when I made a noise or snapped a stick, the shuffling noise would suddenly cease, as if whatever it was were listening. Sometimes I would think it had gone away and would be about to switch on the light, but it always started again, until I crept up and up, closer, and could see it by the moonlight, a ragged white sheet, shifting restlessly over the pieces of fish, and gasping with its greed and eagerness to eat. Now was the moment to switch on.

It was the most horrid thing I have ever seen. For the white sheet was a milling, fighting mass of hermit crabs, and the sound was the sound of their shells rubbing together. Already the fish was a raw mess—a mess covered by these scuttling horrors, a mess of waving hairy legs.

All around were others coming in, converging from all the holes and crannies in the swamp. A nightmare—but I was only too wide awake. I brought my heel down on one that was trying to climb on my boot. It was a pleasure to hear it crush.

I quickly made my way back to our sleeping place. Here I noticed more of these crabs. They must have been around all the time. They seemed to leave the sleeping Norm alone.

"Norm," I said, waking him up, "these awful crabs."

"What did you want to wake me for," he grumbled. "They won't touch you until you're dead."

In a new country it is always the same—that awful ignorance.

We rowed up the muddy river in the first cool light of dawn, approaching each trap with hope and excitement, gliding silently up until we could look into the dark creeks; but each one was empty. Some pelicans came winging upstream, looking like flying boats. No crocodiles appeared, but there was a sudden, powerful swirling in the water which might have been anything—any savage, unseen drama in the murky depths, where danger could surely be detected only by smell, because nothing could see in that dirty river, like living in a yellow fog.

Back in camp, I gave my attention to the radio while Norm cooked breakfast. I had to keep contact with Armand Denis, but toward the end of my five-minute period, I could only make out a faint answer. "Tom, can hear you but cannot understand . . ."

"We must try again tomorrow," I told Norm, "but I think we are too far away to do any good. We are on our own."

It was on the fourth morning, rowing up the river, that we approached a trap—the one that was the most secluded —and saw the tracks of a crocodile going up the mud into the bushes. We quietly turned the boat to the shore and shoved an oar in upright to anchor it. The tracks vanished into the dark hole of the creek, but we could not see the trap, only that the logs were no longer suspended in the trees—so it had at least been sprung. We listened, but there was not a sound.

We got over the side of the boat, once more up to our

knees in the horrid mud, a most vulnerable position if we were suddenly attacked. Then we floundered our way up to the mangrove roots. Here we paused again to listen, but there was still absolute silence.

"We go around to the back," whispered Norm.

"Just a moment while I get my camera set"—a guess at the distance and exposure in case something did happen—the double job to do as usual.

We crawled through the outer fringe of the mangroves and into the dark interior of the swamp. Here were the pools, the rotten wood, and the Gothic arches of the roots holding the trunks above the scum. We climbed from root to root, circling and approaching the trap, until at length we could peer into the creek. The trap was empty.

"Oh, damn, Norm. It got away . . ."

As if I had pressed a trigger, there was a sudden rush through the bushes, a crash, a breaking of sticks, and a huge 'gator came shooting out from the shadows. I jumped, slipped and fell flat on my back in the mud. Out of the corner of my eye I saw a scaly body streak by, but I was too busy fighting with the mud to be frightened. Then as I grabbed a branch and hauled myself out, there was a loud splash. The 'gator had taken to the river.

"Well, that one won't come back here," said Norm, choking with laughter. "Now you'll have a job cleaning your camera." It was an awful mess.

Although we went on hopefully day after day, we had no luck with our trapping, and wanted badly to get through to Armand on our radio to tell him we were running short of food; but all we could hear was that Armand was there, and that he knew we were here.

Part of the radio difficulty was that although we had had a time allocated to us when others were supposed to keep off the air, the women in the stations, hundreds of miles apart but still out for a gossip, would ignore the rules and come roaring in over our faint signals, drowning us out.

"Is that you, Sally? Saw Bill last night, I say, saw your Bill last night. That bitch is here, if I were you I should get him home . . ."

It seemed that half the women in Queensland were checking up on errant husbands either drunk or chasing that rarest outback bird—a *Sheila*.

Once I intercepted a more dramatic message—to the flying doctor service. I did not guess I was to know more about flying doctors later. I was feeling a little off color and put it down to the heat and our diet. Being short of food, we were living mostly on mud crab and malted milk—not a diet recommended for hot weather, and I put my sickness down to this.

After two weeks we decided that since we were running out of water and were having no luck with our trapping, we had better pull out. We would go back to Normanton, re-equip and provision.

By this time I had become quite ill, and suffered acutely while helping with the heavy work of handling our iron boat. To add to our trouble, before we had driven a hundred yards from our camp the truck wheels broke through the surface and sank in soft sand up to the axles. We tried digging, putting down sacks, and pushing—all the usual expedients, but it was no use. Since we had used up our last water in topping up the radiator, the situation would be serious if we failed, and of course our operations had only succeeded in digging the wheels in deeper.

"There's only one way. It'll do it or break the axle," said Norm. "The double back wheels can straddle a tree. We must cut some trees and lay them."

We unpacked the ax and walked back to the swamp. We searched out straight trees, cut them, trimmed the branches, and laid them like railway lines. By this time it was early afternoon, but at the second attempt the truck mounted the logs and began to move forward. We took a chance on the axle, accelerated and kept going. As we bumped off the end of our track, we sank in again, but managed to keep moving until we reached better ground. Then thankfully we tore away over the salt flats, leaving the estuary behind forever—at least so we sincerely hoped.

Next day we crossed the ferry over the Norman River and came into Normanton. After the experiences of the last few weeks this horrid collection of tin shacks seemed like a metropolis—"Now at last for a comfortable bed, a decent meal, and a cool drink," I thought as we drove up that red main street.

chapter 18

THERE WAS a deafening noise coming from the bar. It was the day before the races, and most of the town seemed to be drunk. Whenever I came in sight, a dozen acquaintances shouted at me to have a beer.

"Come on Tom, what's wrong with you?"

I went in there once more because they would not be denied. I had already tipped the barman off to serve me sarsaparilla. It was the same color as beer to a drunk, but now I was feeling so ill that even the sight was nauseating.

"Come on, digger, have another one," a small New Australian of unknown origin hailed me. I had met him on the road at some time, but could not remember where. I recollected the face of his companion as well, a huge gorilla of a man with the figure of a prize bull.

"More beer here," he roared.

"Ow-ky, Bull," said the barman, setting them up.

It would have been sensible for me to lie down, and that was all I wanted to do, but the comforts I had been looking forward to did not exist. The tiny bedrooms were upstairs, under a broiling tin roof. The iron beds sagged and were too small. The furniture was primitive, with cracked water jugs and filthy basins. Partitions did not reach the roof, and one could hear the woman next door washing her neck against a background of screaming children.

It was no better downstairs. In the back was a dining room where one ate quantities of tough Queensland beef (even for breakfast). There were no vegetables because the plane had not had any room, and of course even in Normanton nobody had a garden. There were also as many flies in that dining room as in a Cairo slum. In the yard the earth closet was overflowing. Bits of torn newspaper were blowing about. It was an outback hotel at its worst, and something at which, if I had been an Australian, I should have been up in arms; yet nobody noticed it.

Outside on the wooden veranda a crowd of cattlemen were shooting dice. One of them had just won 100 pounds, and he staggered in with a fistful of notes crumpled up like old paper. He threw them on the bar. "More drinks all around."

I managed to escape outside when nobody was looking. It was just not possible to take when you had a fever which was getting worse every moment. I walked slowly up the street toward Norm's house with a pulse hammering in my head and an ache creeping in my bones. It would be wise to ask about the local hospital and if there was a doctor. Well, there was a hospital, Norm told me, but certainly no doctor, but the flying doctor would come if I really needed him.

"Maybe I'll feel better tomorrow."

I thought, "I've just got to lie down, even under that tin roof." The world was beginning to go around. Maybe it was just too much of this devilish sun. But when I tried to sneak upstairs, a drunk grabbed my arm and pulled me once more into the bar.

"Come on, Tom, just one more . . ."

"Oh, hell . . ."

The counter was running with beer, froth bubbles on the lead top. The glasses seemed to be coming up so fast that in my feverish imagination I could not count them. They just appeared and vanished, sticky, half-finished glasses, already warm. My sarsaparilla tasted like beer, perhaps filled on a half-empty glass, or perhaps it was just the sour smell of the room. Most of the beer was being spilled on the floor, and the barman was shouting because someone had been sick in a corner.

"My bloody oath. Clear it up yourself . . ."

The huge New Australian was now very drunk. His pal, the small fellow, had vanished. I assumed he had passed out.

At first nobody noticed the police sergeant appear at the door. His face was grim.

"There's been an accident—did not close the cab door —fell out of his truck and run himself over."

The small fellow was dead. Or was I just dreaming it all?

"Ow," said the bull, his cobber, letting out a wail. He began to blubber like a child. He downed another glass as if it were medicine to kill the pain. His face was swollen and red. Tears streamed down. "My cobber's dead."

It was sudden and violent—a man drinking and a man dead—no warning of disaster, no breaking it gently. Drunk, and then sobering up under the awful shock. I was sorry for that bull.

But the bull misread my expression and grabbed at me. "I'm going to knock your block off, cobber, for laughing at me."

"I'm not laughing at you."

In answer, he let go of the bar with the other hand to hit me. Even in a fever I could see he worked in slow motion.

"Shut up," someone shouted.

"I won't. My cobber's dead."

"He thinks you're laughing at him because he's crying."

"I'm not."

"Come on, Bull, cut it out, come on . . . come on . . . come on."

A Russian with a large black beard led me out. "You look as if you've got fever. Leave those drunken sods." There

195

was a handsome crocodile hunter—ex.-R.A.F.—and a pretty girl speaking French. They took my temperature.

"You'd better go to the hospital, friend."

The hospital was a collection of shacks just clear of the town. The staff consisted of a matron and a sister, with some aborigines to help.

"We'll radio for the flying doctor," said the matron. "In the meantime *I'll* dose you."

"What with?"

"Never you mind." She offered me some tablets big enough for a horse. "Either you take the medicine you're given, or you get out of the hospital."

The flying doctor, however, was already in town for the races (or maybe they brought me the vet). He did not examine me. He poked a finger in my ribs and said, "Call it gulf fever," and that was that.

It was the only time I saw the doctor, and when his treatment did no good, the matron again took over and gave me penicillin for luck—the great cure-all—but that had no effect either.

Now I began to be frightened—this was the penalty for mucking around in so many tropical swamps. I could not eat. The food was still that Queensland beef, and the only fruit was brought by Jean, the hostess, who visited me when the plane came through. Mostly I existed on fizzy pop which the sister would go and buy from the hotel. It quenched my raging thirst, but I just lay and sweated in the heat, and lost more weight daily.

Somehow I crawled onto a plane for Brisbane, where I met Armand and for a day even tried to break my sickness by will power and work. But it was hopeless. All I could do was totter around, knowing from Armand's face that he was seriously worried that if I continued like this, I should die. The doctors in Brisbane could not tell what was wrong, and in despair I even bought some aureomycin and dosed myself, but to no avail. I just went on getting thinner and thinner.

"Michaela and I have to go back to Paris," said Armand kindly after ten days had passed. "I am afraid you must have proper medical care. You'd better go back to London."

I sat huddled in the airplane as the hours droned by, often unaware where I was or if it was real. Flying from Australia, it is usual to spend one night on the ground in bed, but when we reached Saigon, there was a half-empty plane leaving immediately for Paris. Maybe that was lucky, because if I had gone to bed, I should not have got up again. Something went wrong on take-off, and we only just avoided a crash.

"If it had happened a few seconds later . . ." But I hardly thought of it.

I left tropical Australia in summer, in thin clothes and no overcoat. It was sleeting in Baghdad, snowing in Rome, and snowing all up Europe to Paris. I sat shivering at Orly Airport, waiting for a plane on to London. By now I was so ill, so cold, and so tired that I could only cling to one thing—I must not collapse until I got home. Why home? Why not a hospital? I didn't know, except perhaps that even to wanderers like me, home is home in the final reckoning.

At London Airport I thought I should have to let them call an ambulance, but after a cup of hot Bovril I thought, "I can still make it." So two days after leaving Brisbane, I fell in at my aunt's door and was tucked into bed.

chapter 19

Y O U ' R E not thinking of going on the Everest expedition, are you?" said the nurse with the naughty eyes, imagining she had made a joke. "Come on, try to drink your milk like a good boy. Then I'll come and bathe you."

"Why do you think I might want to go on Everest?"

"Oh, someone from the Everest office called up to ask about you."

"Hell."

"Why? What's the matter?"

"Oh, nothing. I was just trying to keep my illness a secret, and now they have found out, that's all. Now my last chance has gone."

"You *must* be crazy," she said.

Well, I was crazy, because it was futile, to say the least, to be worrying about Everest, the toughest physical test on earth, when I looked like a famine case and could not even wash myself. Even so, it was impossible to avoid some feeling of despair, because it seemed hard to be lying here when the dream of a lifetime had come true.

In this hospital there was no question of poking a finger in the ribs with a "Call it gulf fever" and then going off to the races. Indeed, it was not long before I began to long for such old-fashioned methods of diagnosis. It was astonishing the number of unpleasant things a modern hospital could think of to do to you.

"Stobart. A little more blood . . . a little bone marrow."

The medical student who was taking case notes for the

199

umpteenth time stood aside, gathering up a voluminous pile of papers listing all the things that were *not* wrong with me. "So there you were, in the swamps of Queensland, swallowing aureomycin tablets like sweets . . . and fogging up the diagnosis."

"Yes, but you see it all seemed natural out there. One had to do something . . ."

The climber they had sent down from the Everest office was called Bill Packard, and he was a New Zealander. He was still getting over polio, which he had contracted in the Himalayas, and having endured the disappointment of being mortally sick himself, he understood what I was going through. Even so, I tried to pretend that I was not really bad, sitting up in bed, telling him I hoped to be fit in time, yet secretly knowing I had had it and was not fooling him; praying he would cut his visit short so that I could once more collapse onto the pillows.

However, the student was right. Thanks to the efficient detection of Dr. Dudley Hart, the consultant, the bug was unmasked—but it had taken two more precious weeks. They said I had amebae in the liver, and at last I could feel the medicine doing good. I began to eat again. Even so, I did not really see how I could be ready to go to Everest in time, and I had little incentive to get well.

"If all goes according to plan, we shall get rid of the bugs in three weeks," said Dr. Hart. "Then we shall send you to a convalescent home. You will need to take it easy for several months," he added kindly.

How the devil could I suggest leaving on an Everest expedition only one month after I escaped from his clutches?

"Just ask, old boy," said the fellow in the next bed. "He can only say No."

"That's just what I'm afraid of."

In the end I put the question through someone else.

"What's all this about Everest?" asked Dr. Hart, when next he came on his rounds. "Even if we do cure you in

200

three weeks, you must take it easy for several months. You've been very ill, and going to Everest would be medically *very* inadvisable."

"But is it ever medically advisable to go to Everest?" I asked in despair as he was in the act of moving on to the next bed.

He looked surprised. "No, I don't suppose it is." He gave me a thoughtful look. "So you want to go that much, do you! Well, if you can pass the medical tests, I won't stop you—but you realize the risk you are taking?"

I caught Sister's eye and saw her smile encouragement. Suddenly I had the determination I needed to get well, and I knew I would make it by fair means or foul, "Probably foul," I thought.

That night I passed on the good news.

I was lucky in being in a ward with a long-suffering sister who did not stand rigidly on regulations. People came in droves outside visiting hours and transformed my bedside into a planning office because things had to be got moving.

Still confined to bed, I had plenty of time in which to think—and to worry. As I have said before, I was far from convinced that a film of professional quality could be made of a Himalayan expedition—and least of all of Everest. But perhaps if I could appreciate the lessons I had learned on Nun Kun and in the Antarctic, there was a slim chance I could pull it off. Time somehow makes one more optimistic —one forgets.

When designing a kitchen, a good architect would do well to imagine he was living in the house, scene by scene. "I am a housewife, and the baby is asleep at last, and my arms are full of nappies, and the bedroom door is open, but when the door is open I can't get down the stairs, so I have to close it with my foot, which makes a bang and wakes the baby up, so I'd better design the house so that

I can get down the stairs without having to close the door first."

It is the same when planning an expedition. . . ."It's snowing like hell with a wind, and I want to change the film, but there is no tent and I look in my rucksack for something to keep the snow out but can only find an old sweater which is hairy and the hairs will get in the camera, so what is it I want? A rubber sheet or plastic cloth? But then the wind will blow it away. So perhaps I need a bag I can get my head and shoulders into and kneel on its edge, facing upwind; and I'd better have it dark so that it shades the film from glare; but now I've got the bag and it's torn, so I must have something to repair it with. . . ."

The whole success of planning for an expedition depends on the thoroughness with which you perform this sort of reasoning, because once you leave on an expedition, if you have forgotten anything, you cannot drop into a store and make good your omission. All you can do is hope that someone else has brought something that will enable you to improvise, and you are a fool to rely on this.

There were certain very obvious problems. First, the cold. The theoretical low temperature at the top of Everest —and nothing less would do as a basis for planning—was about 80 degrees of frost. Well, of course ordinary lubricating oils congeal like suet at much less severe temperatures, but special oil or graphite would do the trick. I did not have to worry much about this, because the correct treatment was well known. I had only to check that the job had been done thoroughly.

Weight was a much more serious difficulty. A camera and tripod are not easy to carry on ordinary climbs, and on Everest mobility would be critical. There was no time to monkey with the 16-mm. Bell & Howell cameras I had chosen as my main weapon, but tripods were not so complicated, and could be constructed from a special alloy which would reduce their weight by half. Then I must have two lusty Sherpas to help me. Not only to carry the gear, but also to provide safety in climbing. I must be independent of other climbing parties. If the Sherpas were reasonably intelligent, I might be able to train them as assistants to some extent—at least so they could share the burden of packing up, hand me what I needed, and take some of the back-breaking work out of the operation. But however well I managed, there would be a point beyond which I could not go. It would be dictated by my own strength, by considerations of tent space, food, and logistics. After that the climbing team would have to take over if the rest of the climb (even the final leg to the top) were to be filmed.

I had seen for myself how well little magazine-loading amateur cameras had worked in the Antarctic. Several people had had them. With some doctoring and special selection of magazines (one of their worst features was that part of the important works were in the magazine, which was mass produced), they might do the job. At least they were light and no trouble—I knew that if I asked climbers, exhausted and fuddled by altitude, to go to any trouble, the work would not get done.

To make things easy and comfortable, the metal parts must be covered in fabric. Touch metal at subzero temperatures and it sticks to the fingers like the ice tray of a refrigerator. High up, one would have to work in gloves, so the release must be extended into a trigger that could be worked even in thick overmitts.

Once the film was shot, it would have to be brought back during the monsoon. It must be kept dry. It would have to be able to withstand being dropped in a river by some careless coolie. It is better to use common materials if possible, ones that might be replaced from expedition stores, so I settled on biscuit tins as containers, with strong waterproof adhesive tape to seal the lids and seams.

So far as personal equipment was concerned my main requirements, in addition to the normal expedition issues, would be thin silk gloves so I could load the camera without the cold metal sticking to my fingers. I also asked for antiglare goggles made of the dark neutral viewing filters used to inspect lighting in the studios. Expeditions usually used rosy-tinted glasses on the snow. These have a good psychological effect but are not good for a photographer, as they distort the colors.

The film company which was to make the film was a small company called Countryman Films. Of the three leading spirits, John Taylor, Graham Tharp, and Leon Clore, I already knew the first two well. They were taking an awful gamble, and I often wondered if they realized just what the odds in favor of their losing their stake were. The chances against the expedition climbing Everest this time, after thirty years of failure, were not very good; the chances of getting a film of such an undertaking, even with all this planning, were almost nil. I guessed if they had felt what I had on Nun Kun, they would have packed in then and there.

I had seen films of Everest taken by men with twice the stamina I had. There had been crippling gaps which spoiled the story. Yet whenever I mentioned my doubts, they were brushed aside. "Shut up, Stobart, you're always making alibis," John Taylor would say. "Any fool can walk up Everest. The trouble is, you're getting lazy with all these nurses waiting on you hand and foot." So what was a desperate doubt ended as a laugh, as indeed it should.

My enthusiasm to get well did not always help. As soon as I was out of bed, I ran up five flights of stairs and produced a kick in my pulse chart like an earthquake on a seismograph. As a result I was set back for overdoing it. This led to a rather silly situation.

The men going on the Everest expedition were by now somewhat newsworthy, and of course if there was going to be a film made, there was going to be organized publicity. My sickness was a good line, of course, but there had to be some gimmick attached to it. Someone told the publicity boys about my racing upstairs to get fit, but by the time it reached the press, the story was somewhat distorted.

"Just to check, old boy, you did pick up the sister and carry her up five flights of stairs, didn't you?"

"Goodness, no! You can't have seen the sister. I wouldn't dream . . ."

"Well, it is too late to deny the story completely. Would it be all right if we said you had carried one of the nurses . . ."

"No, it would not. That would be much worse. What sort of a hospital do you think this is, anyway?"

"O.K. We'll think of a way out, but you've got to get used to publicity, you know."

I can only guess at the subsequent conversation. "I say, old boy, that handout we gave you was not quite accurate. He didn't carry the sister up *five* flights of stairs—only four."

"Desperate to prove he was fit for Everest, photographer Tom Stobart swept up the sister and carried her up four flights of stairs. Then he turned to the doctor. "What do you mean, too weak to climb . . ."

The true story of my efforts to prove myself fit was rather more tense. After I had been passed clear of my complaint by Dr. Hart, I had to jump the final hurdle in the shape of Lord Horder, the expedition's medical adviser. I thought a good walk might produce a better color in my cheeks and did a respectable six miles over the downs. Any fool could have told me what would happen if I walked six miles so soon after months in bed. Of course I displaced the bones in my feet and could scarcely walk at all. It was in this state that I had to see Lord Horder for my final medical.

It is very difficult for a doctor to say you are not fit (unless there is something obviously wrong) when to all his questions you answer, "I'm feeling wonderful, I'm feeling fine." But with Lord Horder's very experienced and knowing eye upon me, I was scared he would notice my feet. It was all I could do to walk normally across the room to shake hands. Then I sat on the edge of the examination couch; as he was a short man, this did not seem an unnatural thing to do. I thought, "This is like coping with the Rumanian customs and looked round for a red herring." When I discovered he was interested in taking movies, I knew I was past danger, I could create a diversion. Even so, I was more than relieved to get out. I walked normally the first yards in case he was looking out the window, and then relapsed into my limp.

It was interesting to go the Everest office at the Royal Geographical Society and meet for the first time some of the climbers who were making up the team. I had never met John Hunt before, and I had expected him to give me a close questioning and perhaps even now say he did not like my face. But John was sitting at a desk piled high with papers, and after shaking hands, was obviously mostly concerned with getting me out of the room as quickly as possible. I looked at him with curiosity, because even his name was new to me. Up to the time I had arrived back from Australia, I had still thought Eric Shipton, who had carried out the original reconnaissance of the south side of Everest, would be leading the expedition; but plans had changed. Now, as I looked at this slightly grizzled soldier, I felt there was no doubting the truth of what a friend who had served under him during the war had told me.

"If nobody else can get to the top of Everest, *John will think it necessary to go there himself.*"

Indeed, truer words were never spoken, nor gave a better description of this formidably determined man.

"I suppose I'll be seeing you down at Farnborough when we go into the decompression chamber."

"I think so."

Of course I needn't have gone. Anything to do with

health still meant sticking the neck out, but I could not resist satisfying my curiosity. What exactly was the effect of altitude?

We sat in a boiler-shaped tank under the supervision of a young Air Force doctor. Oxygen masks were adjusted, the door was closed with heavy screws, and the air was pumped out until we were at pressure equivalent to that of the top of Everest, 29,000 feet. There was no sensation except the slight popping of the ears experienced when going up in an airplane.

There was no sensation when we took off the oxygen masks either—no sense of suffocation—everything seemed quite normal, and that was the trouble. You only saw what happened when you watched someone else.

George Band, our youngest member, was sitting opposite. He was given a pad and pencil and told to write his name; to go on doing it as long as he had the mask off. It was interesting to watch his signature gradually deteriorate until it was a drunken scrawl.

"Are you all right, Band?" asked the doctor, at the same time removing George's watch and tie.

"Yes, I'm fine."

But clearly he was not, so the oxygen mask was clapped back over his face. He went on signing his name, the signature slowly returning to normal.

"What time is it?" asked the doctor.

"It's . . . good lord, I must have left my watch behind."

"Did you leave your tie behind as well?" asked the doctor.

"Of course not. I . . ." He felt for his tie and gasped. Everyone laughed.

"That's what is wrong with altitude. You slip into unconsciousness gradually, insidiously, without knowing anything is wrong."

Dr. Griff Pugh, our physiologist, was made the guinea pig for a more alarming demonstration. He was put right out until, with blue lips and spasmodic twitchings, he began to sink to the floor. Most sinister of all was the way he tried to fight off the mask when the doctor was putting it back on. That dangerous anoxic overconfidence—each man is certain that *he* was all right. It was a lesson to all of us to be careful on Everest.

I was surprised to find that I did no worse than anyone else in that chamber, but it was emphasized that it bore no relation whatever to how we should do on the mountain. Indeed, John Hunt (who had to watch from outside on this occasion because of a spell of sinus trouble) had actually been turned down for a previous Everest expedition on the grounds that he could not pass the laboratory tests. It is not surprising that Griff Pugh insisted that no laboratory tests of this nature were relevant in assessing performance in the field. Yet that test had shown one thing. Like a lie detector, decompression had shown the team as made up of most ruthlessly determined characters, filled with an intense spirit of one-upmanship—competitive—a sort of commando. From that moment on I was rather alarmed at the sort of people I had come among.

Before the preparations were completed, I again traveled down to Farnborough, this time to test my own equipment for cold. It was a raw, foggy afternoon, typical of an English winter. I put on a heavy flying suit, boots, and thick mittens. Then, carrying my cameras, film, and a stop watch, I went into a boiler-shaped chamber similar to the one used for decompression tests. But this one was *cold*. A heavy insulated door a foot thick was opened. There was a rumble of machinery; I had just time to notice the pipes sheathed in ice; then the door was banged shut behind me.

This first room was only half as cold as the inner room, and I went on through another insulated door. Inside the frost bit at the nostrils like pepper, and my breath froze to solid ice on the edge of my scarf. There was a small porthole above the bench through which a face stared in to check that I was all right. Too long in here and I would be as stiff as a chicken in a deep freeze.

I opened my cameras, loaded them, and left them on the bench to chill. Then I ran them with a measured length of film against my stop watch, working in thin silk gloves to keep the metal from sticking to my fingers. Miraculously, the large cameras worked normally. The small cameras, however, faltered and ran slow, which was a blow.

If I had now taken the equipment straight into the open air, it would have been sheeted with ice instantly, just as it would on Everest if I took it suddenly into a warm tent. I had special bags into which the equipment could be sealed, but the cold made the adhesive tape lose its stick. As an emergency I put everything in a biscuit tin and shut the lid. Probably not enough air would leak in to do damage. Then I went out into the cold January evening. It felt like walking into a warm greenhouse. The tin became covered with white frost because it was so cold that the condensed moisture turned to ice, which later melted, so that everything was running wet; but when I removed the cameras from the tins after an hour of warming up, I found them perfectly dry.

Unfortunately there was no time to do more to the small cameras. We should just have to hope that it would not be quite so cold on Everest, and that they would work under slightly less rigorous conditions. But other matters, such as the adhesive tape, had to be attended to. The manufacturers set to work and concocted some special tape which would stick even in extreme subzero temperatures. This special tape was to prove vital to the expedition, and luckily, knowing what unscrupulous scroungers expedition members can become, I ordered plenty.

But it was now February, and the P. & O. liner lay waiting for its passengers in Tilbury Docks. What wasn't done would somehow have to be made good on the mountain when we found out. Our few tools, our odds and ends, and our wits would now be all that stood between success and failure.

chapter 20

THE GREATEST OBSTACLE to climbing Everest has always been politics rather than altitude. One cannot imagine that had it been, say, in Switzerland, it would have remained unclimbed so long. Tucked away on the border between Nepal and Tibet, between countries that had their shutters up, it demonstrated the unfortunate truth that the explorer, like everyone else, must more successfully be a person who can pull strings with governments rather than courageous and tough—though preferably both.

Up to the war Nepal was completely closed. If you were a privileged person, you might get to Katmandu, but you would not get any farther. You would not be allowed outside the Nepal Valley in which the capital stands, so the south side of Everest was unknown. Tibet, on the other hand, had let a few expeditions go round to the north side of the mountain, but only after prolonged top-level negotiations. For the ordinary man it was out. Even if you risked being skinned by the Tibetans and just went, you got it in the neck because if the Tibetans did not catch you, the British Government of India did. They had drawn an imaginary 90-mile line beyond which you could not even approach the Tibetan border without permission.

But after the war Nepal underwent long-overdue political changes and for the first time it became possible to travel there. Indeed, it had become almost a Cook's tour. Once only a bridle path led to Katmandu, so that steam rollers, cars and merchandise all had to be carried over the hills, if necessary in pieces, by enormous gangs of coolies. Now in the space of a few years a regular airline hopped the forested ridges and deposited the traveler in this overpopulated and fertile valley without even getting his feet wet. Indian engineer units were even committing the last sacrilege and building a motor road from the plains. There was comfort in the fact that one still had to walk 170 miles over a tremendous mountain switchback to reach the base of Everest itself.

It takes more courage to fly into Katmandu than it does to walk. When I look out of an airplane and see rocks and trees passing alongside instead of clouds and sky, I hope the pilot values his skin as much as I do mine, though I doubt it. Thankfully, this state of affairs does not last long. You soon burst out of the pass and over the great Nepal Valley with terraces that make a decorative Chinese pattern below.

Charles Wylie and I walked over the turf toward a cane-matting customs hut. A crowd of wild-looking Tibetans were leaning on the rails and staring in wonder at the mechanical bird we had arrived in.

My thankfulness at still being alive was not entirely due to our safe arrival on the ground. The sky was blue, there was spring in the air, and apricot trees were in full bloom. I thanked God that I had been given this day, this dream that had at last come true.

The British Embassy was an orange-brown building set among trees and lawns. Many of the trees were in flower. The Union Jack flew from the flagpole and the entrance looked impressive, as it was meant to. It told you to be on your best behavior.

Sir Christopher Summerhayes received us with the mixture of dignity and friendliness expected from one of Her Majesty's ambassadors. I was a little intimidated. There were too many saluting guards and uniformed servants.

The official-looking visitors' book said you were *really* visiting. There was a slight aroma of protocol.

I was shown into an enormous bedroom with three beds draped in mosquito nets. There was a personal bath with quantities of hot water. I thought, "We're going to enjoy this when we get back," and wondered how the Ambassador would react to us when we were bearded, filthy, and lousy on our return. What price the protocol then? Sir Christopher would have to cope with our social rehabilitation. After three or four months in the wilds a man is apt to forget his manners and belch or worse in the drawing room without even noticing he has done so.

Not all the expedition had arrived. Most of us had come out by boat as far as Bombay, then Charles Wylie and I had flown on ahead because Charles, who was a Gurkha officer and spoke Nepali, had the arrangements to make. I was there because I wanted a few days to shoot exotic background material in Katmandu.

Officially the idea of traveling by boat instead of flying was to let the expedition members get to know each other. If this was so, it was a doubtful move, since in my experience there is nothing like a boat journey to make you hate your neighbor. Although we did not, we *might* have stepped off the boat already at loggerheads, and surely we were going to have more than ample opportunity to know each other in the next few months!

The boat journey was really made to save money, which the expedition was very obviously short of, and the whole party traveled tourist. Men who are glad to be going on an expedition don't mind how they get there; they would walk if they had to, and the organizers had fought a noble battle to raise sufficient funds at all. Nevertheless, allowing the members of its first team attempting to climb the world's highest mountain to travel like church mice was a little too characteristic of our country (it might be laudable if it was *only* deliberate humility). Even to exercise the expedition had to jump the barrier and tear around the forbidden part of the ship, to which the P. & O. officers sportingly turned a blind eye. The Germans had an expedition going to study the behavior of elephants. They went first class.

My roommate, who arrived in Katmandu on the second day, was a skeleton, as tall as I was, with a New Zealand accent, a hatchet-thin face, and tied together with steel. I learned that this man was called Ed Hillary. I had just got a rubber torch in pieces and couldn't get it together again. This human vise took charge. "Let's give it a go," he said, using an expression we came to know so well in the following months. It may have meant that he would *try* to fix it, but it did not. Actually it meant he *would* fix it, a subtle but important difference so far as Ed and his fellow countryman, George Lowe, were concerned.

Another fellow arrived who, being a travel agent and knowing the ropes, had come by air. As soon as he opened his mouth I knew that, like myself, he came from the north. He had a habit of blowing air out of his nose—a sniff in reverse. He was around forty, thin and spritely like a cock sparrow, with slightly bowed legs. His favorite phrase, in contrast to Ed's, was "Let's *potter* up and see," but this was also misleading. He also meant he was going to do it—hook or crook. His name was Alfred Gregory—or Greg. Besides being a formidable climber, he was also in charge of the expedition still photography, and therefore it was likely we should be working together to some extent.

While the expedition was organizing and collecting the tons of stores, Greg and I toured the valley, taking photographs. Sometimes we would work outside the town, where the farming was a delight, so intensive and efficient, based on human manure and painstaking hand work. At other times we would go into Katmandu itself, but though the narrow streets with the overhanging carved balconies and the squares with painted dragons were tempting to the eye, they were a penance for the cinematographer. One had only to appear with a tripod to be surrounded by a hoard of sightseers who pushed, jostled, and blocked the view in their efforts to see what was happening.

The Indian engineers building the road most generously helped the expedition transport its stores over the cable railway which was the only alternative to coolie transport for goods into the capital. I went up to the cable station to film the arrival. I had for some years, as a kind of signature, attempted to get some flying birds into my films, and here was a fine chance.

There are certain birds which have adapted themselves to existing with man more than any others in the world. These are sparrows, starlings, and pigeons—and perhaps pigeons most of all. The town pigeon—basically a wood pigeon that has gone slumming—is found in almost every city in the world. Katmandu is no exception. The pigeons there had discovered that sacks of grain were transported on the cable railway. They would settle on the sacks some miles out of the city and ride in, stealing a feed on the way. When the load arrived at the terminus, they would fly back up the wires in search of the next. There was a certain humor in these pigeons taking an aerial ride, and it gave me the first unusual sequence, making the otherwise uninspiring arrival of our gear an event of interest.

There was great activity at the Embassy. Tenzing had arrived with the Darjeeling Sherpas. These were camped with some of their women folk in an outbuilding.

Tenzing was, of course, already famous for his exploits on Everest with Lambert during the Swiss expedition of the previous year. I was immediately struck with his grace of movement, his handsome appearance and beautiful teeth. He had a wonderful flashing smile and a sense of dress which was quite remarkable (and we said he looked more like a Swiss guide than a Swiss guide). There

215

was already an *air* about him which marked him as a man of account.

Of course at that time I could not guess whether our expedition would succeed or not; who among all my companions would be important, or who become the stars. So I had to set out to do the formidable task of filming *everyone*. Suppose, at the worst, there was a sudden disaster and someone got killed! Their pictures would be needed for the story. Or if someone reached the top! They would have to be established as personalities quite early in the film. This increased the work enormously. It was proved impossible, of course, to cover everyone at all times, but luck was with me. Ed Hillary came out of the Embassy and I filmed his introduction to Tenzing. Although I did not know it, I was filming a very historic meeting.

I might have expected something unusual because *I was the thirteenth man on the expedition*—and we set out for Everest on March 10, which was my birthday. I could not repress a slight, though illogical superstition. A crowd had gathered on a parade ground some miles out of town to wish us Godspeed. Ambassador Summerhayes, in a tweed suit and trilby hat, a sort of father to us all. Some of the American colony from the Point Four technical mission, mostly doing as I was and blazing off with movie cameras. Ralph Izzard, the *Daily Mail* correspondent, whom I had not met then, was playing a game of hide-and-seek—what with the expedition's having sold its exclusive story to the London *Times* and Ralph's representing the *Daily Mail*, nobody wanted to oblige him. In fact, they were trying to dodge, which was not a very sensible position in which to be placed.

This cold-shouldering of the press and some mildly face-pushing comments attributed to Tenzing were the first rumblings of the unfortunate situation that was to blossom later. The expedition's press—on the one hand superlative and on the other quite ghastly—was due to a combination

Mukalla, port of the Hadhramaut in Southern Arabia, is one of the places visited by Tom Stobart since he returned from Everest. He is still roving and his cine-camera goes with him.

ABOVE: I photograph Hillary and Tenzing starting off.

LEFT: After their return. Hillary had been my roommate in Katmandu; a skeleton as tall as myself with a New Zealand accent and a hatchet-thin face, he seemed tied together with steel. When he said, "Let's give it a go" he meant simply that he would solve your difficulty for you. Tenzing, a "pocket-Hercules" already famous for his exploits with Lambert, had a wonderful flashing smile and a dress sense that was quite remarkable. We said he looked more like a Swiss guide than a Swiss guide. (*The Mount Everest Foundation*)

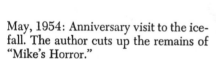

May, 1954: Anniversary visit to the icefall. The author cuts up the remains of "Mike's Horror."

Gyaljen, my personal Sherpa, was taken ill. He was coughing blood and had to be carried down the mountainside. BELOW: That left me to carry my own equipment. Gyaljen is dead, but my memory of him is keen; a gallant young man who would not give up, a fine example of the Sherpa tradition. *(The Mount Everest Foundation)*

RIGHT: At Camp IV, Evans uses my view finder as a telescope. BELOW: Photographing a group of "Tigers" at Camp IV. (*The Mount Everest Foundation*)

The sheer stupendous size of this mountain had somehow to be shown by my camera. The only object of known size was a climber; but looked at from even a little distance, he became a mere speck in the snow, something almost imperceptible. This picture was taken in the Western Corm. *(The Mount Everest Foundation)*

LEFT: Cutting the tunnel to the ice cave which I had constructed at Base Camp. Inside, sheltered from the icy winds, temperature remained constant. Here I could work—and sleep—in comparative comfort. RIGHT: This picture, taken inside a tent at Base Camp, shows Dr. Pugh with George Lowe. George kept everyone in fits of laughter; when all else failed he would take out his false teeth. I am sure that Everest did not realize that behind this clowning exterior it was being stalked by a most determined opponent. (*The Mount Everest Foundation*)

BELOW, RIGHT: Alfred Gregory blew air through his nose—a sniff in reverse. His "Let's potter up and see" meant "Let's do it somehow—by hook or crook." He was in charge of the expedition's still photography. BELOW, LEFT: Camp Three looking toward the Western Cwm; beyond lay the redoubtable Lhotse Face, which was the road to Everest. (*The Mount Everest Foundation*)

Two thousand feet of the icefall. To get an idea of the gigantic size of this maze of ice pinnacles, look at the picture on the right, which shows climbers tackling *one* of the many hundreds of pinnacles. To progress on the ground from the bottom to the top of the photograph would entail a two-day journey. (*The Mount Everest Foundation*)

The pictures on these pages illustrate the immensity of the icefall. The pictures of the climbers were taken within the area pictured at bottom, right.

RIGHT: Mike Ward, personification of confidence, cutting steps up one of the "horrors."

BELOW: To cross this crevasse, the aluminum ladder had been lengthened by lashing on poles. The crossing Sherpa looks downward to the depths of the crevasse. *(The Mount Everest Foundation)*

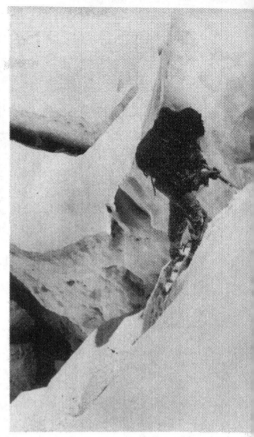

Base Camp sounds like a haven of comfort; actually it is just a place, a gully of sharp stones set in pinnacles of ice over which the thin wind from Tibet blows across the Lho La. It is a cheerless place, a loveless place, even an ugly place, and very far from home. Tents are put up, boxes put in convenient places to sit on, a fire is got going and a mug of tea comes round. Then it all seems much better. Tensing's tent and store boxes are seen under new snow. (*The Mount Everest Foundation*)

Porters on the way to Everest. In the background is Ama Dablam.

ABOVE: On our approach march to Everest we often passed yaks at summer pasture. The yak is the draft animal of the mountain lands of the Himalayas. BELOW, LEFT: At Lobuje, when recovering from pneumonia, I was twice to be visited by a beautiful golden-colored creature the size of a polecat; it enjoys the unbecoming name of yellow-bellied weasel. BELOW, RIGHT: Another, and more frequent, of my visitors at Lobuje was the local mouse hare. It looks like a guinea pig dressed in rabbit fur and is reputed to be the food of the Abominable Snowman.

LEFT: Mrs. Da Tensing, wife of one of our most experienced Sherpas, had the reputation of being a most formidable woman even for a community in which women very much rule the roost. To me she gave much chang—too much! *(The Mount Everest Foundation)* ABOVE: Sherpa boy; what is wrong with rags where rags are no dishonor? BELOW: Sherpa women with chang and more chang for the wedding party.

ABOVE, LEFT: Superstitions still persist, and some Sherpas, though curious, yet fear the camera's "evil eye," but contact with the outside world is broadening the outlook of many of the hill people. ABOVE, RIGHT: Phu Dorje, South Col "Tiger," has his pigtail dressed.

During our stay at Thyangboche, while our stores were sorted and arranged into suitable loads, I took every opportunity to photograph people, both members of the expedition and Sherpas from the neighborhood. BELOW, LEFT: Prayer wheels; you must turn them as you pass. BELOW, RIGHT: An old man tells his beads.

At Thyangboche various men armed with formidable lists went around checking numbered boxes, each seeking his own demesne. One of them, pictured on this page, was Dr. Griff Pugh, our physiologist, a large red-haired scientist of clear-sighted intelligence and traditional absent-mindedness. Of all the expedition, he was the one I liked best to be with. We never ran out of topics for conversation and, like myself, he was a great believer in comfort. ABOVE: He is seen searching for boxes (especially the big one that is missing) and their contents. BELOW, LEFT: With John Hunt, Dr. Pugh is conducting alveoli air tests. BELOW, RIGHT: This Sherpa girl we nicknamed "Cherry Crush" after a popular sweet. (*The Mount Everest Foundation*)

Ten miles under Everest we camped in a meadow of close-cropped golden grass beside Thyangboche Monastery. Here we paid off the coolies and with ropes kept the many spectators from straying among our packages. *(The Mount Everest Foundation)*

To prevent cross-infection with colds, pumps had been provided for inflating the air beds. . . . *(The Mount Everest Foundation)*

Thyangboche Monastery seen from the north. Here we reached the end of the first stage of the expedition. *(The Mount Everest Foundation)*

Sherpa family from Khumjung, a large village near Thyangboche, approached by a variety of paths up a rocky gully. I visited the place to secure pictures of the Sherpas' home life. This was Sherap's village. He and others converged on me with tubs of chang, of which they had already freely partaken. *(The Mount Everest Foundation)*

of circumstances only too clear to an onlooker when considered in the light of events, but not at all so obvious at the time. Yet as we gathered on that parade ground for our departure, there was only one thought in all our minds —after thirty years of failure, could we dare hope to get to the top of Everest? With a queue of countries forming behind us, and if we had unfortunately to regard it as an international prestige race, then it was probably Britain's last chance. Or was Everest just beyond the borders of human endurance after all? Or perhaps I am wrong. Perhaps we just felt overpowered by the excitement and importance of being off and reserved all our questions and doubts until later. I know that my own feelings were mostly a joyous relief because I had wanted passionately to go to Everest ever since I was a kid, and no last-moment mishap had occurred to prevent this lifelong ambition from coming true.

There were some 350 coolies, so our caravan had had to be split in two, the second half following twenty-four hours behind the main body. Even so, it was a formidable gathering to handle. I was glad to see that for now, at least, everyone was not wearing the same attire. I was going to have a difficult enough job distinguishing them without that happening to me as well. The problem is that at a distance a camera does not distinguish between people who are wearing the same clothes. It is this that makes doubling in films possible. It does not take much imagination to realize what a muddle a film audience would be in if everyone dressed in an identical way. For Everest we had all been issued with the same blue windproof clothes, as unvaried as any Army uniform. But for the march everyone seemed to be wearing his own device, and crowning it all was an incredible collection of individual hats. In some cases these represented a femine interest at home, In some cases a rather feminine interest in hats on the part

217

of the individuals themselves. Climbers, like famous generals, are very fashion conscious.

> *"Come, climber, with your scientific hat*
> *And beady gambler's eye, ascend!*
> *He pauses, poses for his camera-man:*
> *'Well-known Climber About to Ascend'."*
>
> —ROBERT GRAVES
> *Collected poems 1914–1947.*

Hunt had a sort of khaki gabardine pork-pie of severe cut; Hillary, a gay cotton helmet with a blue-striped sun flap, like a foreign legionary. It was said to keep the bees out of his ears. George Band had a straw with a black ribbon which made him look like an Italian mule driver until you got down to his large nose with spectacles perched on the end. Greg had a knitted hat with a bobble on the top, quite unfunctional, like a Buddhist chorten, except perhaps it would help him to go bald. Westmacott wore an old Army bush hat, somewhat like my own, and redolent of his days as a sapper in Burma.

"How can I keep all these fellows in sight?" I thought. You would get confused if I named them all, and yet *any* could emerge as the hero of the film.

The loads had been weighed and put in lines and all was ready for the start. Tenzing blew a whistle, and like claim-staking in a gold rush, the coolies dashed to find the lightest box. They quarreled over awkward loads—such as the ladder we were taking to span the crevasses—but at length all was sorted out. I filmed them starting on the long road to Everest. Then I too packed and hurried to catch up. The old disheartening business I knew so well from Nun Kun began again, only this time it was more serious if I could not stand the strain, and how much less was I in a state of health to do so?

I had two Sherpas to carry my gear and help. Strangely enough, one was again called Gyaljen—how the Gyaljens haunt me—a very intelligent fellow, small, sharp and completely reliable. The other, Sherap, who had wanted paid work for the return journey to his homeland, was also bright and intelligent, with a very expressive face, kind and gentle, with mobile eyebrows. He was an old man, a Tibetan, and he loved his booze. We reckoned he was some sort of unfrocked lama. He was one of those old rascals who are so disarming and delightful that one can never be angry with them; so they get away with murder. I liked him, a wonderful cheery companion along the road, but not a serious type and so not much approved of by our leader John Hunt.

The first day led through filthy but picturesque villages, with carved temples and narrow streets full of refuse. It was hot, and in the crowded Nepal Valley people were everywhere. There was no escaping them, even when answering the calls of nature; after trying for a few miles to find a quiet spot, one just gave up and resigned oneself to being watched by a curious crowd of sightseers. It was with relief that on the following morning we began to climb away from the crowded regions.

We most of us suffered from the heat, from soft feet, and from the unaccustomed food. The route lay across the grain of the country, so that we were continually going over a ridge from one river valley into another. These ridges were high, the paths up and up seemed endless, and then when the top was thankfully reached, after perhaps half a day of aching legs, there was a depressing plunge down into yet another wooded valley. The height one had so laboriously gained was lost and the climb started all over again.

We began to form our daily pattern. Just before dawn there would be a sound of stirring Sherpas, and then the flap of the big tent in which we all slept would be pushed open and each man's *personal* Sherpa would come in with a steaming mug of tea. I was glad to see that

Gyaljen was always one of the first. Since washing up was often casual and diseases were prevalent, we all had our names painted on our mugs. Always using the same would avoid cross-infection. The only snag to this bright idea was that the Sherpas could not read. Later, however, the smarter ones learned the *look* of their sahibs' names.

The few like me, who enjoy lying in a warm sleeping bag and watching other people shiver and curse before having to do the same, got short shrift. Sherpas would get in among us and begin stuffing everything into kitbags, so that you knew you would lose your possessions unless you got up and gave an eye to what was going on. It would also amuse the Sherpas to loosen the guy ropes so that the tent fell down before everyone was out.

"Who's got my boots . . ."

"Pemba, where's my new Zealand adjective flashlight?"

"Who's got the toilet paper?"

Then the coolies would come in groups from their little fires and begin roping their loads for the day's march. "Remember what I said about leaving the boxes in the sun . . ." I would hopefully admonish the coolies who carried my own precious packages of film.

Now the sensible ones pushed off along the way to keep ahead of the main body. Coolies soon jammed the narrow paths and made the dawn malodorous with the gasses they had accumulated during the night. "*Om mani padme om,*" muttered the Buddhists to themselves over and over again, in a continuous base growl until, with veins showing in their bulging calves and boxes creaking a protest against going uphill, they became too out of breath to pray.

For perhaps the first hour the light was dim for photography. Greg and I would be able to press on and enjoy the cool morning walk without a care: the wrench of an early rising was soon rewarded by the pleasures of listening to the birds and the beauty of the mountain paths. But then the sun would rise to full power, merciless as it is, and then all thoughts and energies would turn to the job, the hard grind of marching, of filming on the march, of working when others were having fun.

Everyone had their own system. Those bitten with the full spirit of one-upmanship would jostle for the lead like contestants in a walking race. Nor far behind would come pounding the wretched cook, Thondup, with the cookhouse Sherpas clattering under the apparatus for our breakfast. Greg and I would be busy and delayed by our photography, and whatever our position in the caravan to begin with, we would gradually fall toward the rear.

At eight-thirty the leaders would start to look for a breakfast site, somewhere near a clear spring or stream where there was shade. The time was laid down by Greg, who had at first been done out of his breakfast by Tom Bourdillon. Tom had urged the cooking team so far, so fast, and for so long that that day Greg and I never caught up. But now we could work on any flowering rhododendron thicket or any breath-taking view knowing that nobody would press on, carrying our breakfast too far ahead. Sooner or later we would round a corner and find the energetic ones stretched on lie-lows under a tree asleep or reading a book, with their umbrellas up for extra shade, umbrellas being as essential to a Himalayan expedition as to the Stock Exchange, but less smart.

"Hurry up, we've been here over an hour," would shout some lucky fellow reading a book.

"Camera, Sherap, *lal walla*, 'the red lens.'" I had put dabs of different colored paint on them, and Sherap was already becoming quite a good assistant.

"Greg . . . you know what a bind this is . . . I want my tea. But I must get a shot of Wilf Noyce writing in his diary before my good resolutions give out."

"Don't look at me, Wilf, but please suck your pencil again—and go on sucking it."

The walk to Everest is about 170 miles (though how

anyone knows is beyond me, for with all these zigzags it seems like a lot more). It is done at an average of about ten miles a day. That is what the coolies will do, and the stages are governed by where they can buy food and a place to sleep. It is a rather dull walk by Himalayan standards, mostly in the foothills, terraces of young rice or maize, patches of forest and rhododendron, and swing bridges spanning turbulent gray water in muggy hot gorges—muggy because they are low-lying, and also to be avoided as campsites because of malaria.

As day after day we pressed on—Risingo—Those—Junbezi—the main ranges of the Himalayas lay always to the north, and occasionally we glimpsed them from some small pass when the clouds broke. Then there would be long arguments as to which mountain was which; plans for future expeditions and particular scrutiny of the tangle of ice toward the east, where we hoped to see Everest. But it lay behind its neighbors, in a sea of cloud high on the borders of Tibet. True, there were other sights to make up for it, like Menlungtse, which looked all ice but was partly rock, as white as chalk; but it was Everest and Everest alone that we searched the horizon to find.

We knew we were approaching the Sherpa country which lies just to the south of Everest—even those who did not have a map—by the increasing number of *mani* walls and chortens. Chortens are pagodalike towers of stone, often whitened, with eyes painted on them to watch you. They might be tombs, but they are not. You do not understand properly what they are for, but you can feel their powerful medicine. You stand there beside them, looking out over the valley. The steady wind rustles in the grass and in your untidy hair, and the prayer flags flap like the discarded rags of some tramp caught up in the roadside thornbushes.

"Greg, it's fine. Did you ever in all your life . . ." But Greg had been here before.

222

"Come on, hurry up. What exposure are you giving it?"
And then one of Greg's double sniffs.

Once more I would whip myself up to the job I had to do. Others were going to see this one day—if I did my stuff . . . if that camera, which sounded a little rough, had not gone wrong. Perhaps it would cause jitters on the screen and I was just wasting my time. Perhaps my exposures were wrong. . . . The worry was spoiling everything. Down there John Hunt and Mike Westmacott were catching butterflies—bathing in the river—just having a fine holiday—lucky devils.

I often thought what a silly fool I had been to turn the fun of expeditions into work—but at least the work had got me here. I remembered Odell and George Finch lecturing about Everest when I was in school. How we laughed at the mention of bugs and rancid butter in the tea. How I longed to see it for myself, and at eleven even organized my own Everest expedition. The oxygen was lemonade in bottles. . . . "Stobart was leader carrying great boots"—as one boy wrote in the school magazine. I carried the boots because they belonged to my father and were too big.

"Come on, hurry up!" said Greg, breaking in on my thoughts. "Have you finished yet?"

When I started out I had expected to be able to keep up with Greg. He told me he didn't believe in busting himself if it wasn't necessary. "Silly fools . . . keen types." But now I was beginning to change my ideas about him. Pad-pad-pad—his feet in their light gym shoes would move effortlessly up the path just in front of my eyes. I envied the convenience of a still photographer's work as I struggled with tripods and other inventions of the devil, helped by my patient Sherpas.

One of my assistants had bought some Japanese rubber shoes in Those, and he stuck manfully at my side. I wished

223

he had not, because his feet were sweating and it was like being trailed by a Gorgonzola cheese.

We came around a corner one day on an open hillside covered with shaggy grass—and saw a group of our flyers sitting on a wall. It was unusual for them to stop.

"Quickly—the clouds will be over it soon."

And there it was, Everest at last, a pyramid of rock, peering over a gap among other giants, and unmistakably the plume blew twenty miles away from its top.

Was someone trying to get up there? It was crazy. Hopes that our expedition would succeed vanished.

"That little knob there—that's the South Summit."

"What are our chances?"

"We'll give it a go . . ."

I stayed there long after everyone had gone—lining up my big lens—photographing the mountain as if it were the last chance I would ever have, instead of the first. And I thought, "In my film there should be the sound of roaring and tearing wind to go with that distant plume." Even from here you could see the eddies as the blast tore the ice dust off the summit ridge like the trail from the wing tips of a jet, and I was quite certain our expedition would fail, as the others had before.

We camped around the monastery of Taxindu, our coolies sleeping in the outbuildings. The main building had that strange and lovely architecture, the white walls sloping slightly back and the Chinese eaves, but the outbuildings were a slum. There was a smell of sweat, smoke, and old butter, and the open grass was fouled as surely as the grass in a London square. I should have preferred the surrounding forests, though wet with moss and ferns.

"You can have my fruitcake, George—maybe it's good, but every day, and it gives me belly-ache—with due respect to the caterers. That last grind up to the ridge finished me off, I thought it would never end." Some days were hard to endure, I was still not fit, my digestion

224

was always upset, and I wished this chance had come two years before.

The evening mist settled like a silent ghost, like steam drifting through the rhododendrons and breathing life into the orchids of the forest. In a cell the monks began an all-night prayer, droning on and on with rasping bass voices. Down below, perhaps under the clouds, one could hear another voice, the thunderous voice of the Dudh Kosi River, swollen with the day's melt-water from the glaciers of Everest.

The Dudh Kosi, so aptly named the "milk river," though it is milk mingled with green ink, together with its terrifying gorge, is all that Himalayan scenery should be. The gorge rose above in rib and spur; the path was covered with leaves and twisted through the forest. Now and then it dived into a gully where there were rough steps and the rock was wet with spray, so one wondered how man ever got through here before he made this path. And all around the rhododendron and magnolia trees were in full flower, great forest trees smothered in crimson bloom, or floppy and white like wax and as big as your hat. The magnolias are so big that even across the gorge they look like individual white stars against the dark and mysterious tangle underneath. Their scent is sweet. Here if only one had time to search, one would find little red pandas sleeping in the trees, brilliant tragopans, and flying squirrels gliding like kites. The fact was that one felt one could come on any marvel here. I prized off some moss and found a cache of blackberries behind. What creature had put them there? But there was no time to ponder. "Hurry, hurry on toward Everest," was the cry. If only one could come back to examine its fascinating green feet someday.

The problem was to photograph ice peaks through a screen of red flowers—just watch out for the sky—everything else must take care of itself—just find a place with a little sun on the flowers. George Lowe, with an outsized bunch of magnolia in his hat, was decorating a Sherpani bosom with an even larger posy, like a couturier pinning a corsage of orchids on a model. The Sherpas roared with laughter, Tenzing smiled his friendly, patient smile. George Lowe kept everyone in fits. When all else failed, he would take out his false teeth. I am sure that Everest did not realize that behind this clowning exterior it was being stalked by a most determined opponent.

"Mum, mum, mum . . . !" The toothless horror would cause the forest to be split with undignified laughter.

And so we approached Everest up the wonderful Dudh Kosi until that last day when we crossed its tributary river, the Bhote Kosi, on a rickety bridge of branches. Here we were in the deep shadow of the gorge, the wall of which rose in a series of bare rock cliffs with patches of shaggy grass and bushes. I wondered if such steep terrain was the home of the Abominable Snowman; if so, he must be a formidably active climber, for the only animals of any size who habitually live on such slopes are members of the sheep and goat family—the bearded old goat tahr, which looks like the devil.

Our own path pulled steeply up the spur between the two rivers. We were now nearing the Sherpa capital of Namche Bazaar, set in a small amphitheater with rows of stone houses along the slopes; at first glance it looked rather like a Welsh mining village and not very interesting. The word *bazaar* was misleading, for there was not a shop in the place.

Waiting beside the track, come out to meet us, were the families of some of our Sherpas. They offered us chunks of crystallized sugar and half-wasted potatoes, held out in friendly but grubby hands. The potatoes had been kept warm, one felt, under armpits, inside voluminous coats. All carried the ubiquitous brass-bound wooden bottles of chang, a drink which can be like rough cider with an almost unnoticeable cloud, but is usually like sour porridge, as gray and dirty as a chimney sweep's bath water.

With dire warnings from our doctors about dysentery and other forms of belly-ache, I did not feel inclined to drink. Courtesy, however, demanded it. Someone should have warned us that though Sherpa etiquette says your cup be filled at least three times, it is not necessary to finish up before a refill. As a result, having disposed completely of one portion and thankfully handed the cup back, we were compelled to go through the agony twice again.

Many of us, however, became reckless after the first cup; some even liked it and fell for the Sherpa line that it would make us strong.

We camped on a cultivated col above the village. That night the clouds rolled up their blinds and showed that we were in the midst of terrific ice peaks whose hard ragged edges bit into the black of the night sky. The Dudh Kosi River roared in its rocky dungeon below, and the stars shone bright in the frost—stars one knew from home but which somehow one had not expected to find here. We had almost arrived.

The next day we continued on a good path high above the gorge, always toward Everest, which now appeared as the top of a pyramid peeping over the stupendous Lhotse-Nuptse wall. Rather ugly in a way, because the top of the wall is too horizontal for good mountain architecture, and mere size is only realized on closer contact, when you experience that the mounds and dunes at its foot are 19,000-foot peaks.

The eye was chiefly attracted to Ama Dablam, Kangtega, and Thamserku, the former looking like a cathedral spire; and the latter, twin peaks like starched lace, with actual holes through the knifelike ridges. In these the mountain architects have excelled at their building, as if proclaiming to the world that quantity is not always better than quality. A mountaineer can put himself up there in his mind's eye and tremble with terror at the instability—just a touch and——

The path passes below the village of Khumjung. The inhabitants of this too lay in wait for us with chang, holding up the march for an hour and giving me a fine opportunity to catch some of the expedition in their cups. Indeed, they were already getting used to the noise of the camera and had mostly given up either looking at me or backing out of the picture with the slightly girlish modesty the camera-conscious he-man is apt to employ.

I was still having difficulty with the Sherpas, however. They could *not* resist looking at the camera. Of course this effect continually reminds the audience that the camera, like Everest, is there—which is irritating—you usually want them to forget it.

I had now trained Gyaljen, and he had become a very promising assistant director, sometimes even overzealous at shouting directions to his friends. But it was considerably better than my earlier efforts, when I had tried to give directions myself.

I had taken the trouble to learn how to say "Don't look at the camera" in the Sherpa language—which is a dialect of Tibetan—and was feeling rather proud of myself when I first tried it out. The effect, however, was not what I had intended. All my stars had taken me literally and simply turned their backs.

The path below Khumjung dropped to yet another junction of the river—where the Imja Khola joined the Dudh Kosi. The path was bordered by a tangle of wild clematis not yet in flower. The bridge was substantial, to take the lama's ponies, and close by were some small huts containing water-powered prayer wheels. These were broken down due to lack of maintenance, but one could look in at the dark entrance and see the great upright drums covered in blue, red, and gold writing. As they were pushed around by hand, a bell rang to mark each revolution and the moment of the completed prayer shooting up to heaven.

We had cause sometimes to curse the religious zeal of these people, who had invented for themselves a particular kind of torture known as a *mani* wall. This is a wall with tablets of stone inscribed in Tibetan with the invocation, *"Om, mani padme om"* (pronounced omanipamiho), which is translated as "Hail, the jewel in the Lotus" but is perhaps more equivalent to "Hallelujah, praise the Lord!"

Such a wall must be passed on the left; if you do this you also (like the wheel) say a prayer. If you go on the wrong side, you presumably unsay a prayer. The trouble is that it is usually arranged so that passing on the correct side, which is the left, means making a detour uphill, a penance indeed when you are tired. On the way up to Everest, most of us stuck to this "rule of the road"—but on the way back I noticed we were not so careful to keep on the right side of the gods.

When we reached Thyangboche Monastery, which was ten miles under Everest, we camped on a meadow of close-cropped golden grass below the monastery buildings. Here the hundreds of boxes were dumped and the coolies paid off. The first stage of the expedition was over.

chapter 21

THE expedition was distinguished from all other expeditions I had been on by its obtrusive organization along military lines. Everything had been worked out and planned down to the last nail, everyone had his job and his province of responsibility. Some of us regarded this as a bore—which it was. But it is unfortunately also the best way to run a large expedition, and when everyone has his own province and things work efficiently, there is also less tendency to quarrel—and how some expeditions have quarreled!

Armed with formidable lists, the various members went around checking the numbered boxes, looking for their own domain. Boxes were stacked up in walls and pulled down again, looking like a life-size game of mahjong from the vantage point I had taken up on the hill. The air was filled with the sounds of wrenching lids and hammering. Along the side lines, kept back by a rope, wandered groups of lamas and local Sherpas, looking for jobs. There was a grand display of purple robes, red felt boots, and pigtails untidy and in need of combing with more butter. The lamas, of course, were close-shaven.

John Hunt had endless conferences with his selected advisers. There were classes in the use of this or that gadget, and tests of equipment such as oxygen and radio. As I was not directly involved in the attempt on the summit, I did not take much part in these preparations, beyond seeing that I received my full kit and that it fitted. Sometimes I felt a little sad that I was not a climbing member of the expedition and that my job was as a special technician, but this mood soon passed. I was king in my own field, entrusted with a job that meant not only a roving commission around an expedition where I should need all my experience to look after myself and not become a burden, but also the greatest tact to carry it out. It was an unpopular job among people who would be strung up and touchy to a degree and I had no need to feel humble at doing it.

Perhaps what was really annoying me was that I found I was the most expendable body. Of course I was, but that did not make it any better. The first blow I received was when I was told that Gyaljen was too good a man to be tied up as my assistant. I had trained Gyaljen with particular care because Sherap was an old man and could not go on the mountain. Therefore, with the serious part of the expedition just about to begin, I was faced with starting again from scratch.

Worse was to follow. There were flaws in the splendid organization after all. I learned that the two Sherpas I had asked for—they had been among my first requests when I lay in hospital—had not been catered for at all. Not only had the men not been allowed for, which perhaps could be remedied by recruiting local men, but there were no high-altitude clothes for them. This was an incredibly serious blow, because my two personal Sherpas, besides being necessary to help carry the gear, were also vital to give independence of movement on the mountain. It was impossible to film a climbing party well while actually tied to it. I had to have my own little group, and of course it was impossible to move around on the glaciers alone because of the danger from concealed crevasses. I saw the whole of the film project vanishing down the drain and, with it, my reputation for delivering the goods.

To let my annoyance cool off, I went up to film the monastery. The lamas used to perambulate around the walls, always in a clockwise direction, and great banks of prayer wheels were suitably placed for the passing hand to give them a push. The atmosphere was calming until, having filmed a lama spinning the wheels, I wanted him to repeat it for a close-up. I then found that the "clockwise" rule was so rigid that he could not walk back the few yards to the beginning of the row of wheels, but first had to do another complete circuit. Already in a bad mood, I began to curse anything and everything very roundly.

Then I realized I was being very petty. If the monk had the patience to go right round the *gompa* for me each time—and just out of his good nature—then surely I had the patience to wait. I had the patience to wait, and the patience to accept the other mishaps. What right had I to be on the expedition anyway if I flew off the handle; if I expected everything to be as cut and dried as though I were working in a studio? if I could not think up something when plans went wrong?

I sought out Charles Wylie and Tenzing. There had been two Swiss expeditions the year before, and the Sherpas had been allowed to keep all their equipment as a gift. I knew that because it had been a bitter pill for us to be forced to promise the same. The Swiss had established a precedent in the district, and the Swiss, we considered, had more money to spend than we had. They had "spoiled the market." But it was a lucky break for me, because now it seemed possible to raise a man locally who was fully kitted with old but serviceable clothes—if one was prepared to pay extra. Tenzing agreed to pass the word around, which meant there would be action.

In the meantime the expedition was splitting up into climbing parties for the acclimatization period. In time the human body can adapt itself to almost anything, even great heights, if it has a chance to do so gradually. Pilots who need oxygen badly at 17,000 feet are always astonished that climbers can live and do hard work—even over

233

10,000 feet higher. It's because they have spent a period getting used to it. In order that the expedition should not have to spend this time on Everest—and get bored—it was planned that the parties would have a sort of climbing holiday before the really serious business started.

Privately, I was still a little worried about my health. I was not very well. There was not much stuffing in me, and every night I used to sneak out of the tent and into the woods to be sick. I was afraid I would hold back any party I attached myself to and came to the conclusion that I should be more sensible if I did not rush things. In any case, missing the acclimatization parties fitted in with my plans for the film, because I wanted to hold a clear-cut story of Everest, and climbing on another mountain, even though essential to the expedition, would be a red herring in the film. It seemed more profitable for me to visit one of the Sherpa villages and look at their home life. Those who had been with Shipton on the Everest reconnaissance and knew the region advised me to go to Khumjung—the climbers' home away from home.

Khumjung was a large village situated on a bench on the mountainside and was approached by a variety of paths up a rocky gully. The stone houses were in tiers, one row above the other, giving them each a view, and down below, in a hollow of short grass, was a big *mani* wall and a chorten. Behind were some rocky mounds covered with purple dwarf rhododendron. There were a few terraced fields of potatoes.

I pitched my tent in the hollow below the village. Before I had even got my things unpacked, several Sherpa women converged, armed with wooden tubs of chang. My dear friend Sherap, whose village this was and who had gone on ahead, came out of his house, already showing unmistakable signs that he had partaken of drink and would not be a good assistant that day. With him was a pretty young daughter who, to my surprise, had worked for an

234

English family in Darjeeling and spoke the most beautiful English. She spoke rather slowly, and with a charming accent. Indeed, of all foreign people who bring their various accents to English—some ugly and some fascinating—there are no people who sound more attractive than the Tibetans. Their accent has a clear, naïve quality that is completely disarming, and Sherap was originally a Tibetan from the east of Tibet. I discovered, incidentally, that he was not an unfrocked lama at all, as we jokingly made out, but simply a lama who had moved into the Sherpa country and fallen to a lower status by marrying —women even here being slightly sinful! It was difficult for the visitor to sort out quite what was supposed to be correct and what just happened in the Sherpa religion and custom.

Well to the front in the social life of Khumjung was Mrs. Da Tenzing, wife of one of our most experienced expedition Sherpas. She had the reputation of being a most formidable woman, even for a community in which women very much rule the roost. It was quite clear that if I was not very quickly drunk—and drunk for the duration of my stay—she would regard herself as having failed in her hospitality. Somehow I should have to dodge.

"What did you want to say?" asked Miss Sherap.

"I must not drink too much chang before I have finished my work."

When this was translated there was a roar of laughter, because obviously I was making a joke. Previous expeditions had certainly set the standard by coming here for a bat.

I went up onto a small mound from where there was a superb view of Ama Dablam, with prayer flags fluttering in the foreground. Then I took pictures of women hoeing in the fields, and others, helped by their children, who were sorting potatoes out of a pit where they had been stored for the winter. The people were ragged, there were a few cretins, they moved with the peculiar jerky movements of the Tibetan, and the whole scene was indescribably medieval—but one had the overwhelming impression that despite a hard life these were above all a happy people, jolly and carefree in a way one never saw in more civilized climes.

Watching me work was a superior-looking man wearing a tall gold brocade hat with fur ear flaps, so characteristic of the well-to-do Tibetan. As usual, it was asymmetrically placed, as if it had been clapped on in a hurry, but as I have never seen these hats worn otherwise, it must be done on purpose, just as the race-goer tilts his topper. This man was the local lama artist, trained at the Rongbuk Gompa, which everyone who has read of the attempts on Everest from the north has heard of. It was in fact the mother establishment under which all the Sherpa monasteries come.

The artist invited me to his house. It was a typical Sherpa house, of two stories, the bottom one being the barn and the top for living. You go in through the barn, which smells of yak and hay and up some stairs to the living quarters. Having just come in from the light, by the time you reach the top of the stairs you can see nothing, it is so dark, and you are face to face with a trap. If you do not know the layout and walk straight ahead, you are liable to fall down the lavatory. This is a hole in the floor centered over a chamber filled with leaves—a sort of permanent compost heap that is carried out onto the fields yearly.

Knowing the ropes, you turn left, cautiously, although ninety-nine times you will be safe, and enter the main living room. This is well built, beamy, snug, and old-fashioned. There is a small window without glass, a raised platform in front of the window, and to one side an open fire of yak dung. A massive dresser of smoke-darkened wood with shelves for vast copper pots decorated with

236

Tibetan writing fills one side of the room. There is a tea churn—that is a brass-bound wooden cylinder with a plunger—and several metal-bound chests. There is probably also a Sherpa lap dog—or Lahsa terrier—which in many Sherpa homes takes the place of a cat. Cats seem not to be able to stand the altitude.

The artist's wife set about brewing Tibetan butter tea. The tea was brewed in a kettle and poured boiling into the churn, butter and salt were added, and the whole well frothed together by the plunger. The butter should *not* be rancid and should not float on top in globules of fat—this is bad tea. Good Sherpa tea *is* good, and you soon acquire a taste for it—provided you don't expect it to taste like *tea*.

I had come, however, to see the artist's studio. It was both a studio and a shrine, with the walls covered with ornate decorations, like the interior of a temple—a pattern of dragons, flowers, and symbolic clouds painted in shining and violently colored lacquer on a red ground. The work was not yet completed, parts being only sketched in. Obviously it would take several more years to finish the décor.

The artist showed me some completed pictures, commissioned by various *gompas* (monasteries) in this area. One was still on the bamboo frame on which the canvas had been stretched. The apparatus was crude but very workmanlike, and the quality of the draftsmanship superb. The paintings were all of religious subjects, alive with ferocious demons and skulls. I persuaded him to accept a commission from me for a picture, which he was at first reluctant to do—the only man I ever met in Solo Khumbu who had "too much work."

As I left he gave me a paper pattern which he had used in the repetitive borders in his decoration. It was an outline drawing of a dragon on handmade Nepalese paper and had been pricked through along all the lines.

The paper was held in position and a bag of powdered charcoal applied to the back, leaving on the wall a clear design to be painted in.

After two days I was rather thankful to leave Khumjung and escape the excessive hospitality. This went on from first light, when Mrs. Da Tenzing would pull aside the tent flap, without knocking, and thrust in a bowl of hot chang, to the afternoon when I was usually enticed into Sherap's house for a glass of the local firewater called *rakshi.* This tasted like smoky methylated spirits and was pretty powerful poison.

Now I decided I had obtained all that Khumjung had to offer and would join Dr. Griff Pugh and possibly John Hunt's acclimatization party, which was camped some-where in the Chukhung valley round behind Ama Dablam.

I found Griff Pugh settled in a hollow beside a small stream and accompanied by his familiar young sixteen-year-old Mingma. Mingma was the son of Mrs. Da Tenz-ing, who, one gathered, did not much approve of her son following in his father's footsteps.

The main party, Griff told me, was climbing somewhere in the mountains, behind and close under the gigantic Lhotse-Nuptse wall. It was Griff's theory that acclimatiza-tion was better done by going up high in the day and returning to lower altitudes for a good sleep at night, and he did not greatly approve of living so soon in a camp so high. As I had the greatest respect for his opinions, I decided to take his advice and not go on up to the main camp. In any case I could not find this. I went to the top of a rocky peak near by in the hope at least of seeing the camp. All I saw was a complicated wilderness of stones with a large glacier snout sheeted in mist in the distance. Already I had begun to feel the altitude and was gasping for breath. I was a little put out to see young Mingma strolling along beside me, hands in pockets, and kicking a piece of frozen yak dung as casually as a small boy in an alley kicks a tin can.

Dr. Griff Pugh was our physiologist, a large red-haired man who combined the two traditional qualities of the professor—clear-sighted intelligence and absent-mindedness. Of all the members, he was, I think, the one I preferred to be with, because he had that sort of speculative curiosity, wonder, and originality of thought possessed by all the scientific elite. He never became dull, and we never ran out of topics for conversation. So far I had not got really to know him. It was one of the fascinations of the expedition to be for a spell in turn with each member—perhaps sharing a day or a night in a tent—and, because of the stress, getting to know a man in a way one would not hope to in everyday life.

Griff, like myself, was a firm believer in comfort. We both felt, and indeed I am sure it is true, that a man who is uncomfortable uses up a great deal of energy in conquering the discomfort, energy that should be going into the work of the expedition. How, for instance, could we have been at our best on Nun Kun when we had spent the night lying on lumpy ice, wakeful and shivering? Or how can a man be at his best when faced with a sudden, radical change of diet? Indeed, one of the troubles from the past had been that everything was blamed on altitude, when in fact sickness was due partly to other things.

This attitude was regarded by some as heresy and a rationalization, since Griff and I were the most sybaritic members of the team. Yet I had been through the stage of worshiping toughness for toughness' sake—until I had met a few old hands and relegated toughness to its proper place—useful and vital to fall back on only when things go wrong.

"And yet," said Griff, "we know from tests made in the war that men who were toughened in their youth have more stamina and can stand hardship better than those who were not. One must not forget that." From this we went on to discuss topics such as compulsory games at school, the scientific theory of keeping warm, oxygen, dehydration, and boots, ranging over the whole gamut of expedition gear. The only taboo subject—and my only severe criticism of the organization—was as usual the subject of food. Griff had worked it out along very scientific lines, and the packaging was superb; but you cannot chew a package, and there is all the difference between calories and food you can eat. It was not that the food was nasty—it was not—but even the nicest biscuit can become monotonous when eaten every day for several months on end, and the critical, overrestless body like myself would inevitably wonder why it had been thought adequate to bring one kind and no other. Tom Bourdillon's famous dictum, "The important thing about food is that there should be some," would be more usefully changed to "The important thing about food is that there should be *something different*."

Although I had once more failed to bring that great panacea—Worcestershire sauce—I had not come quite unprepared. I had my old stand-by—a nob of garlic and a screw of caraway seed in my pocket—so occasionally I could descend on the cooking and jazz it up a bit. Experiments I had carried out before Nun Kun had shown that a touch of garlic and caraway seed will remove the "canned" taste from food more effectively than anything else.

So Griff and I spent a very pleasant few days acclimatizing and waiting for the more energetic spirits to return. We checked on our acclimatization from time to time by urinating on pieces of litmus paper, watching our slow progress from alkaline, a sign we were not yet acclimatized, back toward the more normal acid. The proceeding was watched in great interest by the Sherpas, whose education hardly extended to the mysteries of hydrogen ion concentration.

Presently the climbing party returned exhausted but happy after some successful ascents. John Hunt looked absolutely whacked and retired straightway to his tent. He had a nasty cough.

"John won't last unless he's careful," said Griff. "He can never learn to do anything except at full blast. At this rate . . ."

It was the first but certainly not the last time we discussed John, shaking our heads and saying that our leader had "had it," but he was always back on the job in the morning, burning into his terrifying reserves of guts and energy, working, planning, and worrying in a dedicated way I have never seen in any other man.

We gathered once more back at Thyangboche, everyone swopping yarns and extolling the virtues of his own party or exploits. Griff had now filled his tent with the most complicated array of glass apparatus, which he had somehow managed to transport here unbroken. It was for gas analysis. He sat in the midst in lordly state, *mirable dictu*, on a chair—the only chair in the expedition—and I must confess that on the few occasions when I managed to sneak into that chair for a short spell I realized how great his foresight had been. We do not usually admit that one of the major discomforts of an expedition is having no chair—nothing softer than a wooden box to sit on for months on end.

Not far away was another tent, the scene of a more spartan activity, one I was glad to have nothing to do with but which brought back certain memories. Dr. Mike Ward, our *official* doctor, was practicing surgery. He was hauling out the abbot's teeth, cold, without an anesthetic. On his way back to the monastery this impressive man in his red robes would pause and spit blood contemplatively, relishing the benefits of modern science. No doubt Mike Ward was a luxury to the Sherpas, and they enjoyed the relief from a toothache that had been going on solidly for several years. But personally I am a coward about dentists and hoped my own fillings would last the trip.

We were now embarking on a second acclimatization period, but one of the parties, under Ed Hillary, was going to spend the time reconnoitering the Everest icefall. Obviously this was part of the direct story of climbing the mountain and I should go with him. Preparations for leaving Thyangboche for good had to be made.

Now I acquired a Sherpa assistant. His name was yet again Gyaljen, but he was quite a different type, a young fellow, not gifted with great mental powers, coupled with a noticeable goiter. Nevertheless, he was both cheerful and willing. He appeared for my inspection one morning, well dressed in a variety of old Swiss expedition clothes and quite serviceable boots. I conferred with Charles Wylie, who agreed that his kit was adequate, and he was taken on. Unfortunately he was not bright enough to be trained as an assistant, but he was an admirable beast of burden and would, I hoped, be strong enough to hold me if I happened to break through into a crevasse. In this I was probably optimistic. He certainly could not have pulled me out.

chapter 22

W E S E T O F F for Everest on a fine morning, sliding down the bare earth through the rhododendron bushes,
not yet in flower at this altitude. We passed a long *mani*
wall and a nunnery. There were a lot of birch trees fes-
tooned with old man's beard and with the bark peeling
off like ragged tissue paper. A raven was nesting under an
overhang above the river.

As the day went on we left the last trees that straggled
up the river and the last cultivated patches of potatoes,
coming into a moorland country with dwarf rhododendron, juniper, and long dry mountain grass. That night
we camped around some yak huts, low stone buildings
with thatched roofs weighed down with stones, which provided shelter for our train of local Sherpas. The women
soon had fires of yak dung going. They seemed tireless.
After a day plodding patiently with a large packing case
slung on a headband, they began cheerfully, with shouts
and smiles, their household chores of making fires and
cooking, little stocky figures tottering like dolls in their
heavy striped woolen skirts and felt boots. They had white
cloths on their heads, tied on with the pigtail, which was
a becoming fashion.

It snowed, which was something we had not bargained
for, and the next day the sun came out, glaring back from
the brilliant tablecloth. We of course had dark goggles,
but we did not have enough for all the coolies. Some tied
their pigtails over their eyes, fraying them out just enough

to see through, but even so it was clear that we would have cases of snow blindness if the snow did not soon melt away.

But the snow did not go, and when we reached the last yak hut before the glacier, a place called Lobuje, the matter had become serious. A few were already blind and obviously could carry no farther. Others had inflamed, running eyes, and going for another day was quite unthinkable. It was just one of the things that nobody had foreseen, and we were stuck. It somehow seemed an ill omen and trying to the patience when we were all agog to set foot on the mountain.

"Some will have to stay behind for the moment," said Ed. "There's nothing else to do."

I had, however, been forced to produce various makeshifts from time to time in my own work and by good chance had several rolls of spare adhesive tape in the photographic kit, so I was able to spark off a small mass-production unit on a rock in the midst of the snow, and soon we had sixty pairs of goggles made and fitted. Once more we could push on toward our goal. The incident stands out in my mind as being one of the few occasions when I could feel I had helped the expedition and not been, when all is said and done, just a nuisance, a man fighting for his own interesting side line, a slightly parasitic sap on the main drive for the summit.

We were now with every step penetrating into the defile of the Khumbu Glacier. At first we mounted piles of loose rocks, shaly and sharp, with patches of frozen mud and large boulders poised to slide down at a touch. It was like range after range of giant slag heaps covered in new snow with a little twisting track stamped to slushy ice by the shuffling feet of our Sherpa girls. Clouds drifted all round, sometimes lifting and thinning so that the sun did not seem far away, and you could see the long trail of bobbing boxes stretching like a slender snake behind and in front;

then the clouds would clamp down so that one could only see the few just ahead, panting, slipping, and occasionally falling where a loose stone lay concealed to trap the unwary.

"Swiss Camp" sounded homely, but it was a dreary hut of mud with a frozen tarn and some ruined walls built for shelter. There was a cold wind with a bitter quality, like a little pain.

Thus far we had kept to the side, but now we had to take to the glacier. Here there were great frozen teeth a hundred feet high, and the stones slid away, showing bottle-hard ice beneath. Many stones had become glacier tables, perched on a column of ice preserved by their own shadow and looking like mushrooms with glass stalks or the stones used to keep rats from a stack.

Whenever the clouds lifted a little, and in between flurries of snow, we could see the feet of giant mountain walls which increasingly shut the glacier in all around, but still there was no view of the icefall, which was so vast and yet gave no sign of its presence. We appeared to be entering a cul-de-sac.

It was not until we were almost at Base Camp that we began to see the staircase of ice blocks tossed down through the cleft in the right-hand ramparts, and we stopped to gaze at the entrance to the Western Cwm—the redoubtable icefall—the road to Everest. I already had vertigo looking at it—imagining it. I began to wonder if I should manage even to get up it, let alone film it. Would I appear faint-hearted among these top-flight experts? They looked like very ordinary men, but they had done routes in the Alps that made an ordinary climber like me shudder even to read about. Moreover, the altitude was already beginning to tell; legs ached, and breathing was against a gag, fighting. This already, so that I had not had the energy to work. I had taken just a few shots, but not enough; all my strength was necessary just to keep up—and keep up with small women carrying loads.

One talks about arriving at Base Camp. Like "Swiss Camp," it sounds like a haven of comfort. Actually Base Camp is just a place—a place where you stop, a gully of sharp stones set in pinnacles of ice. The thin wind from Tibet blows over the Lho La and shuffles the snow about; the clouds are all round, or the air is clear and the sun shines for a moment, which melts the ice. It is a cheerless place, a loveless place, even an ugly place, and very far from home. But somehow it has to be made into a home.

Tents are put up. Stones are laid flat for a floor, but they have sharp edges and are laid on ice, so they shift about and cut the ground sheet. Boxes are put in convenient places to sit on. The Sherpas build a shelter wall for the cook, a fire is got going from some sticks that have been carried up. A mug of tea comes around, and everything seems much better. George Lowe, George Band, Ed Hillary—all our shock troops keep looking up at the icefall, their fingers itching to get hold of it. Tomorrow it will begin.

That night, for the first time but not the last, one could hear the appalling sound of Cheyne-Stokes breathing in the tent. Lying there, warm but unable to sleep, with burning indigestion, with the air bed leaking and the stones just beginning to be felt through—yet unable to face the cold of getting out to blow it up—you hear the awful sound of the sleepers dying all around. The quick accelerated breathing suddenly stops, and as the seconds tick by, you are sure that it has stopped forever. It will never start again, but it does, with a shuddering gasp, and then the cycle begins again, on and on all night. A few have taken sleeping pills, but even some of these are awake. George Lowe has dysentry and keeps on stumbling out into the bitter night, returning so cold you can hear him shiver and pant with the exertion of returning to his bag. It is, however, more comfortable than it was on Nun. The air bed, at least till it leaks down, does keep you warm underneath, and the sleeping bags are superb. Some genius has made them of nylon which slips, so you can turn over without an exhausting struggle.

Yet you lie awake. There are other sounds, sounds from the mountain. A thump followed by the roar of a bursting dam as an avalanche comes pouring down somewhere on Nuptse. Then silence for a spell. Then a crack and groan as the freezing ice shatters with the strain in the heart of the glacier beneath us. Then another rumble of ice and another. From the icefall, from the Lho La, from Nuptse again, and the roar of a Sherpa snoring in the next tent. How long the night seems.

The summit of Everest sailed 10,000 feet above—you flung your head back to look at it and wondered. It was already difficult to breathe here at Base Camp, barely 19,000 feet up, so what would it be like up there? Yet it was not the altitude, nor even the ominous growls of the mountain that made it seem so impossible. It was the awful remoteness, the lonely thrust beyond help that would be necessary to a man reaching that pyramid point. One did not need great imagination to be awed. It was nothing supernatural, nothing even to do with God. It was a simple truth. Anyone up there would be such an awful long way from home, and such a small man on his own.

However, every mountaineer knows that a mountain is made up of a lot of details, and each one must be overcome separately. To look at a whole mountain at once is to be discouraged—it always does look impossible, like any large task, and here before us was the first obstacle, that mammoth icefall, and it was better to keep one's thoughts on that.

This morning the sun was shining, and as we moved up behind Hillary's reconnaissance party all our spirits sang to be setting foot on the mountain at last. The spikes on our crampons bit into the ice with a secure crunching sound. Even though the dry air did whistle in a sore throat that already was too small for the volume one wanted to gulp down, it was nevertheless a pleasure, a day of days, for the hard battle and slogging had not yet set in.

People have described the icefall in all sorts of ways, as a waterfall of ice, a squashed meringue, a staircase of loose cubes of sugar. But nothing could do it justice if one has not seen a big icefall, a glacier bending and sliding over a precipice, and as full of a variety of dangers as unstable ice must always be. And just to spice it up and remind us of that danger, chunks were continually breaking off from the cliffs of the Lho La on our left and thundering down the debris slope beside us. When this happened, the sound of chipping ice axes would cease and everyone would stop to watch, except myself, of course, if I had the camera out. Then I would swing rapidly around and try to catch the scene. But always too late. By the time the sound reached us, the best display was over. Perhaps most maddening of all, the only time I did get a good shot, I ran out of film.

It would have been very nice to enjoy the day. Unfortunately I was working. I can imagine many amateur enthusiasts would feel that being on the lower parts of the icefall, on a bright day, with as much film to blaze off as you could run through your camera, would be a delight. But photography you *have* to do is serious and rather boring work. The continual taking down, packing, and setting up of the camera was infuriating, even though I am practiced quick at it. Moreover, on Everest it was necessary to hold your breath whenever you took a shot, which made the shot steady but built up an oxygen debt which had to be repaid by even more desperate panting.

Although the party was struggling with the difficulties of finding the route, they were moving at a good pace. Often I would spurt and catch them at some obstacle, tear the camera out of the rucksack, set up the tripod, only to find that I was too late and they were moving out of range. It was an awfully disheartening business, fighting a lone battle with everything dissolving away, a sort of nightmare. I should have been hard put to it even if I had been the strongest and fittest member of the team, but as sickness had taken the guts out of me, I could not keep it up for long. The only thing was to expend myself in the first few hours and then return to base.

Yet I did get something. Hillary's Horror held the party up for a few minutes and I managed to shoot off a roll. After that I had to stop to change a film, which I have trained myself to do in less than thirty seconds under good conditions—but not on Everest. Not with a blinding light and snow getting into everything. So I lost the party for the day, going on a bit just for the fun of it and thanking God that it was a war of attrition for the climbers as well as myself. It would go on day after day. Each day they would go a little farther and build up a shade more potential. Each day I should get a few more shots—until in the end, perhaps, success for us all. Perhaps! I was not very hopeful, for there were other difficult problems besides the physical work.

When we slogged down the gullies at the foot of the icefall at the end of that first day, feet soaked in the water that ran down with the hot sun, I took stock of the job ahead. In a light so blinding that one could scarcely bear to look with the naked eye, what were the exposures? Was my estimate quite wrong? The worry nagged like a nail in a new shoe.

There was one comfort—the technical difficulty of the climbing was not beyond what I could easily do, as I had feared it might be. However, this state of complaisance did not last long, and there was soon to come a rude shock to my ego. Griff and I wanted to go as far as the site for Camp II, which had just been chosen in the middle of the icefall, and we followed up the reconnaissance until we were within spitting distance of it. Then we came to the edge of a crevasse. The tracks went on, on the other side, so it must be the place, but it looked too wide to jump; too wide and too high on the other side. Close examination showed a thin flake of ice, little more than a foot thick, which formed a bridge. In the middle of this bridge, as by a miracle, was a footprint. Some maniac had used it!

"Griff I don't know about you, but I . . ."

"Hum."

It was very much "Hum." Just one push and you could be across, but . . . Imagination supplied the rest. A tinkling of a collapsed bridge into the blue depths, rough ice tearing the skin of your knuckles, and then a shattering jerk round the ribs. Gyaljen and Griff would take the strain, but how the devil would they pull me out? I hunted both ways for a place to jump, but there was no alternative.

"Do we risk it?"

"Better not," said Griff, who was wise and had long since conquered the fear of admitting defeat.

I knew he was right, but it went very much against the grain. He was right because our job was to keep strictly out of trouble—not get into it. Later they would bridge it with poles for the Sherpas; just now it was for the reconnaissance boys only, and we must put our self-esteem firmly into the background. Reluctantly we turned away, denying our sporting instincts for the sake of our jobs—and for the sake of the rest of our team.

George Lowe's dysentery had been becoming worse and worse. His face was pinched and thin. In fact he looked so ill that I feared he might be out of the expedition for good. I think George did too, for he was miserable and despondent. For once his cheerful wisecracks ceased. That George was not a man to allow sickness to gain an easy victory, one could very clearly see. For instance, he had a crippled elbow as a result of having once broken his funny bone. I had done the same in a motorcycle accident many years before but had been luckier in my surgeon than George, for he could not straighten his left arm to more than a right angle, which made his climbing at all, let alone his selection for Everest, a real triumph. But dysentery is not a handicap that can just be ignored, and poor George now had to remain at base.

One day Griff and I were returning from the icefall. When we came in sight of camp, we saw a most extraordinary sight. A strange man was sitting on a stone just above our tents. Dressed in a golfing jacket and city shoes, perfectly shaven, we thought we must be dreaming. But on closer inspection our visitor looked exhausted. His lips were blue from lack of oxygen and his eyes were terribly inflamed from walking over the snow without dark goggles.

It was Ralph Izzard, reporter from the *Daily Mail.* The wicked fellow had come up to try to scoop the *Times.*

Maybe it is difficult for people to realize the situation. We had all signed impressive documents in which we had promised not to talk to the press. Moreover, Ralph was regarded as a sinister character because he had dared to write up an interview saying that Tenzing preferred climbing with the Swiss to the British. This article had been seized upon and emphasized by the Indian press, with the result that Ralph was regarded as an archenemy of the expedition—and now he was here.

"Awkward," said Griff with relish, in a way I knew meant, "How lovely—what a lovely situation." Griff was a tolerant man, filled with secret amusement about many things and likely to poke fun.

"We must at least offer him a cup of tea," I said.

"Is George asleep?"

But George was not asleep. George was ignoring Ralph as firmly as an experienced duchess ignores the stray dog that lifts its leg against the platform during prize-giving.

"We just can't send him to Coventry when he has come all the way up here. If it upsets the others, well . . ."

We went over and introduced ourselves. "Would you like some tea?"

"Yes, thank you . . . eh, I would," said Ralph. I felt very sorry for him, knowing what it is like to travel hopefully with no welcome at the end. Over tea we discussed the Abominable Snowman. In an unguarded moment, and perhaps trying overmuch to keep the conversation on this safe topic, I said that I thought an expedition ought to go especially to investigate it.

"Would you go on such an expedition?" asked Ralph.

"Certainly," I said, with more conviction than I felt.

Ralph was exhausted and rapidly becoming snow blind. We watched from a cairn above the camp while he went down the glacier with tired, disappointed steps. It seemed a dreadful thing not to offer him hospitality for the night.

"I hope he makes it," I said to Griff, a little worried.

"He'll make it," said Griff, mentally rubbing his hands. "But what a lovely case of anoxia—absolutely classic symptoms."

I did not know then that I had been meeting a man who was to become one of the best friends of my life.

It was afterward that Ralph told me about his journey. For three weeks he had traveled with no companion but his Nepalese guide—and they did not speak any common language. Improperly kitted, and with an old tent bought in a Calcutta bazaar, he had carefully shaved and washed, cleaned his shoes, and made himself presentable before starting on that last day, in order to show us that "Everest climbers are not so tough after all." It was a very efficient piece of gamesmanship.

When the main body of the expedition arrived, Base Camp was moved a few hundred yards to a better spot, and we set ourselves to make it a little more comfortable. My own worry was to find a place to store my film, safe from the violent temperature fluctuations of day and night. There was often a wind, and snow fell regularly most afternoons, which made the tents crowd up and become difficult to work in. I decided to construct an ice cave for myself.

To begin with, this project was met with a certain amount of mild derision, but as soon as a narrow passage had been driven some ten feet into an ice pinnacle and we had begun to open it into a chamber, more and more people lent a hand. It was something to do in between the growing activity on the icefall and, though exhausting, quite good fun. Later on, when the tent situation at Base Camp became difficult, several other caves were started as living accommodations.

We had a chamber big enough for four or five men to stand in when Tom Bourdillon offered to give a hand, and I shall never forget his first shift. He was a great beefy fellow, without question the strong man of the expedition.

"Let me have a bash," he said, seizing an ax from the nearest Sherpa. He swung back and gave the wall a tremendous wallop. As the ax bit deep, a great crack appeared—there must have been some line of strain—and there was a thunderous boom, alarming in the confined space. Thinking that the roof was coming in, everyone rushed headlong for the door. One blow from Tom was enough to shake the glacier to its foundations.

When the cave was finished, it was entered by a narrow gallery some eleven feet long and six feet high. This led to a chamber eight feet high in the center and about twelve feet in diameter—a nice beehive-shaped room in the ice. The temperature in here stayed constant, just a little below freezing point both day and night, and it was an ideal place to store film. Whatever the conditions outside, the cave remained calm and clean. In the daytime a blue glow filtered in, and at night one candle gave a brilliant light, since the ice reflected back and back like the mirror chamber in the Amber Palace at Jaipur, where a thousand little mirrors lining walls and ceiling make the whole room gay from one tiny lamp.

I moved my belongings in and made this cave my home. It was too dank and uncomfortable to be used for pleasurable sitting about, but it was fine for work such as cleaning my cameras. I had had trouble in the tents, even getting a camera full of beard clippings, about which I was properly enraged.

I even moved into the cave to sleep, and I do not think it did my cough any good. We all suffered from "Sherpa cough" to some degree, and most had dysentery as well. These are some of the curses of high-altitude mountaineering, the coughs, sore throats, and general ill health. Indeed, added to the effects of altitude, it is true to say that Everest is climbed by sick men, and certainly so when compared to the fighting-fit standards of a party in the Alps.

By now the spearhead of the expedition had pushed up the icefall and beyond into the Western Cwm. Other parties were fixing ropes and bridging crevasses. The whole detailed procedure has been described ad nauseam in the many books. To the casual observer it was a busy coming and going, a steady shuffle of stores from camp to camp, a build-up for attack. Now that the novelty had worn off, I began to suffer from a surfeit of that Monday-morning feeling which is so characteristic of life at great altitudes. It was time to bestir myself and to move up to higher camps. Word was coming down from above as to what the Cwm was like, and there were now enough provisions and tents at the top of the icefall at Camp III to make my visit possible.

Climbing up the icefall had now been made easy. It had to be to enable the laden Sherpas to get up. Of danger one did not *know*, one only imagined. At any moment a fall of ice or a collapsing bridge might change what would be a pleasant walk, if it wasn't for the altitude, into a murder. But the day I went up I was too tired to bother.

254

My legs ached and breath came in gasps, punctuated by fits of coughing. All I did was pray for the camp to come in sight.

Camp II was a slightly alarming place, a place where you felt, despite assurances, that something was likely to fall suddenly and in the night. It was also already foul. On account of the danger of walking about unroped, it was impossible to go more than a few paces from the tents in order to answer the calls of nature. This was the curse of all camps and made them unpleasantly sordid. There was also litter. There was our litter and in places the Swiss litter from the previous year. Explorers might well take a lesson from Boy Scouts. We think because the situation is remote that it doesn't matter—that the snow will cover all. It does—but it also melts. An expedition in men per day equals a Bank Holiday crowd—and it shows. It shows in rusty tin cans and bits of paper, an old discarded rag or a packing case, an ugly prospect when met with in the otherwise virgin snows.

As we were settling into camp—which for me meant just collapsing onto a sleeping bag—George Band and party came rattling down out of the mist from above. It gave the feeling of excitement I always get when—I can only say—I penetrate and see for myself. George had been into that mysterious high gorge, the Western Cwm, which, if I were lucky, I should also see on the following day, and so he already had an aura.

The track above Camp II wound in and out of a maze, around blocks, over crevasses all choked with more blocks and icicles, until at the end of the second day we scaled a fifteen-foot rope ladder and came to the top of a slope that led gently to Camp III. It was snowing hard, and Wilf Noyce had arrived down from the Cwm. We stood around, the snow settling on our blue windbreakers, while Sherpas unpacked our sleeping bags and inflated the air beds in the tents. The snow was of the soft half-melting kind that made everything wet. We hoped the Sherpas would not get too much of it into the tents, but being experienced, they knelt down, boots outside and bottoms blocking the entrance.

I was trying to get the plastic wrapping off some boiled sweets when there was a hail from the mist below. It was Hillary and George Lowe, now fully recovered, who had come right up from Base Camp. Having arrived at Camp II, they had felt bored and now were up visiting us at Camp III. Any pride I had in having got here was promptly squashed by such formidable and casual performers.

The Sherpas brewed tea. To brew anything out of tea at this altitude—over 20,000 feet—you have to boil the leaves for several minutes. Even then it is watery because in this reduced pressure water boils at such a low temperature. But the tea was warm. I had thankfully reached for the mug when—damn and blast!—I knew I must at least try to film this. One final effort and the scene would be "in the bag" (just as I would be as soon as it was done)—a typical scene in a snowstorm, and I would never be bothered with it again. Flakes of snow fell on the lens and I had to clean it again and again before I at last got my mug of tea—and it was cold! Wilf Noyce had to go down the slope to connect the radio, and stood shivering for some minutes. It was comforting to see someone else suffer too. Then Ed and George put on their rucksacks and vanished back into the labyrinth of the icefall, so everyone went into the tents, and it was finished. Finished, except that I lay there worrying, as usual, whether anything would possibly come of photographs in this snowstorm; I would not know until it was over and too late to mend.

Next morning I did not feel too well. I had coughed a lot in the night but thought it was the increased altitude and colder air. Then I spat on the dirty rag that was once a handkerchief—and looked. It was red with blood. Panic!

I was given some penicillin chewing gum, which was as much use as a dead fish to a crooner. I went on coughing until the inevitable cry, "Go down, old boy, go down." It was the universal cure, and the only cure, but a hard one too—to turn out when all you wanted to do was lie down warm and just give way.

When I crawled into Base Camp there was already a general move afoot to Lobuje for a rest—Lobuje, the highest yak hut, and a day's march down the glacier. I set off in the company of several sick Sherpas, going very slowly and resting frequently. The pace got slower and slower. We walked in a daze, resting every few steps, and coughing till we made ourselves vomit, but you get there in the end if you go on putting one foot before the other. You think there will come a time when it will be over and you can look back on it, but then, morbidly, that life will be like that too.

Lobuje was in a hollow, two bleak stone huts, grass, a stream, and even a few purple primulas struggling through in the patches between the snow. It was only 16,000 feet more or less, and the relief to the breathing was enormous. Even so, I felt poorly, and lay in my sleeping bag in the sunshine, watching the others come and go. There was a large boulder on which George Band and Tom Bourdillon used to do impossible boulder problems in fierce competition. I was astonished especially at Tom's skill as a rock climber, which was quite incredible for such a heavy man, like an outsize cat with a soft tread. On one occasion George Band fell off on top of a Sherpa shelter that promptly collapsed under his weight, to the consternation of those inside; but if one laughed, one started coughing again.

For two days I was in a semi-coma, and then Griff came down from Base Camp to have a look at me. This was very noble of him because it was not really his job to act as expedition doctor, and he was still suffering from the altitude himself. He listened knowingly to my chest and said I was just recovering from pneumonia. That brought John Hunt down. It meant an extra day's outing, down and back, for him too, and so was an act of kindness and concern, as was Griff's; I shall always remember it. It gave me a sense of belonging which stiffened my determination to get back on the job quickly. The opposite attitude, "Each one for himself and the devil take the hindmost," is apt to discourage the hindmost—which at that moment was me.

The climbers once more returned to the mountain and I was left in the care of the convalescent Sherpas. I was greatly worried that the expedition would have finished with the icefall before I could get back. Although George Lowe had nobly offered to "give it a go" with my cameras and I had given him a little instruction—he was the only member of the expedition who showed interest—I could obviously not rest content on his efforts. However bright he was and however carefully he followed my advice, it was my work and not his.

With Lobuje deserted, and lying silent, I was able to enjoy the entertainment provided by the local mouse hares. Looking like guinea pigs that have somehow got dressed in rabbit's fur, they popped around the rocks, nibbling off the lichen, chasing each other, or just sitting quietly in the sun. On two occasions also I was visited by an animal I had never seen before, the size and shape of a polecat, but a beautiful golden color. On each occasion it sat on a rock and after inspection came quite close to me. Later, when I told the others about this animal, they thought I had seen it in a delirium—but I had not. It was a yellow-bellied weasel, not a romantic name for such a charming companion and friend!

Nine days later I was back up the icefall at Camp III. James Morris, correspondent of the *Times*, was being taken up by Mike Ward, and I was able to dog their party. James had never been on a mountain before, and there was a lot of new snow, making the track difficult. Between the two I was for the first and about the only time able not only to keep up with the party but also to have time to film it. I thought, too, that it would provide a fine opportunity for a non-climber, a man in the street, to report his impressions of Everest, an idea that was subsequently used to great effect in the film.

Even at this slow pace it was hard, grinding work, and many times I thought I would abandon my heavy tripod, because that was the chief devil in my box of tricks; without it the job would be easy, as every professional knows. But that meant abandoning professional standards as well. If only that bastard Mike Ward would *wait*, hang around long enough for a more leisurely pace of work; but nobody would hang around on the icefall, not being concerned with pictures or that hypnotic enthusiasm that makes a photographer keep his head up a little too long in a war—as if he were only an observer and not part of things himself.

"We mustn't hang around here," Mike would say. "You do what you want, but this isn't a good place," and he would go carefully on, vanishing with my prey in the driving snow, and Gyaljen would help me fumble with the maddening packing up.

"Cold?" I asked Gyaljen after a time. "Why don't you put more clothes on?"

"No more clothes, Sahib."

The bloody fool, why hadn't he brought them?

"No more clothes, Sahib. Can Sahib get me some?" he repeated in the mixture of Hindustani and mime with which we communicated.

"But I saw them."

He looked sheepish. "I borrowed them from other Sherpas, now they take them back."

"Well, of all the bloody fools. It's too late now."

259

When the tents of the camp came in sight—dismal snow-covered site and a telling picture—I wanted to get a shot of the party going in—they were some distance ahead and I had run out of film in the camera. Although the camp was little more comfortable than where we were, the temptation to finish the journey was difficult to resist; the temptation to "call it a day"; the temptation to be lazy.

To combat this I used to play a game, like feeding a child with "This one for Daddy, one for Mummy, and the last for Auntie Flo."

"My father would like to see this," I would think. "Or my aunt Molly—or perhaps this will amuse our patron, Prince Philip, or even the Queen." A silly game, perhaps, but I wonder how many of the others did not secretly play such games just to keep themselves going—maybe setting themselves the task of twenty paces or the distance up the bedroom stairs. As my selfsame aunt Molly put it, "They didn't conquer Everest, they conquered their own bleeding flesh."

So once more I knelt upwind in my plastic bag, poking the film into place with frozen fingers, trying to hurry, to keep the snow out of the camera, and yet to do everything carefully right. I could hear poor patient Gyaljen's teeth chattering as I cursed and swore. Why a Sherpa did this, God knew—it was certainly not just the money.

But when I straightened up with the camera again ready, they had already gone into the tents. There was nothing more to be said. It had happened like that so often before.

chapter 23

THE Western Cwm of Everest is around four miles long, a great trench over 20,000 feet high and filled with ice. It rises slowly from the top of the icefall to the bottom of the Lhotse Face. Wide crevasses split it from side to side, and to gain suitable bridges, or sections narrow enough to jump, the path has to zigzag from side to side. But where possible, not too close in under the giant walls, because something unpleasant might fall on your head.

I went out with Greg; we always worked together when he had a spare day, which was of inestimable help. To show the sheer stupendous size of these walls in terms of film was a task that somehow had to be faced. The only object of known size was a climber, but when you looked at one from a distance, he was a mere black speck on the snow. Something an audience could not pick out. One has little inspiration at this height, but it came to me suddenly that the thing to do was to let the audience "climb" the wall in detail, using a telephoto lens and moving the camera gradually. It was a difficult shot to take. By the time I had finished—holding my breath till it burst—I was almost lying under my tripod, tilting the camera up at the fabulous walls that loomed above. These walls of mixed rock and ice shelter the Cwm from winds and reflect the heat, so that being in the Cwm is often sweltering enough to sap all the little remaining energy one has, like being in the bowl of a sun furnace.

When I reached Camp IV it was not complete. A pile

of boxes and gear was stacked in the snow. Although everything was slowly moving up the mountain, we had not yet stripped the lower camps, so there was a shortage of tents. In the meantime my presence caused a slight overcrowding. We were also getting a bit dirty and smelly, not having washed for so long, and our beards were pricking.

Camp IV was a fine grandstand seat. Without moving a muscle one could sit on a box and watch George Lowe and Ag Nyima suffering, trying to blaze a route onward up the Lhotse Face, which was the next major obstacle; but we were so far away that details were invisible and the scene quite impersonal. In the mornings little dots would come out from behind an ice block which screened the tents, and move upward—so slowly, so very slowly. They would get slower and slower until it was no longer profitable to watch. It was like trying to see the movement of the hour hand on a clock. Better only to emerge now and then to see how much more progress they had made—or how little. In between one adopted the "Everest position," which was lying flat on the back, talking, smoking, and reading. It was boring, it was difficult to while away the time, I longed for something to do with my hands, even knitting would have been a good idea. Many had lost all interest in food, so that often we did not even bother to eat; we made jokes, speculating as to whether we had also lost interest in women. One French cat had sent me a teasing photograph of herself in a bikini, stretched on a beach on the Côte d'Azur. It encouraged me to wonder just why I was here instead of enjoying some civilized fun, but a long questionnaire coming by runner from Katmandu and all the way up the icefall gave me the clue. It was from the income tax inspector.

"We are sorry to have disturbed the rarified atmosphere of the Western Cwm," they said afterward, with a flash of unexpected humor.

There was nothing to film around the camp, except an occasional arrival of a convoy from below and the expressions of those around me. John Hunt, for instance, showed obvious signs of being worried—worried by the slow progress—always gazing hopefully upward through fieldglasses. But the core of the story was not here. All that was happening was happening up there on the Lhotse Face, and it was too far away even for my best telephoto lens. Moreover, even if I had had the strength to go there myself, which I did not, it would still have been impossible. To eat precious food and occupy tent space and bedding for anything except the dire needs of the expedition was obviously unthinkable. So where was my film? It was one of the gaps I had feared, one of the basic faults of actuality films. Getting the material without reconstruction was impossible. It seemed possible only to tell the story by the comings and goings from here—how they went out with purpose and came back exhausted with slow steps and lined faces. How we felt, the excitement, the envy, and the mystery of what it was like just over the Geneva Spur and on the South Col itself. That would be easy to convey in studio dialogue—but with pictures alone . . . ?

My only hope was George Lowe, who had one of those little cameras so carefully "hotted up" in London—and he *might* be using it occasionally, and he *might* be doing what I had told him to and not just waving it about, and it *might* work. These cameras had not run to speed in the cold chamber, which was another gamble. I did not tell George this, I thought it might discourage him. I had now set them a little fast, which might counteract any effect of cold on the spring. Later it was to prove that by chance I had done something that paid off.

As if this was not enough to think about, Gyaljen, who had not been well since we had come up the icefall, became definitely sick. Then, after a day's rest, far from improving, he developed alarming symptoms. The poor fellow had gallantly held on until almost too late. When I went over to his tent to see him in the morning, one of the other Sherpas carried out for my inspection an old vegetable tin that had been used as a spittoon. It was full to the brim with liver-colored blood.

I called to Griff Pugh and we hauled Gyaljen out of the tent and into the sunshine.

"Gyaljen is very sick," said Griff, taking the stethoscope out of his ears. "Very near collapse. If we don't get him down he'll die."

"Pneumonia?"

"No, I don't think so, the blood isn't frothy as it usually is from the lungs. I think it comes from his stomach, but I can't make a diagnosis up here. In any case he has to go down, and since he can't walk, he'll have to be carried."

An hour later I said good-by to this faithful fellow. Now glassy-eyed and riding pickaback, head hanging over the shoulder of a friend, he was borne off down the Cwm. I never saw him again. Before we came down the mountain he had returned to his village, apparently recovered, but a year later I heard he had died. Perhaps nobody but myself remembers him now, but he was, in the Sherpa tradition, a gallant young man who would not give up.

My chances of getting a film seemed more slender indeed. In my mind, even amid all the doubts and reservations, I had dreamed of being reasonably fit, with two fighting Sherpas of my own to carry my gear, and trained to help me at least with setting up the tripod and handing me what I required. Maybe I should even scrounge a little oxygen to help on my way. But now I had none of these things. At the luckiest I could borrow a Sherpa who ought to be resting, at worst I should have to carry all thirty pounds of gear myself. At such times one should call upon one's reserves of strength—but I had no reserves. Nearly twelve weeks of fever, improper convalescence, and then pneumonia, and I was just ticking over like a car that is stuck on the slow-running jet.

But if I was going through it, others were doing the same. John Hunt's grizzled red hair was turning a shade white. The little dot that was George Lowe had stopped making progress, and it began to look almost as if we should be driven back ignominiously, without even having reached the South Col, let alone having got enough stores up there to mount an attempt on the summit.

A certain lassitude was setting in. Lying too long in a tent produces a sort of foxhole mentality, and there was also the time factor, because continued residence at this altitude—about 21,000 feet—gradually saps the body, and also because if it's to be done at all Everest has to be climbed during a short period at the end of May, just before the monsoon breaks. It is then that the weather *may* be right.

Weather was crucial. Every day special broadcasts from the Indian Meteorological Department were made to us. If these forecasts of the weather on Everest were mostly wrong—it would have been a miracle if they had not been —at least one could be sure that the movements of the monsoon were correct, and now we heard that it was approaching up the Bay of Bengal. Time was running out.

So faces showed the strain, and we all sat around listening to the radio, mostly the Ceylon commercial, which came in loud, and occasionally the B.B.C. from London, which was faint. They told us about preparations for the Coronation, but it all seemed very remote, and almost unimportant under the shadow of this mammoth mountain we were trying to get up, with its thirty years of cocking a snook at the best efforts of mankind.

"When you're feeling low—*Eno*."

A squeaky female voice would chant the commercial ditty, and we would all join in with feeling, but with due respect to this useful remedy, I doubt if it would have helped just now. George Band, who was a prolific mimic, would then run over his repertoire culled from various meetings we had attended in London.

"We all owe a great debt of gratitude to Mr. X. He has been so busy he has even had to take his secretary home for the weekends."

George Lowe returned, his face fallen in, a man who had sacrificed himself for the expedition. Already it was becoming plain who would, short of misfortune, be the ones selected for the summit. The others had the words "expendable" marked on them like men dying in the breach so that others might cross upon their bodies.

Wilf Noyce was the next on the list. His job was to get to the South Col by hook or by crook, and if possible take a gang of Sherpas with him. We watched the dots move up to Camp VII, as stationary as fly spots on a white wall, not seeming to move at all. And then we waited anxiously to see what would happen the following day.

At first there was no sign—starting seemed delayed till very late—and then only two specks appeared, but these specks went on and up, past the highest point reached by George Lowe, and with mounting excitement we watched them begin on the traverse the Lhotse Face toward the South Col. Excitement reached a climax when we saw them vanish out of sight over the Geneva Spur. Wilf Noyce had reached the Col, itself as high as the top of Annapurna, and things were looking up.

There was now feverish activity. Charles Wylie was organizing a second squadron of Sherpas (we have to stick to military terms), Tom Bourdillon was fixing up the closed-circuit oxygen sets, using my adhesive tape, which seemed to be sticking half the expedition together by now. We were already using it to repair boots and clothes. There was a feeling of buoyancy. The luxury box was raided for more varied foods, which people thought they might tempt themselves to eat higher up. In it were packed a few pounds of everyone's special choice, but they ranged from a laxative cereal which nobody ate—not even the owner on account of the rude remarks passed about it (he did not want to give himself away)—to delicious salami sausages chosen by Greg, which everyone wanted, much to Greg's annoyance. Indeed, with such an arrangement, the sensible thing is to choose something that nobody likes except yourself.

When Charles Wylie took his Sherpas up, I set off with Greg to go as far as possible to film them. Greg had a little oxygen to use up, and I trailed along behind without it. I was also burdened with too much equipment. The man with oxygen does not have to rest, and I was soon in a deplorable state of exhaustion, with the world spinning round, legs aching, and lungs desperately sucking in air. At the first fixed rope on the Lhotse Face, between 22,000 and 23,000 feet, I was glad to pause to set up my camera, going through the motions as a result of long training rather than conscious thought.

By the time the long train of Sherpas had passed through I had recovered somewhat. I should have liked to go on to Camp VI, but it did not seem worth while. I had no hope of catching up. It was useless to photograph from below, and I should have had to get five minutes ahead to find a place from which I could work and then get ready. Moreover, if for any reason I collapsed, I should wreck the whole South Col carry. I should like to be able to say that I turned back reluctantly. I did not. I was very happy to be once more going downhill to Camp V for a cup of tea.

Camp V was a dismal staging post at the bottom of the Lhotse Face. A cold wind seemed always to be flapping the tents, and we did not remain long, but continued on downward to the luxurious accommodations of camp IV.

It was now possible to settle in for grandstand seats. On a memorable day we watched the great train of Sherpas struggle up to the South Col. From here one only cursed their slowness—so much depended on them getting there—and as the day went on, it seemed they would never make it. But each time we came out of our tents, they were a little farther, until they straggled out of sight behind the Geneva Spur. What tragedies, what awful suffering, we did not know—it was hard to realize that these dots were our tough, cheerful little men, doing it for God knows what reason. Not for money, not for honor and glory, but simply because they were men who had that intangible something called *esprit de corps*, a quality which knows no barriers of color or race.

Now the final assault was on. Over the next few days I filmed many departures. There was the last minute checking of rucksacks. The testing of the oxygen gear. Then they would clip on their masks, adjust the regulator, and we would shake their hands and wish them well. They would plod away up the Cwm toward the Face. I would rush around filming them, but in the end all I could do was tilt longingly upward from their retreating figures to the South Col, that mysterious place where a battle would be fought out—it did not look very far away—but a place I should never see.

But two of my little cameras went. One with George Lowe and one with Charles Wylie.

"When anyone goes for the top, see they take one of these cameras. Just try . . ."

"We will if we can." But there was no enthusiasm. One knew that the film did not matter—just getting to the top—and that everything must go into that.

The dots crossed the Lhotse Face and vanished. The dots came back, painfully slow. We counted them and said that must be so-and-so or so. The dots were all there, so everything was all right.

Then they began to come in, haggard, with faces blackened by the frostbite of the icy wind, except for white

268

circles round their eyes and mouth where the goggles and the oxygen masks fitted. You did not have to ask what it was like, the faces were the faces of men who were exhausted to death.

"Bourdillon and Evans have reached the South Summit."

Our jubilation was tempered with a shade of disappointment that they had not reached the top, the disappointment you would feel at winning a million pounds instead of a million and one. Without benefit of an intermediate camp they had almost reached the top from the South Col —*in one*—climbing farther in a day than the Swiss Lambert and Tenzing had previously managed in two.

When Bourdillon returned, he was stumbling with fatigue. I set up my camera to receive him, the ever-present eye, but George stood in front.

"George, blast you, you make a better door . . ."

"Tom asked me to. He doesn't want you to film him like this."

"Tom will never get over it," said someone sadly standing by. "They could have got there—but not there *and* back. I think Tom would almost rather have gone there and *not* come back." It is a pity you do not know what others suffer, only what you suffer yourself. Could you drive yourself until you fell flat every few yards? Could you believe enough? I was sorry to say I could not.

"May 29. Today Ed and Tenzing should be having their bash."

It was a beautiful day and windless in the Cwm. We looked up at the crags of Everest. Were they even now looking down on us from up there? We kept wandering out of the tents and staring upward, but there was nothing to see. John Hunt's face, ever since he got back from the Col, was drawn, fallen in like that of an old man. One suffered just looking at him, such was the strain of this day.

In the evening we expected Wilf Noyce to put sleeping

bags as a signal out on the slopes of the Col. We took turns watching with fieldglasses, but we saw nothing. Nothing but the golden evening light stretching across the crags of Lhotse and a few clouds drifting over the Geneva Spur, with the cold beginning to set in.

"Here is the weather forecast for the British Mount Everest Expedition," said the radio. "The monsoon is . . . Temperature in free air at twenty-eight thousand feet . . ." One could hear the radio from the big tent.

Even now our indefatigable planners were beginning to discuss details for a third attempt, but looking around, I personally did not think we had the power left in us. All over again? They would be rounding up the crocks like me! Even now I guessed many were feeling it would be a relief to get down off the mountain. It had been no exciting cut and thrust, but a long-drawn-out siege.

As soon as the sun had warmed up on the following day, five dots appeared traversing from the Col over the Face toward Camp VII. At least they were safe. We still had no idea of the result, and we expected them to stay when they reached Camp VII. We should have to wait another day.

But after time to brew a cup of tea, three of these dots appeared again, and began the slow journey down. I thought I had better get my camera and go to meet them— just in case.

"John," I said. "If they've done it I'll get in sight of the camp and wave a coat."

"All right, Tom," said John. It was a sign of the times that he did not rush off to meet them himself.

I took some Sherpas and set out. For once I was feeling good and made haste to Camp V. The three dots were descending more rapidly than one would expect for tired men, so leaving the Sherpas to brew tea I pressed on. I hoped to catch them on the last part of the Lhotse Face, but as I was panting up the slope toward it, three figures came over the brow above. They paused and waved their axes in the air.

I was so excited that I began to stumble up toward them at a run.

"Did you do it?" I panted. They all stood there grinning, and George Lowe gave me a silent but oh so expressive thumbs up.

"Ed . . . Tenzing . . . My God, that's wonderful. Congratulations," pant, pant, pant. I was so out of breath and excited I could scarcely take a shot.

"Go on down to Camp V. There's some tea made there. I've just got to go up and wave my coat as a signal to John Hunt, then I'll join you."

"We'd rather tell him ourselves," said George.

"Of course. How stupid of me."

I tied onto their rope; even now, tired as they were, I was afraid they would escape me. I was not going to miss the dramatic scene when the news was broken. How proud can you feel when your own team comes home, as proud as if you had done it yourself—an odd human quirk.

Just before we came over the final slope into Camp IV we stopped for a rest. I unroped in order to be free to move and got the camera ready.

"Please. Nobody give any signal until we are close enough for a picture. Not until I give the word. I will keep my camera hidden under my coat and hold onto the rope pretending I am tied on, so the expedition will get no clue."

As we came in sight of the camp, people began to come slowly to meet us. Mike Westmacott was in front, John Hunt a little behind him. It is a measure of the respect in which we all held him as leader that my eyes were filled with tears just at the thought of how happy he would be. As we approached and yet gave no sign, he obviously thought this attempt had also been a failure. His steps, at first buoyed up with excitement, slowed to those of a hopelessly tired man.

Then I let go the rope, brought up the camera. "Right, George, let it go."

As George gave the thumbs up, everyone stopped for a second, not taking it in, not daring to believe their eyes. Then they began to stumble forward. Flinging arms round the victors' necks, clapping them on the back, everyone talking at once. I was too busy to notice details at the time. Like many hectic moments, I only saw it in the theater afterward.

The anticlimax came when we had all exhausted ourselves. Then they retired to a tent to give the story to Jimmy Morris of the *Times*, who had come up that day to get it. He had now to rush the details to his newspaper.

"Here is the weather forecast for the British Mount Everest Expedition. The monsoon . . ."

But we did not care about that any more. We were filled not only with the joy of success, but also with a great and wonderful relief; we could at last pack up and go down. People started to talk without restraint of the first bottle of beer, of the bath, of the civilized meal, and I think all anticipated the pleasure it would be to tell their climbing friends all about this wonderful success, and maybe other people would be a little interested too.

"I hope the news doesn't arrive at Coronation time," someone said. "We shall get pushed onto the back page."

"There's not much hope of Jimmy getting it back in time, so don't worry."

And nobody did worry except myself, because everyone was happy and relaxed. I was not—not one bit. Ever since about five minutes after I had learned the great news, I had had the coldest feet I had ever had in my life. I was quite sure I had not got a film. Of course everyone had told me that I wouldn't get a film, even the producers agreed it would be all right if I "just did my best"—and yet with all this lip service, I knew that in fact they expected me to get it—and if, as now, this had become not just another Everest expedition but *the* Everest expedition —well, I should be labeled for life: *The man who failed.* There was no getting away from it.

I thought all this as we came down the icefall for the last time. The icefall was bad now, but Everest did not seem disposed to take a last crack at us, except that an aluminum stake anchoring a hand line came loose at the top of "Mike's Horror" and tumbled Wilf Noyce down into our lap in a sudden frantic emergency which luckily came to nought.

chapter 24

O N E O F the striking things about this expedition was that I still liked my companions. With some, of course, I had more in common than with others, but there was no one I watched with hatred as he hung his socks to dry; and, looking round at that happy tentful of men—ordinary men —I remembered the speech from *Henry V* before Agincourts:

> . . . *From this day to the ending of the world,*
> *But we in it shall be remember'd;*
> *We few, we happy few, we band of brothers . . .*

For this was true, and there was not a cloud in the sky, until on Coronation Day the radio gave us the news, "Everest has been climbed . . . Crowds lining the route cheered . . ."

This meant that James Morris had achieved the impossible and got his message back to the *Times* in just over two days from Camp IV to London. It also meant, if we had been smart enough to realize it, that we had become famous, and in the future we had better watch our step.

As for myself, the news came as a nag of extra worry, as at school, when one had not prepared one's homework and discovered that the tolerant young Latin master was sick and the Head would take the class. It made me pack the film the more carefully for its journey home, my own 10,000 feet and the grubby *casettes* full of biscuit crumbs that had come down from the South Col in George Lowe's rucksack.

"Please God," I thought, "let me not have made the gaff of the century." And then my mind once more engaged the cogs. I faced the awful truth, "God helps those who help themselves," and praying would not change the pictures on the film.

"Griff," I said, remembering those desperate ventures on the North Face, "this was a damned boring expedition. Nothing went wrong."

"Don't worry," said Griff. "You will see. The myth will grow."

But it was difficult to cast men in the role of heroes when you had lived with them so long, heard them belch or argue over a last sardine. Even if the exposures were right and the film had not been scratched, nor any one of a thousand other matters gone wrong—even then, what was there? These very ordinary-looking fellows walking or climbing or getting exhausted. Nothing to write home about. Nothing spectacular, like charging lions or icebergs out of control.

A hoard of local Sherpas seized what was left of our gear—much had to be abandoned on the mountain—and we scampered down the glacier. With wonderful relief we breathed in lungfuls of solid air and felt the blood begin to race as it thinned to normal from that black treacle we had developed to snatch the oxygen higher up. It had been so viscous, the heart could scarcely squeeze it around. Then, with renewed circulation, came the awful impatience to get home.

We stumbled back through the opening monsoon, up paths now slippery with mud, and even torrents pouring down where footsteps had worn a track, cutting deeper and deeper gullies as the years went by. We put Methyl Plhalate on our boots to discourage the leeches which waved like groping tentacles from stones and branches as we passed. The Sherpas' legs ran blood where they were bitten. One climbed my sodden umbrella and got between

276

my fingers, so that I suddenly saw an extra black finger, a floppy one without a bone, until in horror I lit a cigarette and burned it. It curled angrily and fell off on the ground.

In camps hastily pitched with soaking tents and bedding wringing wet, I waited anxiously for the coolies carrying the film, worrying about whether my waterproofing had held, looking at the poor man in rags who brought it in and wondering if he realized he was carrying on his back what was now the most valuable part of the expedition. Worth, if I had done my job, 100,000 or 200,000 pounds at a guess. Worth nothing when we set out, but simply because it had been run through cameras, pointed in the right direction, anything; or again that shattering fear—nothing if I had made any mistake at all.

We picked blue poppies as the Sherpas did and ate the stems. They tasted like nuts. We were short of food and so hungry that when we could buy them, each one of us would eat two chickens and a pot of rice; but we could not always buy and often went to bed hungry.

We were thin, so at this altitude we simply fled up the hills, but Ed Hillary, stripped for a bath, looked like a living skeleton, just bones under the skin. We talked incessantly of food and the first glass of beer when we got back. Walking together, Griff and I discussed holidays and going down the Rhine in a canoe—just drinking and eating and sleeping in the sun.

One day, about halfway to Katmandu, we were in a lovely alpine valley, and for once the sun shone. There were wild irises everywhere. Suddenly the mail runners came around a corner carrying their brown canvas sacks.

We cut the seals and sorted out the letters on the grass. To our surprise there were some bottles of champagne inside, but one had come open and spilled into the mail.

"Here," said someone. "Here is a letter addressed to *Sir* Edmund Hillary."

"Ed, you've been knighted."

"No! Stop pulling my New Zealand—adjective leg."

But when he opened the note from John Hunt—who had gone on ahead—it was true.

We poured a carefully rationed inch of champagne into each mug and drank his health.

"Do you know," I told Griff later as we sat around reading the flood of congratulatory telegrams, "the producers of the film say I can have a *bath* in champagne."

"I should take them up on it," said Griff. "And you can invite me to the party." But luxury to us was not champagne. What we dreamed of were simpler needs—a chair, a square meal at a table with fresh vegetables, and above all bread—with a long drink of cold beer. We dreamed, in fact, of what we could afford, a rare and happy state for a civilized man to be in. We had been happy to start out for Everest, we would be even happier to get back, and we did not ask for very much to make our day complete.

Two days out of Katmandu we passed our first flower-garlanded arch, with a notice up in Nepali.

"Hail Tenzing . . ."

It should have been a happy time for Tenzing—and perhaps it was—but politicians, always ready to make capital out of someone else's good fortune, were preparing to cash in. While we, poor innocents, were humbly discussing whether there would be enough money to fly home instead of having the prolonged delay on a ship, they were reckoning exactly what they could make out of it. In spite of congratulatory telegrams and messages from half the world, we were still remembering our tourist-class journey out, and quite unprepared for what was in store; we were about to be given the works.

The local Communist party, having kept back the others by threats at knife point, was the first on the scene. Tenzing, the hero of Asia, must sign this and that manifesto. But if they were the most energetic, the others were quite as ready to secure advantage. There followed first one, then another party and another.

One might have said that poor Tenzing was being taken for a ride—except that it was Tenzing, with his strong legs and his good nature, who was being called upon to do the carrying.

"Tenzing's had it," said Griff. "Poor fellow, he'll never be allowed to move freely again."

"A Tiger in a Golden Cage."

"Maybe. It's certainly time he had something. It will be interesting to see what happens."

We came down a long descent in the early morning and met our first press. There were also my colleagues from the Indian newsreels, on the job as the world over. We shook hands with unspoken understanding.

"Did you get a good film?"

"Really, I don't know yet. I wish I was sure . . ." I did not tell them that I had already sent a telegram expressing my doubts.

Later that day some monkeys were raiding the fields across the valley, and a villager hit the leader with a stone which slowed him up. They then climbed above him and rolled great boulders down. Finally they cornered the wretched animal in a gulley and stoned him till he fell for dead. I looked through my fieldglasses; he lay there covered in blood—but he moved.

"Why don't they finish the monkey off?"

"Because it is against one's religion to kill a monkey—that is just to teach him a lesson," said the Judian correspondent I was walking with.

"A man would have been dead a thousand times."

"Yes, but the monkey will recover, you'll see."

"Or he'll die of starvation with a broken leg. I'm going over to put him out of his misery."

I crossed the valley and reached the apparently dying monkey, but then he got up and set off uphill. He was slow but by no means dead. I did not realize that since we were now famous, even my instinctive gesture of humanity would be the basis for an article in the paper. That from now on it was necessary to watch out and do the right thing.

We were late getting into camp, our last camp, on some short grass on the outskirts of a dirty village. The sign of approaching civilization was a leaking tap in the village square, but whether or not the water was good to drink, nobody knew.

Here under a big tree was John Hunt with his wife Joy, flown out through the generosity of a well-known breakfast cereal company. And to top off our return, several correspondents from several more newspapers. We began to appreciate that as the news of our success had been announced on Coronation morning, far from getting us onto the back page, it had been accepted as a good augur for a new reign and a fine Coronation present for Her Majesty, the Queen.

Next day was walked impatiently and in a rush. The weather was fine, but steamy and hot with the land drying after rain. I wondered whether Joy Hunt could keep up with her flyer of a husband, but she did so without difficulty.

"Do you think the ambassador remembered to bring up the beer?" we asked each other.

"No, I don't suppose he will remember trivial things like that."

But he had. He was waiting for us on top of the last hill, and while the Nepalese began to load Tenzing with the first garlands—and not forgetting us too—we rushed at the nectar with a thankful gasp, and it was out of real glasses, too.

After a short rest we gathered for a triumphal descent into the valley. In addition to garlands of flowers, the

Nepalese had already begun smothering the chief actors in red Holi powder for good luck. This I escaped.

Down in the valley was a tremendous crowd, with lots of fellows standing on stages, decorated, covered in slogans; it looked like a political meeting, and it was. They had that smug platform look, patronizing, self-important, "We are the boys, the boys who make things tick; we *know* Tenzing, without us he could not have done it . . ."

"*Tenzing is an Indian. No, Tenzing is a Nepalese. Tenzing is a Communist. No, Tenzing is a . . .*"

The mob began to howl. There were more garlands, more red powder. Tenzing, Ed, and John were lost in a crowd—just to touch the hem of his garment!

"This is one of the most revolting sights I have ever seen. Why can't they leave us alone? Why can't the world see that the man who gets on the platform is usually . . ."

> *A man of words and not of deeds*
> *Is like a garden full of weeds . . .*

"Come on, let's get the hell out of here. Let's go to the Nepal Hotel for some more beer—cold beer *in a chair.*"

Griff, Greg, and I seized on a friend with a Jeep, and drove off, bumping the twenty miles into Katmandu.

The Nepal Hotel had once been a palace, and stuffed leopards fought in the hall. They were a little the worse for wear, as journalists had been sitting on them to write their copy. The bar was almost empty of hard liquor because so much had been needed to stimulate imagination. For two weeks this had been the center of one of the best contested journalistic battles in history. With smuggled transmitters, telegraph lines tapped, radios monitored, and everyone open to being bribed many times over, correspondents from several dozen newspapers had tried to break the *Times* stranglehold and scoop the news for themselves. Even runners coming back had been waylaid and messages opened by the more unscrupulous, but they had not got much for their efforts. Inaccurate weather forecasts had been used to predict calamity and failure, bizarre rumors had been accepted in lieu of something better, the alcoholic inventions of one had been monitored and spread around by others, and downright, deliberate lies had been told by a few wishing to ferment political trouble. Most vicious of these was the slogan, "Tenzing got to the top first," as we were soon to see. That was invented by one pleasant fellow who is no doubt proud of it.

It is surprising how, having longed for beer on so many hot days of the march—what an awful anticlimax it was— we could actually be satisfied with a couple of glasses and drink the third more because we thought we ought to want it rather than because we really did. The final comfort was sitting in a chair. Oh, what a good invention it is! You know it only when you have been without one for five months.

Later we went out to join the crowds lining the route. Several colonels were trying to keep the mobs back, and everyone was in a holiday mood.

"Tenzing got to the top first, didn't he?" a Nepali shouted at me.

"I don't know, I wasn't there."

"Of course he did." He pointed to a large painting which showed Tenzing pulling Hillary up.

When the procession arrived, going very slowly, you could hardly see the heroes for the officials. They still had the "our boys" expression on their faces while the real boys had only fixed, glassy smiles. Weary eyes looked out from faces smothered in red powder like badly applied rouge. Tenzing, with his friendly smile frozen on, hands pressed together in greeting, bowed from side to side by now in a sort of ritual mime.

The party finished in the King's palace, where the heroes were invested with Stars of Nepal. I could not help feeling how fitting it was that the investiture was made on arrival in hot blood, while most were still in beards and rags.

"Good Lord, Tom, I'm still in my pajamas," shouted Griff, who was absent-minded to the last. "For heaven's sake stand in front of me." It was one of the few times I ever saw Griff out of countenance.

But it didn't matter. Nothing mattered. In spite of the politicians, these very nice people were welcoming us home.

As I said, starting the bogey of, "who got to the top first" was a deliberate act on the part of certain ill-wishing correspondents, and for a short time it broke up the good relations that existed between us all—and they had been good, almost idyllically good. To begin with, we all fell for this trouble-making. Our men were men with a simple mission, climbing Everest, and had not descended to swopping belly punches with people who know how every word can be distorted; people who said, "My line is anti-Indian, or anti-British." It can be any old lie so long as it is anti-something.

There was John Hunt, a very honest and very scrupulous man, and there was Tenzing, a very honest and very straightforward man, being set at loggerheads by people who did not have scruples, or honesty, or straightforwardness.

"There was a spot of bother when you got back?" my friends say. "What was the story? Who *did* get there first?"

When two men get there at last, after all that suffering, how mean to quibble over a few yards on a rope. Someone had to go first to see whether the top was a safe place or the treacherous eaves of a cornice hanging over space and liable to break. It never entered any climbers' head even to ask who was first. It just did not matter.

When the damage was done, we met in the billiard room of the Embassy to agree on a joint story to the world. Publishing that either got there first was playing into the hands

283

of those more at home with an evasion or even a lie, so why let them persuade us it was important?

The truth was that after thirty years Everest had been climbed, and mainly by man's knowledge and technology. For who shall say that our men were tougher than Norton, Mallory and Odell, Smythe, Shipton, Longstaff . . . *ad infinitum*. Norton, who climbed to fantastic heights in a Norfolk jacket. Or Longstaff, whose feats in the Himalayas were a legend. On the other hand, what use is technology alone without men like these—without John, and Tom, and Greg, and George, and Mike . . . Tenzing, Ag Nyima, Annullu . . .

Our main interest in life was now eating, and still more eating. After a long soak in a hot bath, clean clothes, and nervous entry into the ambassador's drawing room (hoping one would remember not to break wind or spit on the floor), eating was all most of us wanted to do.

"It is not often one has endless party food *and* a bottomless appetite."

In Katmandu we sometimes had two teas to eat as well as a lunch and a dinner. In Delhi it was the same story, with receptions by Pandit Nehru, the President, and other high-level functions. Through all these we behaved in a disgraceful manner, leaving the social honors to dutiful John Hunt and making a beeline for the buffet, where we stood and stuffed down the good things without much shame or repentance. Even some young ladies with interesting shapes before and behind failed to draw more than a passing glance away from the sandwiches. Somehow the skeletons would first have to be filled out.

Yet while everyone else was enjoying this unaccustomed life, I was unfortunately still worrying about the film. It was in grave danger from the heat of the Indian summer. It was met at the airport by a fast car and rushed, with a wave from customs, into the cool of the High Commissioner's wine cellar. Then there was the film material ex-

284

posed by the Indian Air Force during a flight they made over Everest's summit. It was excellent, and I sent off a cable to the company, "GET HOLD OF THIS AT ALL COSTS" —because it would at least give an audience a glimpse of the place where Hillary and Tenzing had been.

Of course we were to fly to London. Gone were our humble days, and we should not have been astonished if the airplane had been plated with gold. B.O.A.C. rerouted their Tokyo flight to pick us up, which was an honor we took in stride. We hoped now to be able to relax on the way home, but it was not to be. Someone had kindly passed the word along the route.

A great crowd had gathered in Karachi in the early hours. Greg and I avoided it and headed for the restaurant.

"What! Only sandwiches! Bring us a meal."

Then Bahrein for breakfast, with the oil community offering us whisky. Then Cairo . . .

"B.O.A.C. announces the departure of flight . . . for Rome and London. Will passengers . . ."

"Just time for another—try these, they're good."

Then twenty minutes later a frantic hostess—"Will members of the Everest Expedition *please* board the aircraft?" One felt that the other passengers might be getting less enthusiastic about us than those who made us welcome.

We were due in to London in the early hours of the morning, when this delightful flying binge would come to an end. Luckily the airplane broke down and in Rome, in the midst of yet another party given on the airport balcony, we learned that we should have to stay there the night.

"This is quite the best part of the expedition," said Griff, always ready with the awful truth.

In London we were not straightaway given something more to eat, which was perhaps just as well. As the aircraft swung into its parking position, we could see through the windows a crowd with a barrage of V.I.P.'s, press, newsreel and television cameras.

"Will passengers not part of the Everest Expedition please get off first," said an official from the doorway. And so this final indignity for the wretched passengers. They had to sneak off, running the gantlet of the expectant crowd. They must have been heartily fed up with us indeed.

And then came our turn to face it, standing there on the concrete before the cheering throng, waving to people we knew, watching John doing his stuff, learning fast to give the public and press what they wanted, as any famous general must do—holding up the ice ax with the flags tied to it.

I suppose we were more feted than any group of young men ever were in history. We were entertained by everyone from the government to the Lord Mayor of London, the City Guilds, and even perhaps the most signal honor, Lloyd's rang the Lunine bell for us. There were also the more intimate occasions nearer home, with the Everest Committee and the Alpine Club. In two weeks we must have attended twenty banquets, and we happily ate our way through the lot. Muscles wasted away by altitude were replaced by smoked salmon and caviar. And by fat.

"I wish we could spread all these feasts over a few years," said Griff, getting to the end even of a post-Everest appetite.

"We shall be almost glad when they stop," I observed.

"You won't," said Griff. "When they stop, we'll miss them like hell."

To me, however, there was a reserve throughout the celebrations, and it was the Duke of Edinburgh who put his finger on the tender spot—although he was perhaps only making a joke.

We went to Buckingham Palace for the investiture, which was to follow a garden party. It was raining like a monsoon, and we felt ridiculous in top hats which made our six-foot-plus party look like a herd of giants.

We were late because of the crush and did not have time to be properly instructed in the ceremonial before we found ourselves lined up in the music room. So there was a certain amount of jockeying for position in order not to be first.

The Queen was smiling when she came in, which made the occasion less formidable. The Duke stood behind her while John and Ed received their knighthoods. Tenzing, looking very distinguished in his long black coat and jodhpurs, was there for his decoration. One could not help admiring his perfect dignity and natural good manners. It was now the moment for the rank and file, and in due course it was my turn.

"This is the man who has been taking the film, Ma'm," said John Hunt as I was presented. But just as the Queen was about to hand me the medal, the Duke cracked out like a mind reader, "You'd better not give him the medal until after we've seen the film."

Everyone laughed, but my voice dried in my throat. Maybe I was here under false pretenses! The anxiety had been gnawing at me for over a month, and it was killing.

But at length the technicians at Kodak had finished the work. The day came to see the rushes—the uncut material —for the first time. We sat in the board room of the Film Finance Corporation, George Lane who had helped, and all the people who had bet their money on me.

"I don't know what you've been worrying about," said the producer, John Taylor, after a few minutes. And when to my astonished eyes I also saw George's films from the South Col, bringing to life what I had only observed from a distance, relief flooded in like sunshine on a spring morning.

From now on I could leave it all to other people. I gave what help I could and went away. When you look at a shot and remember that taking it was agony, you cannot bear to do what has to be done—to throw it away on to the cutting-room floor. That is better left to others.

So in the end the night came—my night.

There was a dense crowd outside the theater to see the arrival of the Queen. Inside the guests waited expectantly in a packed house, and my own seat was behind the royal box, so that I could answer questions. I was still sufficiently a small boy to enjoy the fairy story, and I remembered that old school magazine:

"Stobart was leader carrying great boots. . . ." Well, I had not been leader, but a lot of avalanches had fallen since I had carried my father's boots, and time had cast me in a different role.

So once more, amidst flashing diamonds, we made the ascent of Everest, from warm seats, and when we got to the top it seemed a pity that it was all over and that Everest no longer stood as a challenge.

But why worry as long as there were other things to do? Even now Ralph Izzard had telephoned me. "Are you still game to look for the Snowman?" he asked.

"Of course. Do you think I'm going to spend the rest of my life sitting on my fanny?"

CPSIA information can be obtained
at www.ICGtesting.com
Printed in the USA
BVHW010731310821
615580BV00018B/403